THE MICHELIN GUIDE

LONDON

MICHELIN

THE MICHELIN GUIDE'S COMMITMENTS

Whether they are in Japan, the USA, China or Europe, our inspectors apply the same criteria to judge the quality of each and every restaurant that they visit. The MICHELIN Guide commands a **worldwide reputation** thanks to the commitments we make to our readers - and we reiterate these below:

Our inspectors make regular and **anonymous visits** to restaurants to gauge the quality of products and services offered to an ordinary customer. They settle their own bill and may then introduce themselves and ask for more information about the establishment.

To remain totally objective for our readers, the selection is made with complete **independence**. Entry into the guide is free. All decisions are discussed with the Editor and our highest awards are considered at a European level.

The guide offers a **selection** of the best restaurants in every category of style and price. This is only possible because all the inspectors rigorously apply the same methods.

All the practical information, classifications and awards are revised and updated every year to give the most **reliable information** possible.

In order to guarantee the **consistency** of our selection, our classification criteria are the same in every country covered by the MICHELIN Guide. Each culture may have its own unique cuisine but **quality** remains the **universal principle** behind our selection.

Michelin's mission is to **aid your mobility**. Our sole aim is to make your journeys safe and pleasurable.

THE MICHELIN GUIDE'S SYMBOLS

PLEASANT FEATURES • FACILITIES & SERVICES

Particularly interesting wine list
Notable cocktail list
Great view
Outside dining available • Garden or park
Wheelchair accessible
Open for breakfast • Small plates
Vegetarian menu
Private dining room • Air conditioning
Restaurant offering lower priced theatre menu
Credit cards not accepted
Nearest Underground station

Pub serving good food

New establishment in the guide

PRICES

Menu £20/40	Fixed price menu. Lowest / highest price
Carte £20/38	À la carte menu. Lowest / highest price
s	Service included

THE MICHELIN DISTINCTIONS FOR GOOD FOOD

STARS

Our famous One ✿, Two ✿✿ and Three ✿✿✿ Stars identify establishments serving the highest quality cuisine – taking into account the quality of ingredients, the mastery of techniques and flavours, the levels of creativity and, of course, consistency.

✿✿✿ **Exceptional cuisine, worth a special journey!**
Our highest award is given for the superlative cooking of chefs at the peak of their profession. The ingredients are exemplary, the cooking is elevated to an art form and their dishes are often destined to become classics.

✿✿ **Excellent cuisine, worth a detour!**
The personality and talent of the chef and their team is evident in the expertly crafted dishes, which are refined, inspired and sometimes original.

✿ **High quality cooking, worth a stop!**
Using top quality ingredients, dishes with distinct flavours are carefully prepared to a consistently high standard.

BIB GOURMAND

Good quality, good value cooking.
'Bibs' are awarded for simple yet skilful cooking, with 3 courses costing £28 or less.

PLATE

Good cooking.
Fresh ingredients, capably prepared: simply a good meal.

DEAR READER,

We are delighted *to present the 2019 edition of the MICHELIN Guide to London. All of the restaurants within this guide have been chosen first and foremost for the quality of their cooking. You'll find comprehensive information on over 400 dining establishments, ranging from gastropubs and neighbourhood brasseries to internationally renowned restaurants. The diverse and varied selection bears testament to the rich and buoyant dining scene in London, with the city enjoying a worldwide reputation for the range and quality of its restaurants.*

Our most famous *distinctions are our Michelin Stars ✿ but look out too for the Bib Gourmands ☺. These are restaurants where the cooking is still carefully prepared but in a simpler style and, priced at under £28 for three courses, they represent excellent value for money. The rest of the restaurants in our selection are identified by The Michelin Plate 🍽; being chosen by the Michelin Inspectors for inclusion in the guide is a guarantee of quality in itself and the plate symbol highlights restaurants where you will have a good meal.*

Consult the Michelin Guide at
www.viamichelin.co.uk
and write to us at
themichelinguide-gbirl@michelin.com

THERE ARE PLENTY OF HIGHLIGHTS IN OUR 2019 GUIDE!

Two restaurants have been newly awarded Two Stars: **Kitchen Table at Bubbledogs** in Bloomsbury from chef James Knappett and **CORE** by Clare Smyth in North Kensington.

London's vitality and diversity is represented by its new One Stars, which are all so different in their looks, their style and their cuisine. **Brat**, in a room above a converted pub in Shoreditch, is all about cooking over fire, while the highly original **Ikoyi** in St James's introduces diners to the flavours of West Africa. **Hide**, opposite Green Park, was perhaps the most eagerly awaited unveiling of 2018 and marked the return of chef Ollie Dabbous; this bustling, three-storey all-day restaurant bucked the trend for small, intimate places. Many diners were equally thrilled when the team behind Ellory opened their new place, **Leroy**, also in Shoreditch. **Sabor** proves that if you want wonderful tapas you need not travel to Spain and Simon Rogan follows the success of L'Enclume with a Star for his London outpost, **Roganic**.

Relaxed, rustic neighbourhood joints also continue to pull in customers with their good value cooking from all over the world. New Bib Gourmands this year include Thai restaurant **Farang** in Highbury; **Petit Pois** in Hoxton which offers contemporary cooking; **Sorella** in Clapham that specialises in dishes from the Amalfi region; and **Kudu** in Peckham whose cooking exhibits subtle South African influences.

We are committed to remaining at the forefront of the culinary world and to meeting the demands of our readers. Please don't hesitate to contact us, as your contributions are invaluable in directing our work and improving the quality of the information that we provide.

Thank you for your support and happy travelling with the 2019 edition of the Michelin Guide to London.

CONTENTS

CENTRAL LONDON 16

GREATER LONDON 198

INDEXES 272

A CULINARY HISTORY OF LONDON

London, influenced by worldwide produce arriving via the Thames, has always enjoyed a close association with its food, though most of the time the vast majority of its people have looked much closer to home for their sustenance.

Even as far back as the 2nd century AD, meat was on the menu: the profusion of wildlife in the woods and forests around London turned it into a carnivore's paradise, thereby setting the tone and the template. Large stoves were employed to cook everything from pork and beef to goose and deer. The Saxons added the likes of garlic, leeks, radishes and turnips to the pot, while eels became a popular staple in later years.

What a Lark!

By the 13th century, the taste for fish had evolved to the more exotic porpoise, lamprey and sturgeon, with saffron and spices perking up the common-or-garden meat dish. Not that medieval tastes would have been considered mundane to the average 21st century diner: Londoners of the time would think nothing about devouring roasted thrush or lark from the cook's stalls dotted around the city streets. And you'd have been unlikely to hear the cry "Eat your greens!" In the 15th century, the vegetable diet, such as it was, seemed to run mainly to herbs such as rosemary, fennel, borage and thyme.

As commercial and maritime success burgeoned in the age of the Tudors, so tables began to groan under the weight of London's penchant for feasting. No excess was spared, as oxen, sheep, boars and pigs were put to the griddle; these would have been accompanied by newly arrived yams and sweet

potatoes from America and 'washed down' with rhubarb from Asia. People on the streets could 'feast-lite': by the 17th century hawkers were offering all sorts of goodies on the hoof.

Full of beans

All of this eating was of course accompanied by a lot of drinking. Though much of it took place in the alehouses and taverns - which ran into the thousands - by the 18th century coffee houses had become extraordinarily popular. These were places to do business as well as being convenient 'for passing evenings socially at a very small charge'.

Perhaps the biggest revolution in eating habits came midway through the 19th century when the first cavernous dining halls and restaurants appeared. These 'freed' diners from the communal benches of the cook-house and gave them, for the first time, the chance for a bit of seclusion at separate tables. This private dining experience was an egalitarian movement: plutocrats may have had their posh hotels, but the less well-off were buttering teacakes and scones served by 'nippies' at the local Lyons Corner House.

Influenced by post World War II flavours brought in by immigrants from Asia, the Caribbean and Africa – and, more recently, from Eastern Bloc Countries – Londoners now enjoy an unparalleled cuisine alive with global flavours. We're also more confident about waving the flag for Britain these days, with pop-ups, pubs and high end eateries helping us rediscover and celebrate our own culinary heritage.

A. Spatari/Moment/Getty Images (left) • C. Crespo/age fotostock (right)

Xsandra/iStock (left) • sinarp2/iStock (right)

CENTRAL LONDON

fotoVoyager/iStock (bottom) • olaser/iStock (top)

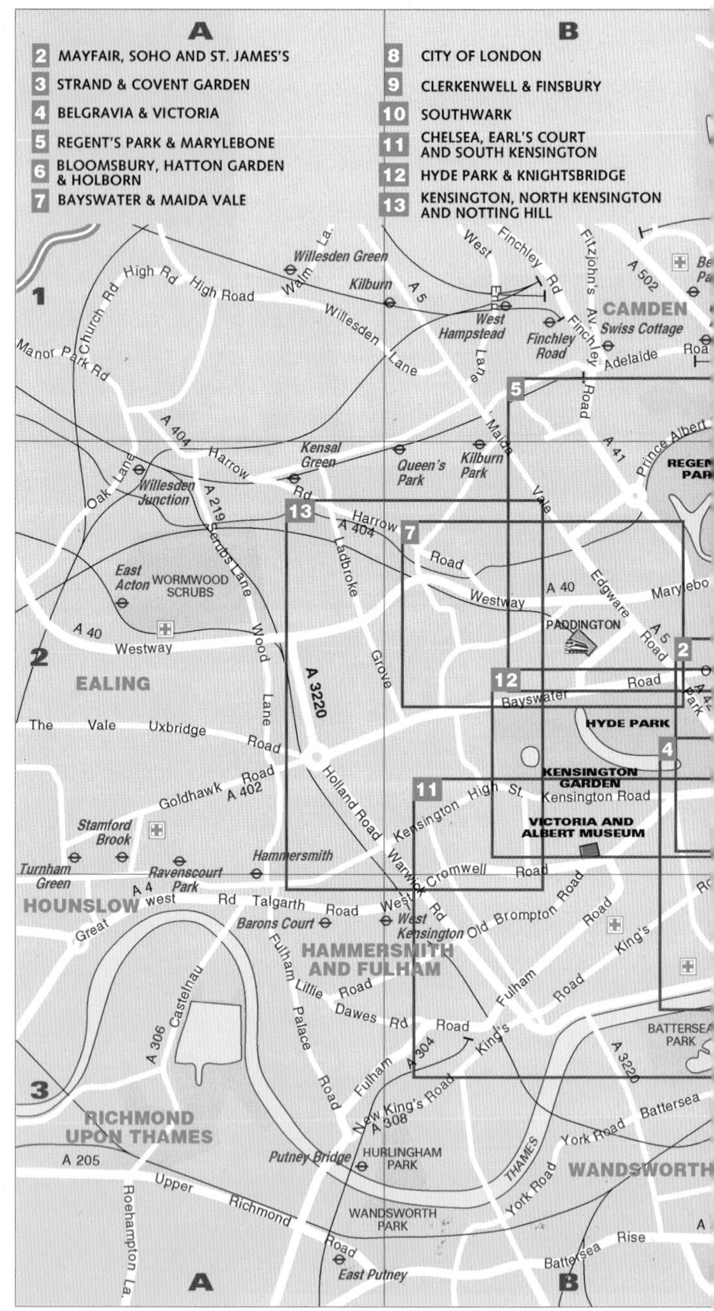
A
B
2 MAYFAIR, SOHO AND ST. JAMES'S
3 STRAND & COVENT GARDEN
4 BELGRAVIA & VICTORIA
5 REGENT'S PARK & MARYLEBONE
6 BLOOMSBURY, HATTON GARDEN & HOLBORN
7 BAYSWATER & MAIDA VALE
8 CITY OF LONDON
9 CLERKENWELL & FINSBURY
10 SOUTHWARK
11 CHELSEA, EARL'S COURT AND SOUTH KENSINGTON
12 HYDE PARK & KNIGHTSBRIDGE
13 KENSINGTON, NORTH KENSINGTON AND NOTTING HILL
CAMDEN
Swiss Cottage
Finchley Road
West Hampstead
Kilburn
Willesden Green
Kensal Green
Queen's Park
Kilburn Park
Willesden Junction
East Acton
WORMWOOD SCRUBS
EALING
PADDINGTON
HYDE PARK
KENSINGTON GARDEN
VICTORIA AND ALBERT MUSEUM
Stamford Brook
Turnham Green
Ravenscourt Park
Hammersmith
HOUNSLOW
Barons Court
West Kensington
HAMMERSMITH AND FULHAM
BATTERSEA PARK
RICHMOND UPON THAMES
Putney Bridge
HURLINGHAM PARK
WANDSWORTH PARK
WANDSWORTH
East Putney
THAMES
1
2
3

Central London Plans

(Plan 1)

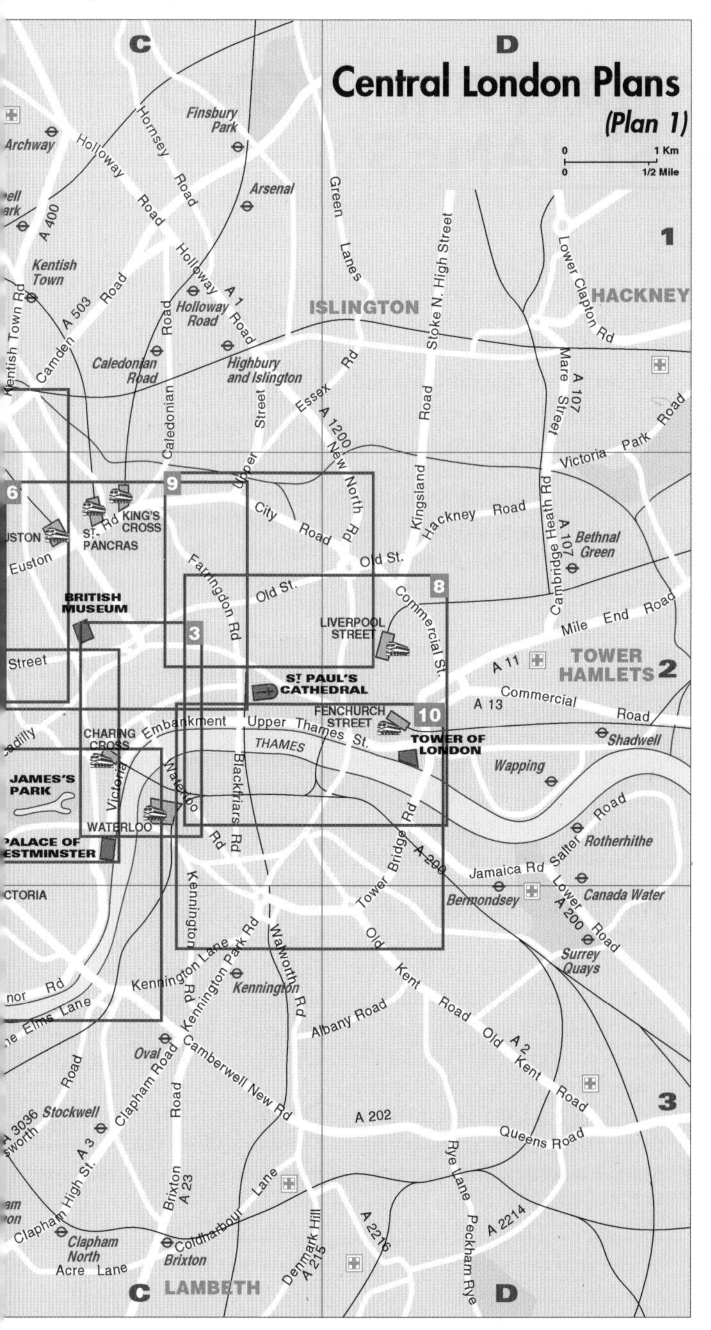

MAYFAIR · SOHO · ST JAMES'S

There's one elegant dividing line between Mayfair and Soho - the broad and imposing sweep of **Regent Street** - but mindsets and price tags keep them a world apart. It's usual to think of easterly Soho as the wild and sleazy half of these ill-matched twins, with Mayfair to the west the more sedate and sophisticated of the two. Sometimes, though, the natural order of things runs awry: why was rock's legendary wild man Jimi Hendrix, the embodiment of Soho decadence, living in the rarefied air of Mayfair's smart 23 Brook Street? And what induced Vivienne Westwood, punk queen and fashionista to the edgy, to settle her sewing machine in the uber-smart Conduit Street?

Mayfair has been synonymous with elegance for three and a half centuries, ever since the Berkeley and Grosvenor families bought up the local fields and turned them into posh real estate. The area is named after the annual May fair introduced in 1686, but suffice it to say that a raucous street celebration would be frowned upon big time by twenty-first century inhabitants. The grand residential boulevards can seem frosty and imposing, and even induce feelings of inadequacy to the humble passer-by but should he become the proud owner of a glistening gold card, then hey ho, doors will open wide. Claridge's is an art deco wonder, while **New Bond Street** is London's number one thoroughfare for the most chi-chi names in retailing. **Savile Row** may sound a little 'passé' these days, but it's still the place to go for the sharpest cut in town, before sashaying over to compact **Cork Street** to indulge in the purchase of a piece of art at one of its superb galleries. Science and music can also be found here, and at a relatively cheap price: the Faraday Museum in **Albemarle Street** explores 200 years of science, and Handel & Hendrix in Brook Street enables you not only to visit the beautifully presented home of the German composer and view his musical scores but also to explore the flat belonging to Hendrix, his 'future' next door neighbour, as it was in 1968-69.

Soho challenges the City as London's most famous square mile. It may not have the money of its brash easterly rival, but it sure has the buzz. It's always been fast and loose, since the days when hunters charged through with their cries of 'So-ho!' Its narrow jumbled streets throng with humanity, from the tourist to the tipsy, the libertine to the louche. A lot of the fun is centred round the streets just south of **Soho Square,** where area legends like The Coach & Horses ('Norman's Bar'), Ronnie Scott's and Bar Italia cluster in close proximity, along with 80s favourite, the Groucho Club. The tightest t-shirts in town are found in **Old Compton Street,** where the pink pound jangles the registers of gay-friendly bars and restaurants. To get a feel of the 'real' Soho, where old engraved signs enliven the shop fronts and the market stall cries echo back to the 1700s, a jaunt along **Berwick Street** is always in vogue, taking in a pint at the eternally popular Blue Posts, an unchanging street corner stalwart that still announces 'Watney's Ales' on its stencilled windows.

Not a lot of Watney's ale was ever drunk in **St James's;** not a lot of ale of any kind for that matter. Champagne and port is more the style here, in the hushed and reverential gentlemen's clubs where discretion is the key, and change is measured in centuries rather than years. The sheer class of the area is typified by **Pall Mall's** Reform Club, where Phileas Fogg wagered that he could zip round the world in eighty days, and the adjacent **St James's Square,** which was the most fashionable address in London in the late seventeenth century, when dukes and earls aplenty got their satin shoes under the silver bedecked tables.

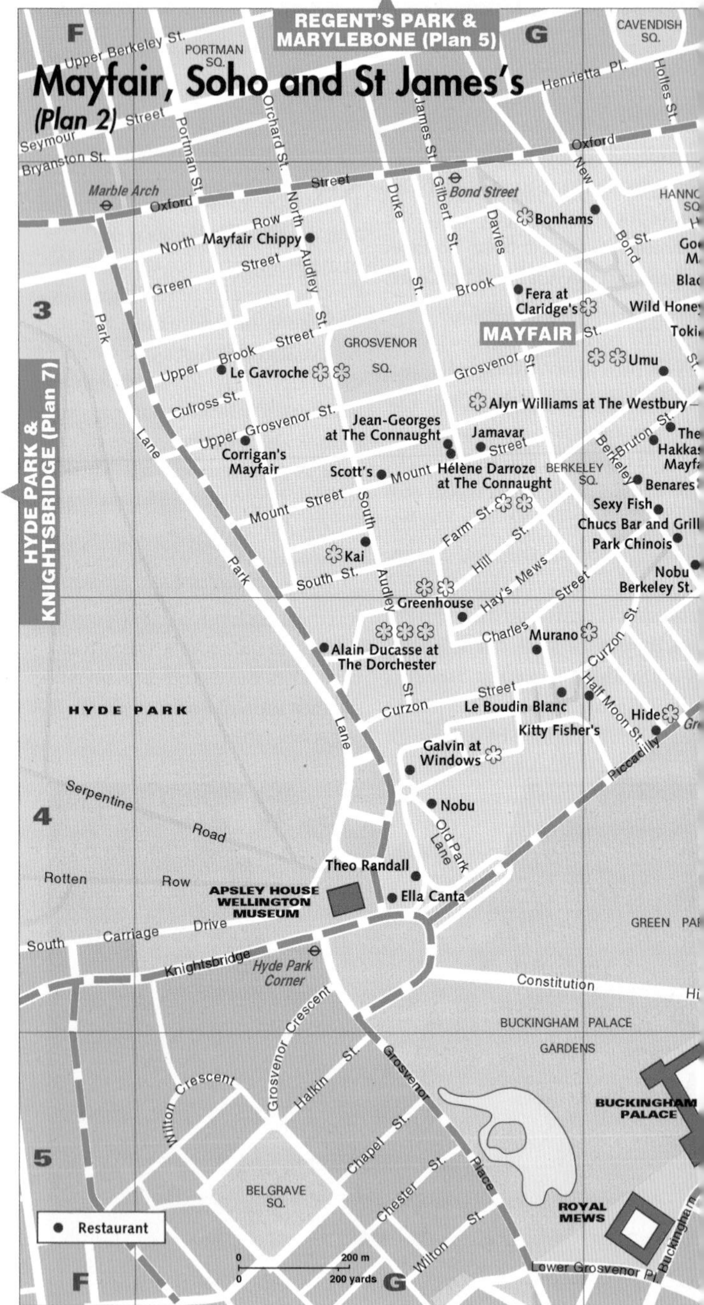

Mayfair, Soho and St James's
(Plan 2)
REGENT'S PARK & MARYLEBONE (Plan 5)
HYDE PARK & KNIGHTSBRIDGE (Plan 7)
MAYFAIR
Mayfair Chippy
Bonhams
Fera at Claridge's
Wild Honey
Umu
Le Gavroche
Alyn Williams at The Westbury
Jean-Georges at The Connaught
Jamavar
Corrigan's Mayfair
Scott's
Hélène Darroze at The Connaught
Benares
Sexy Fish
Chucs Bar and Grill
Park Chinois
Kai
Nobu Berkeley St.
Greenhouse
Murano
Alain Ducasse at The Dorchester
Le Boudin Blanc
Kitty Fisher's
Hide
Galvin at Windows
Nobu
Theo Randall
Ella Canta
APSLEY HOUSE WELLINGTON MUSEUM
HYDE PARK
GREEN PARK
BUCKINGHAM PALACE GARDENS
BUCKINGHAM PALACE
ROYAL MEWS
BELGRAVE SQ.
GROSVENOR SQ.
BERKELEY SQ.
PORTMAN SQ.
CAVENDISH SQ.
Marble Arch
Bond Street
Hyde Park Corner
Restaurant
0 200 m
0 200 yards

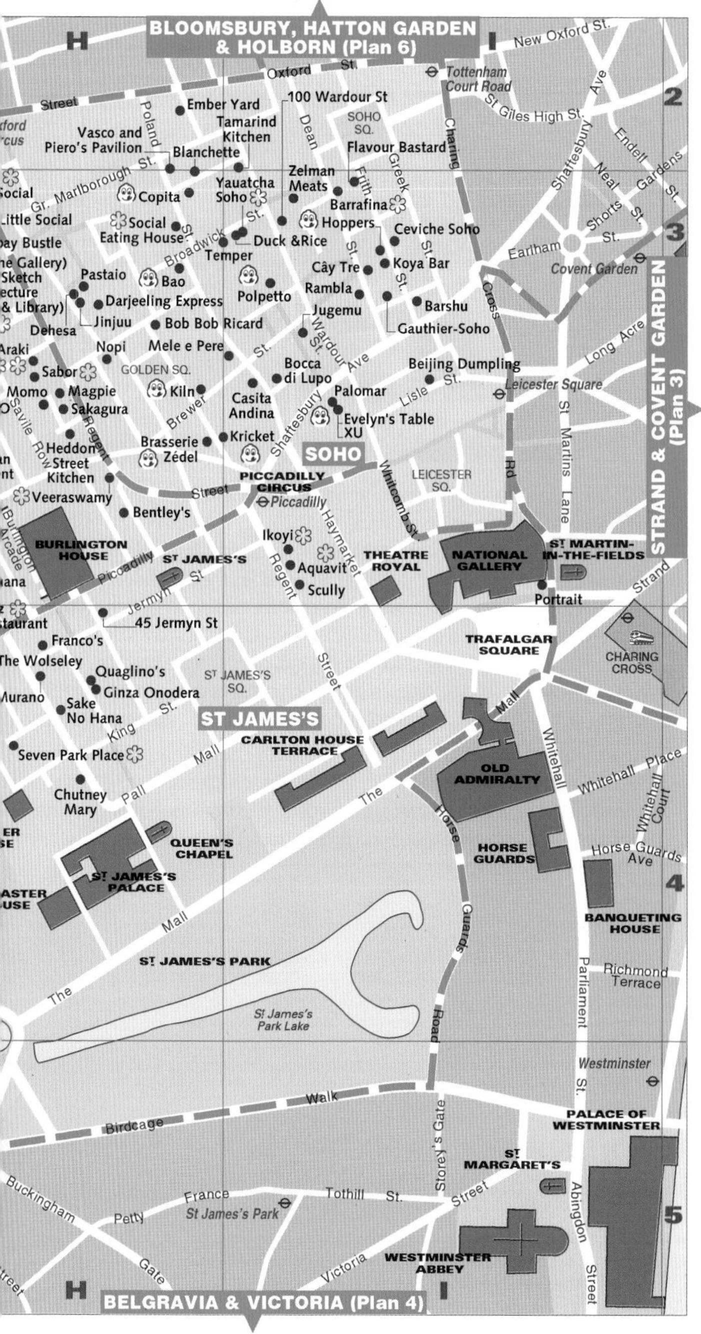
BLOOMSBURY, HATTON GARDEN & HOLBORN (Plan 6)
Ember Yard
100 Wardour St
Tamarind Kitchen
Vasco and Piero's Pavilion
Blanchette
SOHO SQ.
Flavour Bastard
Zelman Meats
Yauatcha Soho
Copita
Barrafina
Hoppers
Ceviche Soho
Social Eating House
Duck &Rice
Temper
Koya Bar
Cây Tre
Pastaio
Bao
Polpetto
Rambla
Barshu
Darjeeling Express
Jugemu
Jinjuu
Bob Bob Ricard
Gauthier-Soho
Dehesa
Nopi
Mele e Pere
Bocca di Lupo
Beijing Dumpling
Sabor
GOLDEN SQ.
Palomar
Momo
Magpie
Kiln
Casita Andina
Sakagura
Evelyn's Table
XU
Kricket
Brasserie Zédel
Heddon Street Kitchen
SOHO
PICCADILLY CIRCUS
Piccadilly
LEICESTER SQ.
Leicester Square
Veeraswamy
Bentley's
Ikoyi
BURLINGTON HOUSE
ST JAMES'S
THEATRE ROYAL
NATIONAL GALLERY
ST MARTIN-IN-THE-FIELDS
Aquavit
Sculty
Portrait
45 Jermyn St
Franco's
The Wolseley
TRAFALGAR SQUARE
CHARING CROSS
Quaglino's
ST JAMES'S SQ.
Ginza Onodera
Sake No Hana
ST JAMES'S
CARLTON HOUSE TERRACE
Seven Park Place
OLD ADMIRALTY
Chutney Mary
QUEEN'S CHAPEL
HORSE GUARDS
ST JAMES'S PALACE
BANQUETING HOUSE
ST JAMES'S PARK
St James's Park Lake
Richmond Terrace
Westminster
PALACE OF WESTMINSTER
ST MARGARET'S
WESTMINSTER ABBEY
St James's Park
STRAND & COVENT GARDEN (Plan 3)
Tottenham Court Road
Covent Garden
BELGRAVIA & VICTORIA (Plan 4)
Oxford St.
New Oxford St.
St Giles High St.
Shaftesbury Ave
Charing Cross Rd
Long Acre
Whitehall
The Mall
Pall Mall
Birdcage Walk
Horse Guards Road
Parliament St.
Tothill St.
Victoria Street
Abingdon Street

ALAIN DUCASSE AT THE DORCHESTER ✿✿✿

French • Elegant

Alain Ducasse's elegant London outpost understands that it's all about making the diner feel at ease – as Coco Chanel said "Luxury must be comfortable, otherwise it is not luxury". Thanks to their charm and professionalism, the service team's attentiveness is never overbearing nor does their confidence ever cross the line into haughtiness. The kitchen uses the best British or French produce to create visually striking dishes, including some that showcase the flavours of Southern France. Dishes like 'Sauté gourmand' of lobster are much loved perennials while others, such as Anjou pigeon with sardine, prove that the kitchen is not averse to taking risks. For dessert, it's hard to resist the signature Rum Baba.

The exemplary wine list includes an impressive selection of Domaine de la Romanée Conti and Château d'Yquem. The best tables are in the main room – those on the raised dais can feel a little detached from the action. Luminaries wanting a semi-private experience should book the 'Table Lumière' which is wrapped in a shimmering curtain.

FIRST COURSE	MAIN COURSE	DESSERT
Dorset crab, celeriac and caviar. • Confit duck foie gras with cherry and basil.	Halibut with oyster and seaweed. • Farmhouse veal medallion with sweetbreads and carrots.	'Baba like in Monte Carlo'. • Baked apple, crème fraîche and saffron.

Dorchester Hotel, Park Ln ✉ W1K 1QA **MAP: 2-G4**
✆ 020 7629 8866 — **www**.alainducasse-dorchester.com
⊖ Hyde Park Corner

Menu £70/105
Closed 3 weeks August, first week January, 26-30 December, Easter, Saturday lunch, Sunday and Monday – booking essential

ALYN WILLIAMS AT THE WESTBURY ✿

Modern cuisine • Design

Peep inside this restaurant within the Westbury Hotel and the impression you get is one of considerable formality but the good news is that it's a long way from being one of those whispering shrines to gastronomy. Granted, it's a very comfortable room, with rosewood panelling and well-spaced, smartly laid tables but the reason the atmosphere never strays into terminal seriousness is largely down to the staff, who exude genuine warmth and sincerity. Their willingness to please can also take one by surprise – for instance, they'll happily let you mix and match the à la carte with the weekend tasting menu. The other reason for its appeal is the relative value for money when one considers the quality of the ingredients and the skill of the kitchen. Alyn Williams' team has an innate understanding of flavours; dishes are colourful and quite elaborate constructions but the combinations of textures and tastes marry happily together.

FIRST COURSE	MAIN COURSE	DESSERT
Orkney scallop with yuzu caramel, white asparagus, morels and seaweed. • Herdwick lamb shoulder with English pea velouté and asparagus.	Roasted halibut with fennel compote, cashews and coconut. • Pork jowl with fennel, pickled rhubarb and pollen.	Gariguette strawberry tartlet, lemon, vanilla curd and basil. • 'Walnut Whip'.

Westbury Hotel, 37 Conduit St ✉ W1S 2YF **MAP: 2-H3**
✆ 020 7183 6426 — **www**.alynwilliams.com
⊖ Bond Street

Menu £30/90
Closed first 2 weeks January, last 2 weeks August, Sunday and Monday

AQUAVIT ✿

Scandinavian • Brasserie

The original Aquavit has been a luminous feature of the New York dining scene for over twenty years but the owners sensibly decided to resist the temptation of making their London outpost a carbon copy. Instead, they created a large brasserie with plenty of marble, wood and leather that's much warmer, more informal and accessible.

The cooking is also different: instead of a tasting selection full of intricate dishes, you can expect a menu of more familiar Scandinavian influences – and it's all immensely appealing. Kick things off by heading straight to the smörgåsbord section and some wonderful herring or shrimp; follow up with venison tartare or smoked eel and then for a main course consider fish again: the whole trout will make you forget all the heinous culinary crimes committed in its name over the years. The ingredients are exemplary and there's a vitality to the food that leaves you feeling good about life.

FIRST COURSE

Crab with rye brioche and fennel. • Veal tartare with dill, cauliflower and parmesan.

MAIN COURSE

Turbot with horseradish, beetroot and Sandefjord sauce. • Swedish meatballs with lingonberries and pickled cucumber.

DESSERT

Douglas fir panna cotta with queen's sorbet and sorrel. • Norwegian omelette with sea buckthorn and vanilla.

St James's Market, 1 Carlton St ✉ SW1Y 4QQ **MAP: 2-13**
☎ 020 7024 9848 – **www.**aquavitrestaurants.com
⊖ Piccadilly Circus

Menu £24 (lunch) - Carte £34/58
Closed 23-27 December

THE ARAKI ✿✿✿

Japanese • Intimate

It wasn't a straightforward move when Mitsuhiro Araki packed up his Three Star sushi restaurant in Tokyo's Ginza district and sailed for London in 2014. He wanted a challenge so instead of merely importing produce from Tsukiji fish market, he set himself the task of using largely European fish and shellfish and spent time adjusting his Edomae methods and techniques accordingly – the results are extraordinary.

There are two sittings at his 9-seater counter, at 18.00 and 20.30, and payment is taken in advance. Only an omakase menu is served – it doesn't come cheap, but the best things in life rarely do. His exquisite nigiri comes in manageable sizes and you can expect, for example, tuna and mackerel from Spanish waters, salmon from Scotland and caviar from Cornwall. The rice, grown by his father-in-law back in Japan, is extraordinary; it is served at near body temperature, with every grain discernible in the mouth.

FIRST COURSE	MAIN COURSE	DESSERT
Tuna tartare. • Cornish squid with albino caviar.	Nigiri sushi. • Salmon roe with seaweed.	Wagashi. • Japanese rice cake with red bean paste and macadamia.

12 New Burlington St ✉ W1S 3BF **MAP: 2-H3**
020 7287 2481 — **www**.the-araki.com
Oxford Circus

Menu £300
Closed last 2 weeks August, Christmas-first week January and Monday – booking essential – (dinner only) – (tasting menu only)

A/C

BAO

Asian • Simple

There are some things in life worth queueing for - and that includes the delicious eponymous buns here at this simple, great value Taiwanese operation. The classic bao and the confit pork bao are standouts, along with 'small eats' like trotter nuggets. There's also another Bao in Windmill St.

53 Lexington St W1F 9AS **MAP: 2-H3**
020 3011 1632 — **www**.baolondon.com
Tottenham Court Road
Carte £17/27
Closed 24-26 December, 1 January and Sunday dinner - bookings not accepted
A/C

BARSHU

Chinese • Exotic décor

The fiery and authentic flavours of China's Sichuan province are the draw here; help is at hand as the menu has pictures. It's well run and decorated with carved wood and lanterns; downstairs is better for groups.

28 Frith St. W1D 5LF **MAP: 2-I3**
020 7287 8822 — **www**.barshurestaurant.co.uk
Leicester Square
Carte £19/53
Closed 24-25 December
A/C

BEIJING DUMPLING

Chinese • Neighbourhood

This relaxed little place serves freshly prepared dumplings of both Beijing and Shanghai styles. Although the range is not as comprehensive as the name suggests, they do stand out, especially varieties of the famed Xiao Long Bao.

23 Lisle St WC2H 7BA **MAP: 2-I3**
020 7287 6888
Leicester Square
Menu £17/25 - Carte £14/38
Closed 24-25 December - bookings not accepted
A/C

BARRAFINA ✿

Spanish • Tapas bar

The owners – the Hart brothers – sliced their Quo Vadis restaurant into two to accommodate Barrafina when it moved from Frith Street and, apart from it now sitting beneath one of the famous neon signs of this Soho landmark, you can't see the join. This site is brighter and roomier, although the number of seats at the L-shaped counter is actually the same as before, and the queues are still here if you don't arrive early enough.

The menu is also reassuringly familiar and supplemented by an appealing little blackboard menu of the day's best produce – from which it's well worth ordering a few dishes like crisp anchovies or octopus with capers. The dishes burst with flavour, leave a lasting impression and are easy to share, although you'll find yourself ordering more when you look around and see what your neighbours are having. As well as hiring delightful staff, another thing they get right here is that once you've got your seats you won't be hurried out of them too quickly.

FIRST COURSE	MAIN COURSE	DESSERT
Ham croquetas. • Morcilla Ibérica with quails' eggs.	Chorizo, potato and watercress. • Chargrilled John Dory.	Santiago tart. • Pears in white wine.

26-27 Dean St ✉ W1D 3LL
020 7440 1456 — **www**.barrafina.co.uk
⊖ Tottenham Court Road

MAP: 2-13

Carte £20/40
Closed bank holidays - bookings not accepted

A/C

BENARES ✿

Indian • Chic

No Indian restaurant in London enjoys a more commanding location or expansive interior than Benares. You'll be greeted at the foot of the stairs before being escorted up past the flower-filled pool and busy bar into the cleverly textured and warmly lit restaurant – you won't even notice the lack of windows.

The influences here are many and varied. The use of British ingredients like Scottish scallops and New Forest venison is to be applauded and there is certainly no doubting their skill when it comes to spicing: flavours are judiciously layered and expertly balanced. Presentation isn't as elaborate or ornate as it once was and the dishes are all the better for it. The lunch menu offers good value and there is an evening tasting menu but the kitchen's strength lies with the à la carte. If you're coming in a group consider booking the Chef's Table, with its close-up views of all the action in the kitchen.

FIRST COURSE

Crispy soft shell crab with puy lentil salad, kasundi and honey dressing. • Chargrilled saddle of Andhra spiced marinated rabbit and pickled carrot.

MAIN COURSE

Venison, kale and chestnut mushroom biryani with butternut purée. • Pan-fried halibut with grilled asparagus, edamame purée and kokum curry.

DESSERT

Peanut butter parfait, with almond cake, cumin marshmallow and jaggery ice cream. • Spiced chocolate cherry lava cake with white chocolate sorbet.

■ 12a Berkeley Square House, Berkeley Sq. **MAP: 2-H3**
✉ W1J 6BS
✆ 020 7629 8886 — **www**.benaresrestaurant.com
⊖ Green Park

■ Menu £29 (lunch and early dinner)/98 - Carte £50/79
Closed lunch 25 December,1 January and Sunday lunch

BENTLEY'S

Seafood • Traditional décor

This hundred year old seafood institution comes in two parts: upstairs is the more formal and smartly dressed Grill, with seafood classics and grilled meats; on the ground floor is the Oyster Bar which is more fun and does a good fish pie.

11-15 Swallow St. W1B 4DG — **MAP: 2-H3**
020 7734 4756 — **www**.bentleys.org
Piccadilly Circus

Carte £39/93
Closed 25 December, 1 January, Saturday lunch and Sunday

BLACK ROE

World cuisine • Trendy

Poke, made famous in Hawaii, is the star here. You can choose traditional ahi over the sushi rice or something more original like scallop and octopus. Other options include dishes with assorted Pacific Rim influences, along with others cooked on the Kiawe wood grill.

4 Mill St W1S 2AX — **MAP: 2-H3**
020 3794 8448 — **www**.blackroe.com
Oxford Circus

Carte £26/66
Closed Sunday

BLANCHETTE

French • Simple

Run by three frères, Blanchette takes French bistro food and gives it the 'small plates' treatment. It's named after their mother - the ox cheek Bourguignon is her recipe. Tiles and exposed brick add to the rustic look.

9 D'Arblay St W1F 8DR — **MAP: 2-H3**
020 7439 8100 — **www**.blanchettelondon.co.uk
Oxford Circus

Menu £20 (lunch and early dinner) - Carte £18/49
Booking essential

BOB BOB RICARD

Traditional British • Vintage

Small but perfectly formed, BBR actually sees itself as a glamorous grand salon; ask for a booth. The menu is all-encompassing - from pies and burgers to oysters and caviar. Prices are altered depending on how busy they are, with up to a 25 % reduction at off-peak times.

1 Upper James St ✉ W1F 9DF **MAP: 2-H3**
020 3145 1000 — **www**.bobbobricard.com
Oxford Circus
Carte £38/86

BOCCA DI LUPO

Italian • Tapas bar

Atmosphere, food and service are all best when sitting at the marble counter, watching the chefs at work. Specialities from across Italy come in large or small sizes and are full of flavour and vitality. Try also their gelato shop opposite.

12 Archer St ✉ WID 7BB **MAP: 2-I3**
020 7734 2223 — **www**.boccadilupo.com
Piccadilly Circus
Carte £26/63
Closed 25 December and 1 January – booking essential

Ⓝ BOMBAY BUSTLE

Indian • Fashionable

Tiffin tin carriers on Mumbai's railways inspired Jamavar's second London restaurant. A charming train theme runs through it; the ground floor is the livelier; downstairs is more 'first class'. Before a curry, biryani or dish from the tandoor order some tasting plates, made from family recipes.

29 Maddox St ✉ W1S 2PA **MAP: 2-H3**
020 7290 4470 — **www**.bombaybustle.com
Oxford Circus
Menu £16 (lunch) - Carte £29/42
Closed 25-25 December and 1-2 January

BONHAMS ✿

Modern cuisine • Minimalist

Established in 1793, Bonhams is one of the world's largest auctioneers of fine art and antiques. The last renovation added this modern, crisply decorated restaurant with floor to ceiling windows, which is tucked away at the back of the building.

The succinct lunch menu with four choices per course is an appealing document governed by what's in season. The dishes are elegantly presented and quite delicate in appearance yet there's real clarity to the flavours thanks to their French base being combined with Scandic-style simplicity. There's also a very good wine list, which is no surprise when you find that it is compiled by Bonhams' own wine department. It includes some terrific older vintages and some of the finest wines at quite generous prices, including by the glass and carafe. Service is assured and professional and while the restaurant can get busy on sales days, it provides a relaxing environment.

FIRST COURSE	MAIN COURSE	DESSERT
Devon crab with bone marrow royale, green apple and horseradish. • Rose veal tartare with smoked eel, white asparagus and cornichons.	Saddle of Welsh hogget with smoked pomme purée, artichoke and grelot onions. • Dover sole with grapes, coastal herbs and crab bisque.	Gariguette strawberry, rice crème, rhubarb and rose meringue. • Chocolate sabayon tart L'Ambroisie with Madagascan vanilla ice cream.

101 New Bond St ✉ W1S 1SR **MAP: 2-H3**
✆ 020 7468 5868 — **www**.bonhamsrestaurant.com
⊖ Bond Street

Menu £42/70

Closed 2 weeks Christmas, 2 weeks mid-August, Saturday, Sunday, dinner Monday-Thursday and bank holidays

LE BOUDIN BLANC

French • Rustic

Appealing, lively French bistro in Shepherd Market, spread over two floors. Satisfying French classics and country cooking are the draws, along with authentic Gallic service. Good value lunch menu.

5 Trebeck St W1J 7LT — MAP: 2-G4
020 7499 3292 — **www**.boudinblanc.co.uk
Green Park
Menu £19 (lunch) - Carte £28/57
Closed 24-26 December and 1 January

BRASSERIE ZÉDEL

French • Brasserie

A grand French brasserie, which is all about inclusivity and accessibility, in a bustling subterranean space restored to its original art deco glory. Expect a roll-call of classic French dishes and some very competitive prices.

20 Sherwood St W1F 7ED — MAP: 2-H3
020 7734 4888 — **www**.brasseriezedel.com
Piccadilly Circus
Menu £11/20 - Carte £18/43
Closed 25 December

CAFE MURANO

Italian • Fashionable

Angela Hartnett and her chef have created an appealing and flexible menu of delicious North Italian delicacies - the lunch menu is very good value. It's certainly no ordinary café and its popularity means pre-booking is essential.

33 St. James's St SW1A 1HD — MAP: 2-H4
020 3371 5559 — **www**.cafemurano.co.uk
Green Park
Menu £23 (lunch and early dinner) - Carte £30/42
Closed Sunday dinner - booking essential

CASITA ANDINA

Peruvian • Rustic

Respect is paid to the home-style cooking of the Andes at this warmly run and welcoming Peruvian picantería. Dishes are gluten-free and as colourful as the surroundings of this 200 year old house.

31 Great Windmill St ✉ W1D 7LP — **MAP: 2-13**
020 3327 9464 — **www**.andinalondon.com/casita
Piccadilly Circus
Carte £18/37

CÂY TRE

Vietnamese • Minimalist

Bustling Vietnamese restaurant offering specialities from all parts of the country. Dishes are generously sized and appealingly priced; their various versions of pho are always popular. Come in a group to compete with the noise.

42-43 Dean St ✉ W1D 4PZ — **MAP: 2-13**
020 7317 9118 — **www**.thevietnamesekitchen.co.uk
Tottenham Court Road
Menu £25 - Carte £14/27
Closed 25 December

CEVICHE SOHO

Peruvian • Friendly

This is where it all started for this small group that helped London discover Peruvian food. It's as loud and cramped as it is fun and friendly. Start with a pisco-based cocktail then order classics like tiradito alongside dishes from the grill such as ox heart anticuchos.

17 Frith St ✉ W1D 4RG — **MAP: 2-13**
020 7292 2040 — **www**.cevicherestaurants.com
Tottenham Court Road
Carte £17/29
Closed 24-26 December and 1 January - booking essential

CHUCS BAR AND GRILL

Italian • Elegant

Like the shop to which it's attached, Chucs caters for those who summer on the Riviera and are not afraid of showing it. It's decked out like a yacht and the concise but not inexpensive menu offers classic Mediterranean dishes.

- 30b Dover St. ✉ W1S 4NB **MAP: 2-H3**
  ✆ 020 3763 2013 — **www**.chucsrestaurant.com
  ⊖ Green Park
- Carte £36/69
  Closed 25-26 and dinner 24 and 31 December, 1 January and bank holidays – booking essential

---

CHUTNEY MARY

Indian • Elegant

One of London's pioneering Indian restaurants, set in the heart of St James's. Elegant surroundings feature bold art and Indian artefacts. Spicing is understated, classics are done well, and some regional dishes have been subtly updated.

- 73 St James's St ✉ SW1A 1PH **MAP: 2-H4**
  ✆ 020 7629 6688 — **www**.chutneymary.com
  ⊖ Green Park
- Menu £29 (lunch) – Carte £39/70
  Closed 25 December

COPITA

Spanish • Tapas bar

Perch on one of the high stools or stay standing and get stuck into the daily menu of small, colourful and tasty dishes. Staff add to the atmosphere and everything on the Spanish wine list comes by the glass or copita.

- 27 D'Arblay St ✉ W1F 8EP **MAP: 2-H3**
  ✆ 020 7287 7797 — **www**.copita.co.uk
  ⊖ Oxford Circus
- Carte £20/41
  Closed Sunday and bank holidays – bookings not accepted

CORRIGAN'S MAYFAIR

Modern British • *Elegant*

Richard Corrigan's flagship celebrates British and Irish cooking, with game a speciality. The room is comfortable, clubby and quite glamorous and feels as though it has been around for years.

28 Upper Grosvenor St. W1K 7EH **MAP: 2-G3**
020 7499 9943 — **www**.corrigansmayfair.com
Marble Arch
Menu £28 (lunch and early dinner) - Carte £42/76
Closed 25-26 December, 1 January, Saturday lunch, Sunday and bank holidays

---

DARJEELING EXPRESS

Indian • *Brasserie*

With Royal Mughlai ancestry and a great love of food gained from cooking traditional family recipes, the owner couldn't be better qualified. Her open kitchen is run by a team of housewives; the influences are mostly Bengali but there are also dishes from Kolkata to Hyderabad. Lively and great fun.

Top Floor, Kingly Ct. Carnaby St W1B 5PW **MAP: 2-H3**
020 7287 2828 — **www**.darjeeling-express.com
Oxford Circus
Carte £22/29
Closed 25-26 and 31 December, 1 January and Sunday - booking essential

---

DEHESA

Mediterranean cuisine • *Tapas bar*

Repeats the success of its sister restaurant, Salt Yard, by offering flavoursome and appealingly priced Spanish and Italian tapas. Busy, friendly atmosphere in appealing corner location. Good drinks list too.

25 Ganton St W1F 9BP **MAP: 2-H3**
020 7494 4170 — **www**.dehesa.co.uk
Oxford Circus
Menu £15 (weekday lunch) - Carte £20/35
Closed 25 December

DUCK & RICE

Chinese • Intimate

Something a little different - a converted pub with a Chinese kitchen - originally set up by Alan Yau. Beer and snacks are the thing on the ground floor; upstairs, with its booths and fireplaces, is for Chinese favourites and comforting classics.

90 Berwick St ✉ W1F 0QB **MAP: 2-I3**
020 3327 7888 — **www.**theduckandrice.com
Tottenham Court Road

Carte £21/49
Closed 25 December

ELLA CANTA

Mexican • Design

Martha Ortiz is one of Mexico's most celebrated chefs and she now has a London outpost here at the InterContinental. The cooking draws on themes of history, philosophy and fantasy to create dishes that are colourful, creative and original. Great drinks list and charming staff.

InterContinental London Park Lane Hotel, 1 Hamilton Pl, Park Ln ✉ W1J 7QY **MAP: 2-G4**
7318 8715 — **www.**ellacanta.com
Hyde Park Corner

Menu £25 (weekday lunch) - Carte £34/63
Closed Sunday dinner and Monday lunch

EMBER YARD

Mediterranean cuisine • Tapas bar

Those familiar with the Salt Yard Group will recognise the Spanish and Italian themed menus - but their 4th fun outlet comes with a focus on cooking over charcoal or wood. There's even a seductive smokiness to some of the cocktails.

60 Berwick St ✉ W1F 8DX **MAP: 2-H2**
020 7439 8057 — **www.**emberyard.co.uk
Oxford Circus

Carte £29/48
Closed 25-26 December and 1 January

N EVELYN'S TABLE

Modern cuisine • Simple

A former beer cellar of a restored 18C inn - much is made of the whole cramped, underground, speakeasy thing. Watching the chefs behind the counter is all part of the appeal; their modern European dishes are designed for sharing, with fish from Cornwall a highlight.

The Blue Posts, 28 Rupert St ✉ W1D 6DJ — **MAP: 2-I3**
www.theblueposts.co.uk
⊖ Piccadilly Circus
Carte £25/43
Closed 25-26 December and Sunday - (dinner only)

N FLAVOUR BASTARD

Fusion • Brasserie

Here it's about "London on a plate" - food that celebrates our truly international capital. The 'Small' and 'Tiny' sharing plates fuse influences from Asia to the Caribbean, Europe to South America; in fact, nowhere is off-limits. Do try 'Cloud of curds' and 'TFC' (tandoori-fried chicken).

63-64 Frith St ✉ W1D 3JW — **MAP: 2-I3**
020 7734 4545 — **www**.flavourbastard.com
⊖ Tottenham Court Road
Menu £15 (lunch) - Carte £27/33
Closed 25 December, Sunday and bank holidays

45 JERMYN ST

Traditional British • Brasserie

Style and comfort go hand in hand at this bright, contemporary brasserie. The menu is a mix of European and British classics; the beef Wellington and lobster spaghetti are finished off at your table. Sodas, coupes and floats pay tribute to its past as Fortnum's Fountain restaurant.

45 Jermyn St. ✉ SW1 6DN — **MAP: 2-H4**
020 7205 4545 — **www**.45jermynst.com
⊖ Piccadilly Circus
Menu £26 (early dinner) - Carte £30/67

FERA AT CLARIDGE'S ✿

Creative British • Elegant

Fera is set in one of the most striking rooms in the capital, in the delightful and ever-so-British surroundings of Claridge's Hotel. Muted tones of green give it an almost herbaceous feel, which is juxtaposed by touches of art deco and magnificent detailing – yet the grandeur of the room is tempered by the refreshing lack of pomposity or mannered formality in the service. The 'wild' of Fera may refer to the influence of nature but this is intricately planned and highly refined cuisine.

There's an impressive purity and a natural, unforced style to Matt Starling's cooking that is evident on the plate, yet the wonderfully well-balanced and textured dishes deliver multi-dimensional layers of flavours. Lesser-known ingredients might include hyssop, mead, meadowsweet and pickled pine; choose the tasting menu to best appreciate the kitchen's skills. The weighty wine list offers an intelligent mix of the classic and the more esoteric.

FIRST COURSE	MAIN COURSE	DESSERT
Roasted quail with hazelnut, carrot and juniper. • Scallops with oyster, dill and celeriac.	Aged Dexter beef sirloin with ox cheek, salsify and thyme. • Halibut cooked in pine with bone marrow, peas and whey.	Chocolate, whiskey and pine. • Strawberries with Jersey milk ice cream and sorrel.

■ Claridge's Hotel, Brook St ✉ W1K 4HR **MAP: 2-G3**
✆ 020 7107 8888 — **www.**feraatclaridges.co.uk
⊖ Bond Street
■ Menu £42 (lunch) - Carte £63/85

FRANCO'S

Italian • Traditional décor

Have an aperitivo in the clubby bar before sitting down to eat at one of London's oldest yet rejuvenated Italian restaurants. The kitchen focuses on the classics and they live up to expectations; the regulars, of whom there are many, all have their favourites.

61 Jermyn St ✉ SW1Y 6LX **MAP: 2-H4**
020 7499 2211 — **www**.francoslondon.com
Green Park
Menu £32 - Carte £36/64
Closed Sunday and bank holidays - booking essential

GAUTHIER - SOHO

French • Intimate

Detached from the rowdier elements of Soho is this charming Georgian townhouse, with dining spread over three floors. Alex Gauthier offers assorted menus of his classically based cooking, with vegetarians particularly well looked after.

21 Romilly St ✉ W1D 5AF **MAP: 2-I3**
020 7494 3111 — **www**.gauthiersoho.co.uk
Leicester Square
Menu £30/75
Closed Sunday, Monday and bank holidays except Good Friday

GINZA ONODERA

Japanese • Elegant

Re-fitted and re-launched in 2017 on the site of what was Matsuri for over 20 years. A staircase leads down to the smart restaurant and the three counters: for sushi, teppanyaki and the robata grill. The emphasis is on traditional Japanese cuisine and top-end ingredients.

15 Bury St ✉ SW1Y 6AL **MAP: 2-H4**
020 7839 1101 — **www**.onodera-group.com
Green Park
Menu £23 (lunch) - Carte £29/70
Closed 25 December and 1 January

GALVIN AT WINDOWS ✿

Modern cuisine • Friendly

The lift may take time to drop off its cargo of Hilton hotel residents as it makes its way up to the 28th floor but the wait will be worth it as the views from up here are spectacular – it's worth arriving early for a drink in the adjacent bar. The restaurant has been cleverly laid out to make the most of the three sides of views and, if you can't secure a window table, the elevated section in the middle of the room is a good compromise. Service is relaxed and friendly which softens some of the formality of the room, although a little more passion would dispel some of the corporate blandness that pervades the atmosphere.

The food provides worthy competition to the views. British ingredients like Cornish lamb, Cumbrian beef and Dorset crab proudly feature on the various menus – the Menu du Jour draws in plenty of customers at lunch as it's a steal for this postcode. There's a classical base to the boldly flavoured dishes, which come with a pleasing degree of flair and innovation.

FIRST COURSE	MAIN COURSE	DESSERT
Cured Loch Fyne salmon with brown crab mousseline and celeriac remoulade. • Marinated Iberico pork with mooli and pickled mushrooms.	Fillet of beef and short-rib beignet with ox tongue and red wine jus. • Pan-fried red mullet with shellfish raviolo, aioli and spinach.	Pavlova with exotic fruit salsa and coconut ice cream. • Pear soufflé with warm salt caramel fudge and cinnamon ice cream.

London Hilton Hotel, 22 Park Ln (28th floor) ✉ W1K 1BE
✆ 020 7208 4021 — **www**.galvinatwindows.com
⊖ Hyde Park Corner

MAP: 2-G4

Menu £37 (weekday lunch)/82
Closed Saturday lunch and Sunday dinner

LE GAVROCHE ✿✿

French • Intimate

You don't get to celebrate 50 years – as Le Gavroche did in 2017 – without doing something right. Anyone with any interest in Britain's post-war culinary history will be aware of this restaurant's significance, not just because of its celebration of French cuisine but also because of all the chefs who have passed through its kitchen over the years.

In an age of hectoring health-consciousness and tedious calorie counting there is something exhilarating about Michel Roux and head chef Rachel Humphrey's unapologetically extravagant French dishes. The ingredients are of the highest order, whether that's the huge scallops or the succulent Goosnargh duck. Everyone has their favourite dish but if the soufflé Suissesse or omelette Rothschild ever came off the menu there'd be riots, albeit polite ones, in Upper Brook Street. The cheese board is one of London's best. You're guided gracefully through the meal by a charming team and the hum of satisfaction that pervades the room says it all.

FIRST COURSE	MAIN COURSE	DESSERT
Artichoke with foie gras, truffles and chicken mousse. • Grilled scallops with clam minestrone.	Butter poached lobster with white wine, asparagus and claw tart. • Roast saddle of rabbit, with crispy potato and parmesan.	Apricot and Cointreau soufflé. • Strawberry shortbread and sorbet with Madagascan vanilla cream.

43 Upper Brook St ✉ W1K 7QR — **MAP: 2-G3**
020 7408 0881 — **www**.le-gavroche.co.uk
⊖ Marble Arch

Menu £70/175 **s** - Carte £68/197 **s**
Closed 2 weeks Christmas, Saturday lunch, Sunday, Monday and bank holidays - booking essential

GOODMAN MAYFAIR

Meats and grills • Brasserie

A worthy attempt at recreating a New York steakhouse; all leather and wood and macho swagger. Beef is dry or wet-aged in-house and comes with a choice of four sauces; rib-eye the speciality.

26 Maddox St W1S 1QH **MAP: 2-H3**
020 7499 3776 — **www**.goodmanrestaurants.com
Oxford Circus
Carte £31/107
Closed Sunday and bank holidays - booking essential
A/C

HEDDON STREET KITCHEN

Modern cuisine • Brasserie

Gordon Ramsay's follow up to Bread Street is spread over two floors and is all about all-day dining: breakfast covers all tastes, there's weekend brunch, and an à la carte offering an appealing range of European dishes executed with palpable care.

3-9 Heddon St W1B 4BE **MAP: 2-H3**
020 7592 1212 — **www**.gordonramsayrestaurants.com
Oxford Circus
Menu £23 (lunch and early dinner) - Carte £26/63
A/C

HOPPERS

South Indian • Simple

Street food inspired by the flavours of Tamil Nadu and Sri Lanka features at this fun little spot from the Sethi family (Trishna, Gymkhana). Hoppers are bowl-shaped pancakes made from fermented rice and coconut - ideal with a creamy kari. The 'short eats' are great too, as are the prices, so expect a queue.

49 Frith St W1D 4SG **MAP: 2-I3**
020 3011 1021 — **www**.hopperslondon.com
Tottenham Court Road
Menu £20 (lunch) - Carte £15/30
Closed 25-27 December and 1-3 January. - bookings not accepted
A/C

GREENHOUSE ✿✿

Creative • Fashionable

The Greenhouse has many charms and one of them is its setting. You enter via a mews, through a little bamboo garden, and this pastoral theme continues inside with a pale green colour scheme and leaf-etched glass. The restaurant is bright and airy during the day, and warm and intimate by night. If it wasn't for the fact that your fellow diners are an immaculately robed, international crowd, you would scarcely believe you were in the heart of the city.

The cooking here has always been underpinned by a sound classical French base. A variety of menus provide plenty of choice and the sourcing finds the best produce from around the UK, whether that's seafood from Cornwall and Scotland or lamb and venison from Wales. The wine list features the good and the great and an exceptional breadth of vintages: Château Lafite back to 1870, Château Latour to 1900, Château Haut Brion to 1945, 15 vintages of La Tâche and 37 of Penfolds Grange.

FIRST COURSE	MAIN COURSE	DESSERT
Native lobster with chicken, kohlrabi and cardamom leaf. • Veal sweetbread with pineapple, black sesame and ginger.	Welsh lamb with aubergine, gomasio, harissa and soya. • Brill with onion, banana, kaffir lime and dukkah.	'Ajuba Head' - chocolate with walnut and nutmeg. • Chestnut with mandarin and granola.

27a Hay's Mews ✉ W1J 5NY — **MAP: 2-G4**
020 7499 3331 — **www.**greenhouserestaurant.co.uk
⊖ Hyde Park Corner

Menu £45/100
Closed Saturday lunch, Sunday and bank holidays

GYMKHANA ✿

Indian • Fashionable

If you enjoy Trishna then you'll love Gymkhana. Inspired by Colonial India's gymkhana clubs, the interior is full of wonderful detail and plenty of wry touches, from the hunting trophies and ceiling fans to the glass wall lamps and Grandma Sethi's barometer. If you're on the ground floor ask for one of the booths but it's worth a little persistence to ensure you're seated downstairs, where the beaten brass topped tables, leather banquettes and the dimmest of lighting add to the intimate atmosphere.

There's an array of dishes inspired by the flavours of North India – don't procrastinate, just go straight for the 6 courser; included could be wild tiger prawns that show what a charcoal grill can do; kid goat methi keema with a pleasing richness and well-judged spicing; suckling pig vindaloo with complex flavours; or wild muntjac biryani, a triumph of flaky pastry.

FIRST COURSE

Dosa, Chettinad duck and coconut. • Amritsari shrimp and queenies with dill raita.

MAIN COURSE

Wild muntjac biryani with pomegranate and mint raita. • Chicken butter masala.

DESSERT

Saffron and pistachio kulfi falooda. • Black carrot halwa tart with gulab ice cream.

42 Albemarle St ✉ W1S 4JH **MAP: 2-H4**
✆ 020 3011 5900 — **www**.gymkhanalondon.com
⊖ Green Park

Menu £25 (weekday lunch) - Carte £25/67
Closed 1-3 January, 25-27 December and Sunday - booking essential

HAKKASAN MAYFAIR ✿

Chinese • Minimalist

You can usually spot the neophytes – they're the ones walking up and down Bruton Street trying to find the discreet entrance. Once in, they'll feel nicely cocooned from the outside world and transported somewhere infinitely more exotic. This branch may be a little more corporate in feel than the Hanway Place original, but it can still deliver a healthy dose of glamour. If you're here for lunchtime dim sum, then the ground floor is perfectly fine; for dinner, ask for a table in the lower floor as it is markedly sexier, thanks to its flattering lighting and energising atmosphere.

All the classics that have made the reputation of this group are here, like silver cod and jasmine tea smoked chicken, but there are also dishes specific to this branch, like delicious wok-fried pork belly in lychee sauce, Szechuan-style langoustine and, for dessert, yuzu and sesame vacherin. The simplest and least expensive dishes can also be the best, like salt and pepper tofu or golden soft shell crab.

FIRST COURSE	MAIN COURSE	DESSERT
Soft shell crab with red chilli. • Smoked beef ribs with jasmine tea.	Pan-fried Wagyu beef in spicy Sichuan sauce. • Stir-fried Alaskan king crab in XO sauce with shimeji mushrooms.	Apple and sesame croustillant. • Chocolate and cherry.

17 Bruton St ✉ W1J 6QB — MAP: 2-H3
✆ 020 7907 1888 — **www**.hakkasan.com
⊖ Green Park

Menu £42 (lunch and early dinner)/120 - Carte £38/115
Closed 24-25 December - booking essential

HÉLÈNE DARROZE AT THE CONNAUGHT ✿✿

Modern cuisine • Luxury

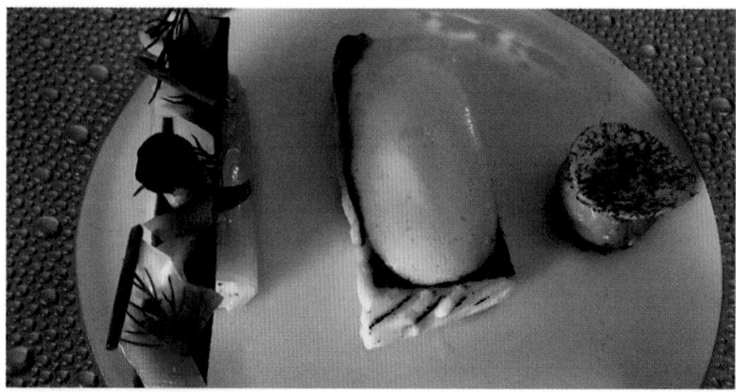

When it's time to choose what you're going to eat you'll be handed a Solitaire board featuring 13 marbles, each bearing the name of a single ingredient – you choose 5, 7 or 9 (courses). The board is accompanied by a menu showing the other components of the dishes in question, which are delivered in any order you wish. Some will love this game, others will hate it, but at least it highlights the fact that the dishes are built around a stunning main ingredient and allows Hélène Darroze to shine a light on her wonderful French and British suppliers. Her cooking is largely informed by her homeland but she's not averse to using the occasional unexpected flavour, be it Asian or Indian, if she feels it brings something to the dish; she is also aware of the modern diners' preference for a lighter, less elaborate style of cooking.

The wood-panelled room is comfortable and elegant and credit must go to the service team who keep the atmosphere light, relaxed and never overbearingly formal.

FIRST COURSE

Foie gras with black truffle, apple, celery and brioche. • Scallop with black pudding, Jerusalem artichoke and sorrel.

MAIN COURSE

Venison with Sarawak pepper, butternut, grapes and Stichelton. • Sea bass with clams, girolles and lemongrass.

DESSERT

Chocolate, cardamom and vanilla. • Chestnut with kumquat and grapefruit.

Connaught Hotel, Carlos Pl. ✉ W1K 2AL **MAP: 2-G3**
✆ 020 7107 8880 — **www**.the-connaught.co.uk
⊖ Bond Street

Menu £55/105
Booking essential

Ⓝ HIDE ✿

Modern British • Design

One of the most eagerly anticipated restaurant openings of 2018 was this collaboration between Hedonism Wines and chef Ollie Dabbous, occupying some prime real estate facing Green Park. Indeed, the park provides the inspiration between the decorative theme of this three-floored restaurant: 'Above' is decorated with light oak to represent the branches of the tree; 'Ground' is slightly darker to signify the trunk; while the bar 'Below' is darker still and represents the roots. 'Above' is where to book if you have more time and wish to experience the full repertoire of this talented kitchen as only tasting menus are offered here. Ground is a slightly more casual, all-day affair but shares the same vision: to bring out the natural flavours of the ingredients, in light and immaculately crafted dishes. The service team are clued up and charming and, needless to say, the wine list offers unparalleled depth.

FIRST COURSE	MAIN COURSE	DESSERT
Celeriac, avocado and angelica seed. • Steamed day-boat turbot with crushed nasturtium broth.	Slow-roast goose with birch sap and kale. • BBQ octopus with moscatel grapes, lovage and white miso.	Jasmine and wild pea flower religieuse. • Hide strawberry millefeuille.

85 Piccadilly ✉ W1J 7NB — **MAP: 2-H4**
✆ 020 3146 8666 — **www**.hide.co.uk
⊖ Green Park

Menu £42/95 - Carte £42/72
Closed 25 December

Ⓝ IKOYI ✿

Creative • Simple

The somewhat colourless development that is St James's Market is the unlikely setting for one of the most innovative and original restaurants to open in the capital in recent times. It is named after the most prosperous neighbourhood in Lagos, Nigeria which gives a clue as to its USP: the two owners, friends since childhood, have put together a kitchen that uses home-grown ingredients enlivened with flavours from West Africa.

There is nothing gimmicky here – it' all about using ingredients with which many diners will be unfamiliar while still ensuring that the main constituent of the dish, be it monkfish, duck or scallops, remains the star of the show. Kick off with Moin Moin with prawns or the buttermilk-soaked plantain with a Scotch Bonnet dip – they will certainly get your taste-buds in the mood. Jollof rice is a must and here it comes with crab – when the lid is lifted you'll find the smoky aromas intoxicating. The relatively small room is decorated in a warm and stylish way, while service is charming and helpful.

FIRST COURSE	MAIN COURSE	DESSERT
Mushroom suya, malted barley and pine. • Squid and coffee shito.	Duck, uda, candied bacon and bitter leaf. • Fish pepper soup, squash and shiso.	Black benne and blackcurrant. • Groundnut and zobo.

■ 1 St. James's Market ✉ SW1Y 4AH **MAP: 2-13**
✆ 020 3583 4660 — **www**.ikoyilondon.com
⊖ Piccadilly Circus

■ Menu £35 (lunch and early dinner)/60 - Carte £36/51
Closed 25 -26 December, 1 January and Sunday - booking essential
♿ A/C

Ⓝ INDIAN ACCENT ⑩

Indian • Elegant

The third branch, after New Delhi and NYC, is set over two levels, with a bright, fresh look. The kitchen takes classic dishes from all regions of India and blends them with European and Asian notes and techniques. The resulting dishes are colourful, sophisticated and full of flavour.

16 Albemarle St ✉ W1S 4HW **MAP: 2-H3**
020 7629 9802 — **www**.indianaccent.com
Green Park
Menu £30/55
Closed Christmas, New Year, Sunday and bank holidays
A/C

JAMAVAR ⑩

Indian • Exotic décor

Leela Palaces & Resorts are behind this smartly dressed Indian restaurant. The menus, including vegetarian, look to all parts of India, with a bias towards the north. The 'small plates' section includes Malabar prawns, and kid goat shami kebab; from the tandoor the stone bass tikka is a must; and biryanis are also good.

8 Mount St ✉ W1K 3NF **MAP: 2-G3**
020 7499 1800 — **www**.jamavarrestaurants.com
Bond Street
Menu £24 (lunch and early dinner) - Carte £32/54
Closed 25-26 December, 1 January and Sunday - booking essential at dinner
A/C

Ⓝ JEAN-GEORGES AT THE CONNAUGHT ⑩

Modern cuisine • Intimate

Low-slung bespoke marble-topped tables and comfy sofas make this room at the front of The Connaught hotel somewhere between a salon and a restaurant. It has something for all tastes, from Asian-inspired dishes to fish and chips. The truffle-infused pizza is a best seller.

Connaught Hotel, Carlos Pl. ✉ W1K 2AL **MAP: 2-G3**
020 7107 8861 — **www**.the-connaught.co.uk
Bond Street
Carte £57/88
A/C

JINJUU

Asian • Design

American-born celebrity chef Judy Joo's restaurant is a celebration of her Korean heritage. The vibrant dishes, whether Bibimbap bowls or Ssam platters, burst with flavour and are as enjoyable as the fun surroundings. There's another branch in Mayfair.

15 Kingly St W1B 5PS **MAP: 2-H3**
020 8181 8887 — **www**.jinjuu.com
Oxford Circus

Menu £14 (weekday lunch) - Carte £27/57
Closed 1 January and 25 December

JUGEMU

Japanese • Simple

Like all the best izakaya, this one is tucked away down a side street and easy to miss. It has three small tables and a 9-seater counter from where you can watch the chef-owner at work. Popular with a homesick Japanese clientele, it keeps things traditional; the sashimi is excellent.

3 Winnett St W1D 6JY **MAP: 2-H3**
020 7734 0518
Piccadilly Circus

Carte £10/50
Closed Christmas, New Year and Sunday - (dinner only)

KILN

Thai • Simple

Sit at the far counter to watch chefs prepare fiery Thai food in clay pots, woks and grills. The well-priced menu includes influences from Laos, Myanmar and Yunnan - all prepared using largely British produce. The counter is for walk-ins only but parties of four can book a table downstairs.

58 Brewer St W1F 9TL **MAP: 2-H3**
www.kilnsoho.com
Piccadilly Circus

Carte £10/22
Bookings not accepted

KAI ✿

Chinese • Intimate

Both the owner and his long-standing chef Alex Chow are Malaysian and, while the cooking features dishes from several provinces in China, it is the southern region of Nanyang which is closest to their hearts. The addition of subtle Malaysian influences results in a light, fresh style of cooking.

The menu comprises 20% traditional dishes and 80% where a little innovation has been blended with some less familiar ingredients. However, the flavours remain true, balanced and refined and the dishes are vibrant and colourful. The lunch menu offers further proof that this isn't your typical Chinese restaurant: instead of dim sum, they call their smaller versions of the dinner specialities 'Little plates of loveliness'. Vegetarians are well catered for and desserts are given a bigger billing than one usually sees. The unashamedly glitzy look of the restaurant is as eclectic as the food and the service team are switched on and fully conversant with the menu.

FIRST COURSE	MAIN COURSE	DESSERT
Seared scallop with spicy XO sauce, lotus root crisp and stir-fried vegetables. • Pork belly 'Open Bao', BBQ glaze.	Kagoshima Wagyu with foie gras, sesame ginger paste and Wagyu infused rice. • Steamed Chilean sea bass with sweet lime, chilli and lemongrass sambal.	Coconut parfait with chocolate and mango sorbet. • Durian and vanilla soufflé with salted caramel.

65 South Audley St ✉ W1K 2QU **MAP: 2-G3**
✆ 020 7493 8988 — **www.**kaimayfair.co.uk
⊖ Hyde Park Corner

Carte £51/199
Closed 25-26 December and 1 January - booking essential

KITTY FISHER'S

Modern cuisine • Bistro

Warm, intimate and unpretentious restaurant - the star of the show is the wood grill which gives the dishes added depth. Named after an 18C courtesan, presumably in honour of the profession for which Shepherd Market was once known.

10 Shepherd Mkt ✉ W1J 7QF **MAP: 2-H4**
✆ 020 3302 1661 — **www**.kittyfishers.com
⊖ Green Park
Carte £36/70
Closed Christmas, New Year, Easter, Sunday and bank holidays - booking essential

---

KOYA BAR

Japanese • Simple

A simple, sweet place serving authentic Udon noodles and small plates; they open early for breakfast. Counter seating means everyone has a view of the chefs; bookings aren't taken and there is often a queue, but the short wait is worth it.

50 Frith St ✉ W1D 4SQ **MAP: 2-I3**
✆ 020 7494 9075 — **www**.koya.co.uk
⊖ Tottenham Court Road
Carte £14/32
Closed 25 December and 1 January - bookings not accepted

KRICKET

Indian • Simple

From Brixton pop-up to a permanent spot in Soho; not many Indian restaurants have a counter, an open kitchen, sharing plates and cocktails. The four well-priced dishes under each heading of 'Meat, 'Fish' and 'Veg' are made with home-grown ingredients. Bookings are only taken for groups of 4 or more at the communal tables downstairs.

12 Denman St ✉ W1D 7HH **MAP: 2-I3**
✆ 7734 5612 — **www**.kricket.co.uk
⊖ Piccadilly Circus
Carte £20/27
Closed 25-26 December, 1 January and Sunday - bookings not accepted

LITTLE SOCIAL

French • Bistro

Jason Atherton's lively French bistro, opposite his Pollen Street Social restaurant, has a clubby feel and an appealing, deliberately worn look. Service is breezy and capable and the food is mostly classic with the odd modern twist.

5 Pollen St ✉ W1S 1NE **MAP: 2-H3**
020 7870 3730 — **www**.littlesocial.co.uk
Oxford Circus
Menu £25 - Carte £38/65
Closed Sunday and bank holidays - booking essential

MAGPIE

Modern cuisine • Fashionable

From the same team as Hackney's Pidgin. Sharing plates using an eclectic array of ingredients make for some original flavour pairings. This former gallery has an open feel and benefits from a large glass roof at the back; ask for one of the side booths.

10 Heddon St ✉ W1B 4BX **MAP: 2-H3**
020 3903 9096 — **www**.magpie-london.com
Oxford Circus
Menu £25 (lunch) - Carte £25/38
Closed Sunday dinner and bank holidays

MAYFAIR CHIPPY

Fish and chips • Vintage

There are chippies, and there is the Mayfair Chippy. Here you can get cocktails, wine, oysters, starters and dessert but, most significantly, the 'Mayfair Classic' - fried cod or haddock with chips, tartar sauce, mushy peas and curry sauce.

14 North Audley St ✉ W1K 6WE **MAP: 2-G3**
020 7741 2233 — **www**.eatbrit.com
Marble Arch
Carte £19/38
Closed 25 December and 1 January

MELE E PERE

Italian • Friendly

There's a small dining room on the ground floor but all the fun happens downstairs, where you'll find a large vermouth bar with vintage posters and plenty of seating in the buzzy vaulted room. The rustic Italian dishes hit the spot and the pre-theatre menu is great value.

46 Brewer St W1F 9TF **MAP: 2-I3**
020 7096 2096 — **www**.meleepere.co.uk
Piccadilly Circus

Menu £20 (lunch and early dinner) - Carte £22/39
Closed 25-26 December and 1 January

MOMO

Moroccan • Exotic décor

An authentic Moroccan atmosphere comes courtesy of the antiques, kilim rugs, Berber artwork, bright fabrics and lanterns - you'll feel you're eating near the souk. Go for the classic dishes: zaalouk, briouats, pigeon pastilla, and tagines with mountains of fluffy couscous.

25 Heddon St. W1B 4BH **MAP: 2-H3**
020 7434 4040 — **www**.momoresto.com
Oxford Circus

Menu £20 (weekday lunch) - Carte £32/49
Closed 25 December

NOBU

Japanese • Fashionable

Nobu restaurants are now all over the world but this was Europe's first and opened in 1997. It retains a certain exclusivity and is buzzy and fun. The menu is an innovative blend of Japanese cuisine with South American influences.

Metropolitan by COMO Hotel, 19 Old Park Ln W1Y 1LB **MAP: 2-G4**
020 7447 4747 — **www**.noburestaurants.com
Hyde Park Corner

Carte £24/73
Closed 25 December - booking essential

MURANO ✿

Italian • Fashionable

For some chefs, attaining a certain level of success means they all but abandon their stoves for the more glitzy existence of TV and travel. Not so Angela Hartnett, who is very much in evidence at her restaurants and none more so than at her flagship, Murano: the elegant yet understated restaurant named after the famous Venetian glassware.

Seasonal, Italian-inspired dishes – like baked potato gnocchi with homemade coppa and curly kale or Carnaroli risotto with Cornish crab – have their roots in the love of food and cooking engendered by her Italian grandparents, who came from Bardi in the heart of Emilia-Romagna. Angela's cooking exhibits an appealing lightness of touch, dishes are uncluttered and balanced, and flavours assured and defined. The well-organised service team strike the right balance between friendliness and formality.

FIRST COURSE

Scallops, whipped cod's roe, dill, cucumber and horseradish. • Spring vegetable tortellini with peas, broad beans and Rove des Garrigues.

MAIN COURSE

Lamb saddle, crispy shoulder, morels and wild garlic. • Dry-aged beef with celeriac.

DESSERT

Blood orange polenta cake with cream cheese sorbet. • Lemon parfait, eucalyptus, yoghurt and mint sorbet.

20 Queen St ✉ W1J 5PP **MAP: 2-G4**
✆ 020 7495 1127 — **www**.muranolondon.com
⊖ Green Park

Menu £28/70
Closed Christmas and Sunday

♿ A/C

NOBU BERKELEY ST

Japanese • Fashionable

This branch of the glamorous chain is more of a party animal than its elder sibling at The Metropolitan. Start with cocktails then head upstairs for Japanese food with South American influences; try dishes from the wood-fired oven.

15 Berkeley St. W1J 8DY **MAP: 2-H3**
020 7290 9222 — **www**.noburestaurants.com
Green Park
Carte £30/92
Closed 25 December - booking essential

NOPI

Mediterranean cuisine • Design

The bright, clean look of Yotam Ottolenghi's charmingly run all-day restaurant matches the fresh, invigorating food. The sharing plates take in the Mediterranean, the Middle East and Asia and the veggie dishes stand out.

21-22 Warwick St W1B 5NE **MAP: 2-H3**
020 7494 9584 — **www**.ottolenghi.co.uk
Piccadilly Circus
Carte £31/49
Closed 25-26 December, 1 January and Sunday dinner

---

100 WARDOUR ST

Modern cuisine • Contemporary décor

For a night out with a group of friends, this D&D place is worth considering. At night, head downstairs for cocktails, live music (well, this was once The Marquee Club) and a modern, Med-influenced menu with the odd Asian touch. During the day, the ground floor offers an all-day menu.

100 Wardour St W1F 0TN **MAP: 2-I3**
020 7314 4000 — **www**.100wardourst.com
Tottenham Court Road
Menu £42 - Carte £31/58
Closed 25-26 December and Sunday-Monday

PALOMAR

World cuisine • *Trendy*

A hip slice of modern-day Jerusalem in the heart of theatreland, with a zinc kitchen counter running back to an intimate wood-panelled dining room. Like the atmosphere, the contemporary Middle Eastern cooking is fresh and vibrant.

34 Rupert St W1D 6DN — **MAP: 2-I3**
020 7439 8777 — **www**.thepalomar.co.uk
Piccadilly Circus
Carte £17/40
Closed dinner 24-26 December

PARK CHINOIS

Chinese • *Exotic décor*

Old fashioned glamour, strikingly rich surroundings and live music combine to great effect at this sumptuously decorated restaurant. The menu traverses the length of China, with dim sum at lunchtimes and afternoon tea at weekends.

17 Berkeley St W1J 8EA — **MAP: 2-H3**
020 3327 8888 — **www**.parkchinois.com
Green Park
Menu £26 (lunch) - Carte £53/124
Closed 25 December - booking essential

PASTAIO

Italian • *Osteria*

Get ready to queue and even share a table - but at these prices who cares? This buzzy spot, a stone's throw from Carnaby Street, is all about pasta. It's made in-house daily by the all Italian team, with short and long semolina pasta extruded through bronze dies. The tiramisu is great too.

19 Ganton St W1F 9BN — **MAP: 2-H3**
020 3019 8680 — **www**.pastaio.london
Oxford Circus
Carte £24/28
Closed 25 December and 1 January - bookings not accepted

POLLEN STREET SOCIAL ✿

Creative • Fashionable

Pollen Street Social is where it all started for Jason Atherton when he went solo and, even though he now has an impressive international portfolio of restaurants to his name, it's clear it remains his flagship operation. Top quality British produce lies at the heart of a menu which offers a hugely appealing selection of modern dishes; the cooking is clearly undertaken with great care and the confident kitchen brings out the best in those ingredients. There are moments of originality and innovation, even the occasional little playfulness, but never for its own sake. The à la carte prices can get a little dizzying but there's a decent value lunch menu.

The wine list has impressive breadth and is rooted in the classic regions – and the care and consideration customers receive from the sommeliers is another of the restaurant's strengths. Think twice if you're offered a table in the bar area rather than in the main room, as you end up feeling a little detached from proceedings.

FIRST COURSE	MAIN COURSE	DESSERT
Slow-cooked Copper Maran egg with turnip purée, parmesan, sage and kombu crumb. • Crab salad with apple, coriander and brown crab on toast.	Lake District lamb loin & fillet with peas, broad beans and seaweed. • Roast sea bass with shellfish fondue and crushed potatoes.	Pistachio soufflé with 70% chocolate and vanilla ice cream. • Lemon, lime & olive oil sponge with honey crackling.

■ 8-10 Pollen St ✉ W1S 1NQ **MAP: 2-H3**
✆ 020 7290 7600 — **www.**pollenstreetsocial.com
⊖ Oxford Circus

■ Menu £37 (lunch) - Carte £64/78
Closed Sunday and bank holidays - booking essential

POLPETTO ☺

Italian • Simple

Order a negroni at the bar then start ordering some of those Italian-inspired small plates. Look for the daily specials on the blackboard but don't forget old favourites like the pork and beef meatballs. It's fun, busy and great for a quick bite.

■ 11 Berwick St ✉ W1F 0PL **MAP: 2-I3**
✆ 020 7439 8627 — **www**.polpo.co.uk
⊖ Tottenham Court Road
■ Carte £14/24

PORTRAIT ꙮ

Modern cuisine • Contemporary décor

Set on the top floor of National Portrait Gallery with views of local landmarks. Carefully prepared modern European food; dishes are sometimes created in celebration of current exhibitions. Good value pre-theatre and weekend set menus.

■ National Portrait Gallery (3rd floor), St Martin's Pl. ✉ WC2H 0HE **MAP: 2-I3**
✆ 020 7312 2490 — **www**.npg.org.uk/portraitrestaurant
⊖ Charing Cross
■ Menu £20/33 - Carte £37/87
Closed 24-26 December - booking essential - (lunch only and dinner Thursday-Saturday) XX

QUAGLINO'S ꙮ

Modern cuisine • Design

This colourful, glamorous restaurant manages to be cavernous and cosy at the same time, with live music and a late night bar adding a certain sultriness to proceedings. The kitchen specialises in contemporary brasserie-style food.

■ 16 Bury St ✉ SW1Y 6AJ **MAP: 2-H4**
✆ 020 7930 6767 — **www**.quaglinos-restaurant.co.uk
⊖ Green Park
■ Menu £33 - Carte £36/52
Closed Easter Monday and Sunday dinner

Ⓝ RAMBLA

Spanish • Tapas bar

The owner's childhood in Barcelona is celebrated here with an interesting range of Catalan-inspired dishes, which are punchy in flavour and designed to be shared. It's a simple unpretentious place dominated by an open kitchen; the best seats are at the counter.

64 Dean St W1D 4QQ **MAP: 2-I3**
020 7734 8428 — **www.**ramblalondon.com
Tottenham Court Road
Carte £22/39
Closed Christmas

SAKAGURA

Japanese • Exotic décor

A contemporary styled Japanese restaurant part owned by the Japan Centre and Gekkeikan, a sake manufacturer. Along with an impressive drinks list is an extensive menu covering a variety of styles; highlights include the skewers cooked on the robata charcoal grill.

8 Heddon St W1B 4BS **MAP: 2-H3**
020 3405 7230 — **www.**sakaguralondon.com
Oxford Circus
Carte £21/53
Closed 25 December

SAKE NO HANA

Japanese • Minimalist

A modern Japanese restaurant within a Grade II listed '60s edifice - and proof that you can occasionally find good food at the end of an escalator. As with the great cocktails, the menu is best enjoyed when shared with a group.

23 St James's SW1A 1HA **MAP: 2-H4**
020 7925 8988 — **www.**sakenohana.com
Green Park
Menu £34 (lunch and early dinner)/45 - Carte £39/123
Closed 25-26 December, Sunday and bank holiday Mondays

RITZ RESTAURANT ✿

Modern British • Luxury

Tyneside-born Executive Chef John Williams MBE has enjoyed an illustrious career over many years but the way he has developed the cooking at The Ritz will always be his crowning achievement. His traditionally structured kitchen has taken classic dishes, including some Escoffier recipes, and by using enormous skill and adding its own touches of modernity and finesse has lifted those dishes to new heights, while still respecting their spirit and heritage. Unsurprisingly, the ingredients used are from the far end of the ledger marked 'extravagant' and, along with a 'Menu Surprise' and the à la carte, are dishes for two on the 'Arts de le Table' menu that could include Beef Wellington and Gateaux St Honoré finished off at the table.

There is no restaurant in London grander than The Ritz. The lavish Louis XVI decoration makes this the place for the most special of special occasions – so it should come as no surprise that they insist on a jacket and tie.

FIRST COURSE

Artichoke royale with truffle, pear and Ragstone cheese. • Veal sweetbread with wild garlic, almonds and Madeira.

MAIN COURSE

Native lobster with broad beans, almond and lemon verbena. • St Brides chicken with truffle, leeks and suprême sauce.

DESSERT

Apple mousseline with marigold and buttermilk sorbet. • Vanilla mousse with strawberries and clotted cream.

■ Ritz Hotel, 150 Piccadilly ✉ W1J 9BR **MAP: 2-H4**
✆ 020 7300 2370 — **www**.theritzlondon.com
⊖ Green Park

■ Menu £57/67 - Carte £73/123

Ⓝ SABOR ✿

Spanish • Tapas bar

Heddon Street may not quite resemble a side street in Seville but it is one of those hidden alleys that can sometimes lead to serendipitous discoveries. Sabor is the brainchild of chef Nieves Barragán Mohacho, formerly of Barrafina, and she has created something authentic and truly joyful. Co-owner José Etura runs the front-of-house and has assembled a charming team.

There are three distinct areas: on the ground floor is the bar and opposite a counter serving tapas from all over Spain – start by ordering the pan con tomate. Upstairs is El Asador, the only area for which bookings are taken; here you sit at communal tables enjoying specialities from Galicia and Castile. There are two must-haves: succulent Segovian suckling pig – quartered, halved or whole – and roasted in the specially built oven and the melt-in-the-mouth octopus cooked in vast copper pans. You'll be licking your lips for hours.

FIRST COURSE	MAIN COURSE	DESSERT
Pulpo a feira. • Caldeira de raya.	Segovian suckling pig. • Frit Mallorquín.	Cuajada de turrón with oloroso cream. • Bombas de tres chocolates.

35-37 Heddon St ✉ W1B 4BR — **MAP: 2-H3**
✆ 020 3319 8130 — **www**.saborrestaurants.co.uk
⊖ Oxford Circus

Carte £24/40
Closed 24-26 December, 1-2 January, Sunday dinner and Monday
A/C

SCOTT'S

Seafood • Fashionable

Scott's is proof that a restaurant can have a long, proud history and still be fashionable, glamorous and relevant. It has a terrific clubby atmosphere and if you're in a two then the counter is a great spot. The choice of prime quality fish and shellfish is impressive.

20 Mount St ✉ W1K 2HE **MAP: 2-G3**
020 7495 7309 — **www**.scotts-restaurant.com
⊖ Bond Street
Carte £39/66
Closed 25-26 December

SCULLY

World cuisine • Friendly

The eponymous chef-owner's travels and family heritage inform his style of food. The small plates feature an array of international influences and the bold, diverse flavours give them an appealing vitality. The kitchen makes good use of the shelves of pickles and spices.

4 St James's Market ✉ SW1Y 4AH **MAP: 2-I3**
020 3911 6840 — **www**.scullyrestaurant.com
⊖ Piccadilly Circus
Carte £21/46
Closed dinner Sunday and bank holidays - booking essential

SEXY FISH

Seafood • Design

Everyone will have an opinion about the name but what's indisputable is that this is a very good looking restaurant, with works by Frank Gehry and Damien Hirst, and a stunning ceiling by Michael Roberts. The fish comes with various Asian influences but don't ignore the meat dishes like the beef rib skewers.

Berkeley Sq. ✉ W1J 6BR **MAP: 2-H3**
020 3764 2000 — **www**.sexyfish.com
⊖ Green Park
Carte £44/58
Closed 25-26 December

SEVEN PARK PLACE ❁

Modern cuisine • Cosy

You might have to breathe in a little to squeeze past the narrow bar on the way in to this restaurant at St James's Hotel and Club, but once you're settled into this gilded little box, you'll find yourself warming to the discreet and intimate setting. There are just nine tables so you can expect nods of appreciation from your fellow diners for discovering this secret little jewel.

2019 will see William Drabble celebrate 10 years in charge of the kitchen and it's a rare night if he's not at the stove. He trained and worked in some significant kitchens before joining the hotel and his style of food is unapologetically classic, both in the make-up and flavour combinations of his dishes but also in the techniques he uses to create them. Sauces are a particular strength but at the heart of his philosophy is the sourcing of great ingredients, like Rhug Estate chicken and Lune Valley lamb.

FIRST COURSE	MAIN COURSE	DESSERT
Lobster tail with cauliflower and truffle butter sauce. • Warm salad of quail with sweetbreads, foie gras, orange and hazelnuts.	Fillet of turbot with chestnut purée and wild mushrooms. • Assiette of rabbit with langoustines, young leeks and rosemary.	Dark chocolate ganache with caramelised banana. • Pineapple with rum and coconut sorbet.

St James's Hotel and Club, 7-8 Park Pl — **MAP: 2-H4**
✉ SW1A 1LS
020 7316 1615 — **www.**stjameshotelandclub.com
⊖ Green Park

Menu £28/95
Closed Sunday and Monday - booking essential
A/C

SKETCH (THE GALLERY) 🍴

Modern cuisine • Trendy

The striking 'Gallery' has a smart look from India Mahdavi and artwork from David Shrigley. At dinner the room transmogrifies from art gallery to fashionable restaurant, with a menu that mixes the classic, the modern and the esoteric.

9 Conduit St ✉ W1S 2XG — **MAP: 2-H3**
020 7659 4500 — **www**.sketch.london
Oxford Circus
Carte £43/86
Closed 25 December and 1 January - booking essential - (dinner only)

STREETXO 🍴

Creative • Trendy

The menu at Madrid chef David Muñoz's London outpost is inspired by European, Asian and even South American cuisines. Dishes are characterised by explosions of colour and a riot of different flavours, techniques and textures. The quasi-industrial feel of the basement room adds to the moody, noisy atmosphere.

15 Old Burlington St ✉ W1S 2JL — **MAP: 2-H3**
020 3096 7555 — **www**.streetxo.com
Oxford Circus
Menu £25 (weekday lunch) - Carte £45/68
Closed 23-26 December, 1 January and Monday lunch

TAMARIND KITCHEN 🍴

Indian • Exotic décor

A more relaxed sister to Tamarind in Mayfair, this Indian restaurant comes with endearingly earnest service and a lively buzz. There's a nominal Northern emphasis to the fairly priced menu, with Awadhi kababs a speciality, but there are also plenty of curries and fish dishes.

167-169 Wardour St ✉ W1F 8WR — **MAP: 2-I2**
020 7287 4243 — **www**.tamarindkitchen.co.uk
Tottenham Court Road
Menu £18 (lunch) - Carte £22/35
Closed 25-26 December, 1 January

SKETCH (THE LECTURE ROOM & LIBRARY) ✿✿

Modern French • *Luxury*

We all need a little luxury in our lives from time to time – so praise be for Mourad Mazouz and Pierre Gagnaire's 18C funhouse. As you're whisked past the braided rope and up the stairs to the Lecture Room & Library, you'll feel your expectations rise with every step. The room is lavishly decorated in a kaleidoscope of colours and the impeccably set tables are so far apart they're virtually in different postcodes. The staff are unfailingly polite and professional and it appears that nothing is too much trouble.

The French cooking bears all the Pierre Gagnaire hallmarks: the main 'plate' comes surrounded by a number of complementary dishes and at first you don't quite know what to focus on – now is the time to relax into that comfortable armchair and just enjoy the variety of textures and tastes, the complexity and depth of flavours and the quality of the ingredients.

The wine list is a tome of epic proportions; take the sommeliers' advice; they know what they're talking about. And do make sure you order the array of treats that make up the 'grand dessert' – pudding it ain't.

FIRST COURSE	MAIN COURSE	DESSERT
Live langoustines. • Red mullet with coastal aromatics.	Organic rack of pork with sage, mango vinegar and seasonal fruit. • Pan-roasted veal sweetbreads with angelica.	Pierre Gagnaire's 'Grand Dessert'. • Millefeuille with Tahitian vanilla mousseline.

■ 9 Conduit St (1st floor) ✉ W1S 2XG **MAP: 2-H3**
✆ 020 7659 4500 — **www**.sketch.london
⊖ Oxford Circus

■ Carte £102/131

Closed 25 December, 1 January, 2 weeks late August-early September, Sunday, Monday and lunch Tuesday-Thursday. – booking essential

A/C

SOCIAL EATING HOUSE ✿

Modern cuisine • Fashionable

The coolest joint in Jason Atherton's stable comes with distressed walls, moody lighting and a laid-back vibe – it also has a terrific speakeasy-style bar upstairs. The serving team may look as though they've just been chopping wood outside but they know the menu backwards, offer great advice and contribute enormously to the overall fun of the place.

The 'Sampler' menu is an easy way of experiencing the full breadth of the kitchen's talents, although the à la carte also shows the modern cooking style to full effect. Influences are international, with effective combinations of flavours being punchy and well-judged. Food miles from the largely British suppliers are shown on the reverse of the menu. Cumbrian steaks are a speciality and are 40, 45 or 60 day aged, expertly cooked on the Josper grill and rested. The well-chosen wine list includes some eclectic choices by the glass.

FIRST COURSE	MAIN COURSE	DESSERT
Truffled Royal Legbar egg, Iberico de Bellota with Jerusalem artichoke. • Seared mackerel with cider, green apple, cauliflower and curry oil.	Slow-cooked rump of salt marsh lamb with olive oil mash, pickled turnips and sauce niçoise. • Brown butter poached cod with peas cucumber and mussel cream.	Peanut butter parfait with cherry sorbet, almond and griottine cherry. • Butternut crème brûlée with lemon thyme ice cream and yoghurt.

58 Poland St ✉ W1F 7NR — **MAP: 2-H3**
✆ 020 7993 3251 — **www**.socialeatinghouse.com
⊖ Oxford Circus

Menu £27/36 - Carte £49/60
Closed Christmas, Sunday and bank holidays
♿ A/C 🍸

THE SQUARE ✿

Creative French • Elegant

This landmark restaurant wasn't just refurbished and re-launched - you really sense that a new era has begun. At the helm in the kitchen is Clément Leroy, a proud Frenchman who's also respectful of the UK and keen to celebrate the country's produce. Cornish mackerel and lobster, Lincolnshire eel, Scottish langoustines and Cumbrian beef all feature on his menu, albeit with the occasional imaginative or even playful twist - his Orkney scallops, for example, come with coffee and Marsala. The pastry section is headed up by Japanese-born Aya Tamura, who is Clément's wife; her desserts display the occasional Asian note and are equally intriguing and refined.

The room has a sleeker, more contemporary look these days and more is made of the artwork. Service remains as polished and attentive as ever and the wine list has enormous depth.

FIRST COURSE	MAIN COURSE	DESSERT
Orkney scallop with coffee and marsala. • Smoked Lincolnshire eel with caviar.	Aged Herdwick lamb 'earth and sea'. • Crisp red mullet with black pepper sauce.	St John's Wood honey with grapefruit and sweet potato. • Harlequin soufflé with cascara frappé

6-10 Bruton St. ✉ W1J 6PU — MAP: 2-H3
✆ 020 7495 7100 — **www**.squarerestaurant.com
⊖ Green Park

Menu £37/85
Closed 24-26 December and Sunday

TEMPER

Barbecue • Contemporary décor

A fun, basement restaurant all about barbecue and meats. The beasts are cooked whole, some are also smoked in-house and there's a distinct South African flavour to the salsas that accompany them. Kick off with some tacos - they make around 1,200 of them every day.

25 Broadwick St W1F 0DF — MAP: 2-H/13
020 3879 3834 — **www**.temperrestaurant.com
Oxford Circus
Carte £20/40
Closed 25-26 December and 1 January

THEO RANDALL

Italian • Classic décor

There's an attractive honesty about Theo Randall's Italian food, which is made using the very best of ingredients. The somewhat corporate nature of the hotel in which it is located can sometimes seem a little at odds with the rustic style of food but the room is bright, relaxed and well run.

InterContinental London Park Lane Hotel, 1 Hamilton Pl, Park Ln W1J 7QY — MAP: 2-G4
73188747 — **www**.theorandall.com
Hyde Park Corner
Menu £29 (weekday lunch) - Carte £35/63
Closed 25 December

TOKIMEITĒ

Japanese • Chic

Yoshihiro Murata, one of Japan's most celebrated chefs, teamed up with the Zen-Noh group to open this good looking, intimate restaurant on two floors. Their aim is to promote Wagyu beef in Europe, so it's understandably the star of the show.

23 Conduit St W1S 2XS — MAP: 2-H3
020 3826 4411 — **www**.tokimeite.com
Oxford Circus
Menu £25 (lunch) - Carte £40/106
Closed Sunday and bank holidays

UMU ✿✿

Japanese • Fashionable

The kaiseki menu is the best way to truly experience chef Yoshinori Ishii's cuisine – he trained at Kitcho in Kyoto, a bastion of tradition where the central tenets and philosophy of kaiseki are preserved and celebrated. Here at Umu he has steadily been shifting the food away from a Western idea of Japanese food to a more authentic base, which means that flavours are more delicate and subtle than many expect. It hasn't always been easy: to get hold of fish in the right condition he went out with Cornish fishermen himself to teach them the ikejime method of killing fish – and you'll see the benefit in the firmer texture of the tsukuri. But that's not to say he's trying to replicate what happens in Kyoto – he wisely acknowledges that this is a London restaurant by incorporating the best of the UK's larder as well as dropping in an occasional playfulness.

Instead of tatami rooms you'll find a neatly laid out restaurant making good use of warm woods and natural materials.

FIRST COURSE

Cornish cuttlefish with bottarga and tosazu sauce. • Homemade tofu with ginger and spring onion.

MAIN COURSE

Wagyu tataki with vegetables and a sesame and ponzu sauce. • Lightly grilled tuna back and belly.

DESSERT

Japanese seasonal tiramisu with matcha tea and ginjo sake. • Warm chocolate sponge with genmaicha ice cream.

14-16 Bruton Pl. ✉ W1J 6LX **MAP: 2-H3**
✆ 020 7499 8881 — **www**.umurestaurant.com
⊖ Bond Street

Menu £45/155 - Carte £46/151
Closed Christmas, New Year and Sunday
A/C

VASCO AND PIERO'S PAVILION

Italian • Friendly

Regulars and tourists have been flocking to this institution for over 40 years; its longevity is down to a twice daily changing menu of Umbrian-influenced dishes rather than the matter-of-fact service or simple decoration.

15 Poland St W1F 8QE **MAP: 2-H2/3**
020 7437 8774 – **www**.vascosfood.com
Oxford Circus

Carte £28/48
Closed Saturday lunch, Sunday and bank holidays - booking essential at lunch

---

WILD HONEY

Modern cuisine • Design

The elegant wood panelling and ornate plasterwork may say 'classic Mayfair institution' but the personable service team keep the atmosphere enjoyably easy-going. The kitchen uses quality British ingredients and a French base but is not afraid of the occasional international flavour.

12 St George St. W1S 2FB **MAP: 2-H3**
020 7758 9160 – **www**.wildhoneyrestaurant.co.uk
Oxford Circus

Menu £35 (lunch and early dinner) - Carte £33/59
Closed 25-26 December, 1 January, Sunday and bank holidays except Good Friday

---

THE WOLSELEY

Modern cuisine • Fashionable

This feels like a grand and glamorous European coffee house, with its pillars and high vaulted ceiling. Appealing menus offer everything from caviar to a hotdog. It's open from early until late and boasts a large celebrity following.

160 Piccadilly W1J 9EB **MAP: 2-H4**
020 7499 6996 – **www**.thewolseley.com
Green Park

Carte £25/76
Booking essential

VEERASWAMY ✿

Indian • Design

The traditionally attired doorman sets the tone for the restaurant itself which is decorated in a subtle yet colourful style, thanks largely to the glass lanterns and chandeliers. London's oldest surviving Indian restaurant may have opened in 1926 but it's always full of life – as soon as you get out of the lift, you're aware of the bustle and the vitality. It is also run with enormous charm by an enthusiastic team – even when there's a mass exodus in the early evening by those heading to the theatre they display a reassuring calmness.

You can opt for royal recipes like Pista Ka Salan (chicken with pistachio and aniseed) or Patiala Shahi Raan (slow-cooked lamb shank) or for dishes from various regions of the country. The Hyderabadi lamb biryani has been on the menu since opening day but, like all the dishes, boasts a fresh, invigorating taste thanks to the judicious spicing.

FIRST COURSE

Venison mutta kebab with tamarind glaze. • Angara chicken tikka with garam masala and mace.

MAIN COURSE

Goan roast duck vindaloo. • Travancore prawn curry with coconut and kokum flowers.

DESSERT

Rasmalai with tandoori fruit. • Chocolate ganache with chilli and lime crème.

Victory House, 99 Regent St
(Entrance on Swallow St.) ✉ W1B 4RS
020 7734 1401 — **www**.veeraswamy.com
⊖ Piccadilly Circus

MAP: 2-H3

Menu £26/45 - Carte £40/76

XU

Asian • Chic

They've squeezed a lot into the two floors to create the feel of 1930s Taipei, including an emerald lacquered tea kiosk and mahjong tables. Don't miss the numbing beef tendon and classics like Shou Pa chicken. Tofu is made in-house and Chi Shiang rice is flown in from Taiwan.

30 Rupert St ✉ W1D 6DL — MAP: 2-13
020 3319 8147 — **www**.xulondon.com
Piccadilly Circus
Menu £18 (lunch) - Carte £22/38
Closed 25-26 December - booking essential
A/C

ZELMAN MEATS

Meats and grills • Rustic

Those clever Goodman people noticed a lack of affordable steakhouses and so opened this fun, semi-industrial space. They serve three cuts of beef: sliced picanha (from the rump), Chateaubriand, and a wonderfully smoky short rib.

2 St Anne's Ct ✉ W1F 0AZ — MAP: 2-13
020 7437 0566 — **www**.zelmanmeats.com
Tottenham Court Rd
Carte £18/49
Closed Monday lunch and bank holidays

Remember, stars ✿ are awarded for cuisine only! Elements such as service and décor are not a factor.

YAUATCHA SOHO ✿

Chinese • Design

One of Soho's grandees, the original Yauatcha may have been here fifteen years, but thanks to subtle changes it still manages to feel fresh and contemporary. The bright ground floor is home to well-spaced tables, a bar and a patisserie offering chocolates and macaroons to take home, while downstairs offers a moody basement with low banquettes, an aquarium bar and a sparkly star-lit ceiling.

The extensive à la carte means there's something for everyone, from seafood to excellent ribs, and over-ordering is easy to do. Cooking is undertaken with care and consistency and dishes are colourful and attractive with strong flavours and excellent texture contrasts. Stand-outs include the scallop shui mai, the duck roll and the wonderfully light venison puff. Dishes arrive at a good pace and prices are pretty good when you consider how much food you get for your money. Tea is the natural choice when it comes to what to drink – but the cocktails are definitely worth exploring too.

FIRST COURSE	MAIN COURSE	DESSERT
Scallop shu mai. • Wagyu beef puff.	Stir-fried rib-eye beef. • Spicy steamed sea bass with pickled chilli.	Chocolate pebble. • Lemon sesame tart.

15 Broadwick St ✉ W1F 0DL — **MAP: 2-13**
✆ 020 7494 8888 — **www**.yauatcha.com
⊖ Tottenham Court Road

Carte £25/65
Closed 25 December

THE LION KING
Crispins FOOD
Raza Sayang

STRAND · COVENT GARDEN

It's fitting that Manet's world famous painting 'Bar at the Folies Bergère' should hang in the **Strand** within a champagne cork's throw of theatreland and Covent Garden. This is the area perhaps more than any other which draws in the ticket-buying tourist, eager to grab a good deal on one of the many shows on offer, or eat and drink at fabled landmarks like J.Sheekey or Rules. It's here the names already up in lights shine down on their potential usurpers: celeb wannabes heading for The Ivy, West Street's perennially fashionable restaurant. It's here, too, that Nell Gwyn set up home under the patronage of Charles II, while Oscar Wilde revelled in his success by taking rooms at the Savoy.

The hub of the whole area is the piazza at **Covent Garden,** created by Inigo Jones four hundred years ago. It was given a brash new lease of life in the 1980s after its famed fruit and veg market was pulled up by the roots and re-sown in Battersea. Council bigwigs realised then that 'what we have we hold', and any further redevelopment of the area is banned. Where everyone heads is the impressive covered market, within which a colourful jumble of arts and crafts shops gels with al fresco cafés and classical performers proffering Paganini with your cappuccino. Outside, under the portico of St Paul's church, every type of street performer does a turn for the tourist trade. The best shops in Covent Garden, though, are a few streets north of the market melee, emanating out like bicycle spokes from Seven Dials.

For those after a more highbrow experience, one of London's best attractions is a hop, skip and *grand jeté* from the market. Around the corner in **Bow Street** is the city's famed home for opera and ballet, where fire – as well as show-stopping performances – has been known to bring the house down. The **Royal Opera House** is now in its third incarnation, and it gets more impressive with each rebuild. The handsome, glass-roofed Paul Hamlyn Hall is a must-see, so enjoy a drink in the Champagne Bar before curtain up or during the interval. At the other end of the Strand the **London Coliseum** offers more opera, this time all performed in English. Down by Waterloo Bridge, art lovers are strongly advised to stop at **Somerset House** and take in one of London's most sublime collections of art at the Courtauld Gallery. This is where you can get up close and personal to Manet's barmaid, as well as an astonishing array of Impressionist masters and twentieth century greats. The icing on the cake is the compact and accessible eighteenth century building that houses the collection: real icing on a real cake can be found in a super little hidden-away café downstairs.

Of a different order altogether is the huge **National Gallery** at Trafalgar Square which houses more than two thousand Western European pieces (it started off with 38). A visit to the modern Sainsbury Wing is rewarded with some unmissable works from the Renaissance. It can get just as crowded in the capital's largest Gallery as in the square outside, so a good idea is to wander down **Villiers Street** next to Charing Cross station and breathe the Thames air along the Victoria Embankment. Behind you is the grand Savoy Hotel; for a better view of it, you can head even further away from the crowds on a boat trip from the **Embankment,** complete with on-board entertainment. And if the glory of travel in the capital, albeit on the water, has whetted your appetite for more, then pop into the impressively renovated Transport Museum in Covent Garden piazza, where gloriously preserved tubes, buses and trains from the past put you in a positive frame of mind for the real live working version you'll very probably be tackling later in the day.

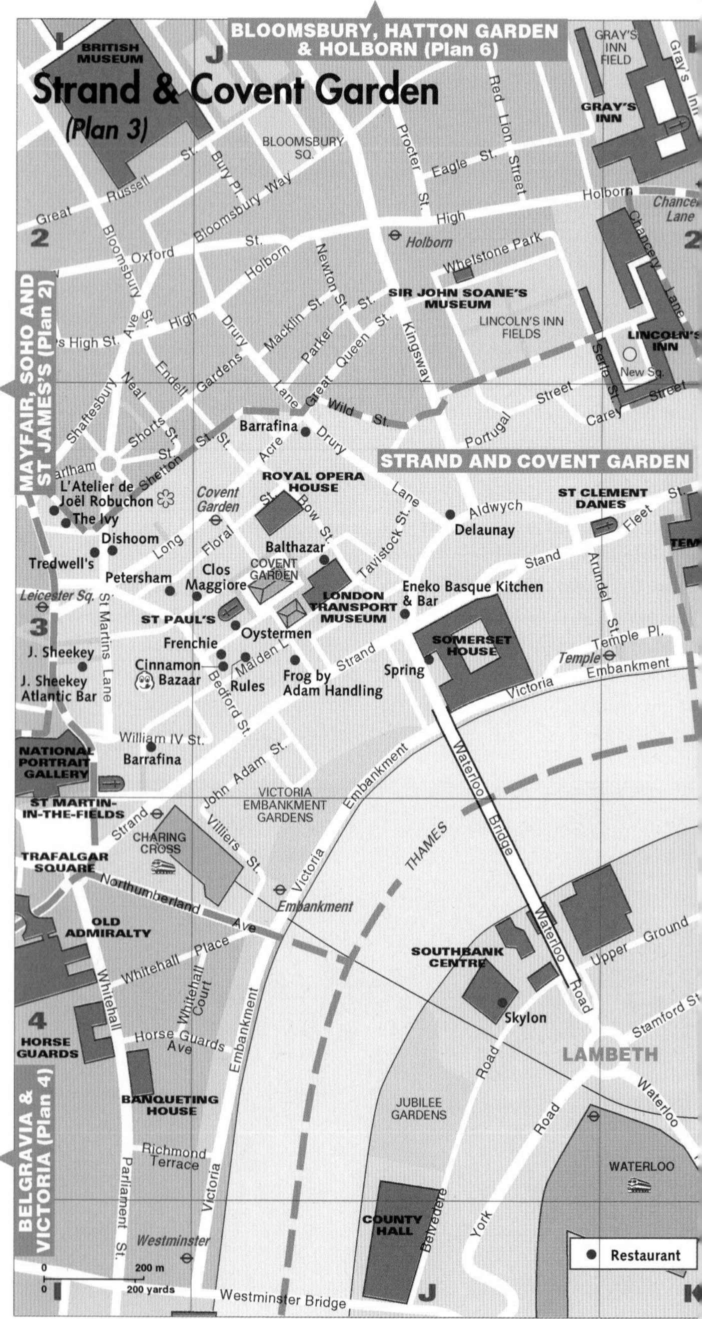

Strand & Covent Garden
(Plan 3)
BLOOMSBURY, HATTON GARDEN & HOLBORN (Plan 6)
MAYFAIR, SOHO AND ST JAMES'S (Plan 2)
BELGRAVIA & VICTORIA (Plan 4)
STRAND AND COVENT GARDEN
BRITISH MUSEUM
BLOOMSBURY SQ.
GRAY'S INN FIELD
GRAY'S INN
SIR JOHN SOANE'S MUSEUM
LINCOLN'S INN FIELDS
LINCOLN'S INN
New Sq.
ROYAL OPERA HOUSE
COVENT GARDEN
LONDON TRANSPORT MUSEUM
ST PAUL'S
ST CLEMENT DANES
SOMERSET HOUSE
NATIONAL PORTRAIT GALLERY
ST MARTIN-IN-THE-FIELDS
TRAFALGAR SQUARE
CHARING CROSS
VICTORIA EMBANKMENT GARDENS
OLD ADMIRALTY
HORSE GUARDS
BANQUETING HOUSE
SOUTHBANK CENTRE
LAMBETH
JUBILEE GARDENS
COUNTY HALL
WATERLOO
THAMES
Holborn
Covent Garden
Leicester Sq.
Temple
Embankment
Westminster
Barrafina
L'Atelier de Joël Robuchon
The Ivy
Dishoom
Tredwell's
Petersham
Clos Maggiore
Balthazar
Delaunay
Eneko Basque Kitchen & Bar
Oystermen
Frenchie
Cinnamon Bazaar
Rules
Frog by Adam Handling
Spring
J. Sheekey
J. Sheekey Atlantic Bar
Skylon
Great Russell St.
Bury Pl.
Bloomsbury Way
Oxford St.
Bloomsbury St.
High Holborn
Newton St.
Procter St.
Red Lion Street
Eagle St.
Whetstone Park
Chancery Lane
Kingsway
Macklin St.
Parker St.
Great Queen St.
Drury Lane
Endell St.
Neal St.
Shaftesbury Ave
Shorts Gardens
Wild St.
Portugal Street
Serle St.
Carey Street
Shelton St.
Long Acre
Floral St.
Bow St.
Tavistock St.
Aldwych
Strand
Fleet St.
Arundel St.
Temple Pl.
Victoria Embankment
St Martins Lane
Maiden L.
Bedford St.
William IV St.
John Adam St.
Villiers St.
Northumberland Ave
Whitehall Place
Whitehall Court
Whitehall
Horse Guards Ave
Richmond Terrace
Parliament St.
Westminster Bridge
Waterloo Bridge
Waterloo Road
Upper Ground
Stamford St.
Belvedere Road
York Road
Restaurant
200 m
200 yards

L'ATELIER DE JOËL ROBUCHON ✿

French • Elegant

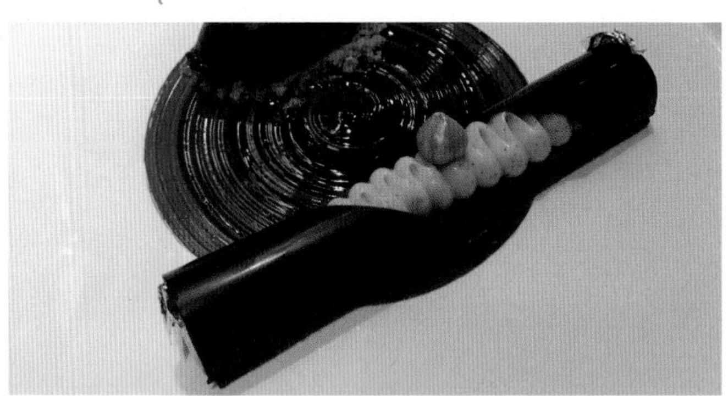

For a special night out in the West End, this restaurant should be on everyone's list; it's sexy and lively, with intensely flavoured cooking, confident, capable staff and an atmospheric top floor bar. It differs from many of the Ateliers around the world as it features two dining experiences under one roof: on the ground floor is the moody red and black L'Atelier, with its counter dining and open kitchen, while upstairs monochrome La Cuisine offers table dining in an intimate setting just a few nights a week. Apart from a few wood-fired dishes upstairs, the menus are largely similar.

Those here to celebrate should go all out with the 8-course menu découverte. Cooking is assured and accomplished, with an emphasis on the Mediterranean; dishes are creative and well-balanced, and there's a pleasing simplicity to their presentation – despite the fact that there are over thirty chefs in the building.

FIRST COURSE	MAIN COURSE	DESSERT
Langoustine and truffle ravioli with Savoy cabbage. • Poached egg with wild mushrooms, sherry and crispy bacon.	Oxtail braised with chestnuts, bone marrow and black truffle. • Lightly-smoked sea trout with spring forage and buttermilk.	Exotic fruit soufflé with coconut ice cream. • Creamy Manjari chocolate mousse with cookie crumb.

13-15 West St. ✉ WC2H 9NE — **MAP: 3-13**
✆ 020 7010 8600 — **www.**joelrobuchon.co.uk
⊖ Leicester Square

Menu £45 (lunch and early dinner) - Carte £65/117
Closed 25 December

BALTHAZAR

French • Brasserie

Those who know the original Balthazar in Manhattan's SoHo district will find the London version of this classic brasserie uncannily familiar in looks, vibe and food. The Franglais menu keeps it simple and the cocktails are great.

4-6 Russell St. WC2B 5HZ **MAP: 3-J3**
020 3301 1155 — **www**.balthazarlondon.com
Covent Garden
Menu £23 (lunch and early dinner) - Carte £31/73
Closed 25 December - booking essential

BARRAFINA

Spanish • Tapas bar

The second Barrafina is not just brighter than the Soho original - it's bigger too, so you can wait inside with a drink for counter seats to become available. Try more unusual tapas like ortiguillas, frit Mallorquin or the succulent meats.

10 Adelaide St WC2N 4HZ **MAP: 3-I3**
020 7440 1456 — **www**.barrafina.co.uk
Charing Cross
Carte £27/52
Closed Christmas, New Year and bank holidays - bookings not accepted

---

BARRAFINA

Spanish • Tapas bar

The third of the Barrafinas is tucked away at the far end of Covent Garden; arrive early or prepare to queue. Fresh, vibrantly flavoured fish and shellfish dishes are a real highlight; tortillas y huevos also feature.

43 Drury Ln WC2B 5AJ **MAP: 3-J3**
020 7440 1456 — **www**.barrafina.co.uk
Covent Garden
Carte £27/52
Closed 25-26 December, 27 May and 26 August - bookings not accepted

CINNAMON BAZAAR

Indian • Exotic décor

Vivek Singh's latest venture provides relaxed, all-day contemporary Indian dining in the heart of Covent Garden, with a bright, colourful interior evoking a marketplace. Menus are influenced by the trade routes of the subcontinent, with twists that encompass Afghanistan, the Punjab and the Middle East.

28 Maiden Ln ✉ WC2E 7JS — **MAP: 3-J3**
020 7395 1400 — **www**.cinnamon-bazaar.com
⊖ Leicester Square
Menu £17/24 - Carte £20/38

CLOS MAGGIORE

French • Classic décor

One of London's most romantic restaurants - but be sure to ask for the enchanting conservatory with its retractable roof. The sophisticated French cooking is joined by a wine list of great depth. Good value and very popular pre/post theatre menus.

33 King St ✉ WC2E 8JD — **MAP: 3-J3**
020 7379 9696 — **www**.closmaggiore.com
⊖ Leicester Square
Menu £30 (weekday lunch)/37 - Carte £44/64
Closed 24-25 December

DELAUNAY

Modern cuisine • Elegant

The Delaunay was inspired by the grand cafés of Europe but, despite sharing the same buzz and celebrity clientele as its sibling The Wolseley, is not just a mere replica. The all-day menu is more mittel-European, with great schnitzels and wieners.

55 Aldwych ✉ WC2B 4BB — **MAP: 3-J3**
020 7499 8558 — **www**.thedelaunay.com
⊖ Temple
Carte £31/70
Closed 25 December - booking essential

DISHOOM

Indian • Trendy

Expect long queues at this group's original branch. It's based on a Bombay café, of the sort opened by Iranian immigrants in the early 20C. Try vada pau (Bombay's version of the chip butty), a curry or grilled meats; and finish with kulfi on a stick. It's lively, a touch chaotic but great fun.

MAP: 3-I3

12 Upper St Martin's Ln ✉ WC2H 9FB
020 7420 9320 — **www**.dishoom.com
Leicester Square

Carte £14/28
Closed dinner 24 December, 25-26 December and 1-2 January - bookings not accepted

---

ENEKO BASQUE KITCHEN & BAR

Basque • Design

Set in the One Aldwych Hotel, this stylish, ultra-modern restaurant features curved semi-private booths and a bar which seems to float above like a spaceship. Menus offer a refined reinterpretation of classic Basque dishes.

One Aldwych Hotel, 1 Aldwych ✉ WC2B 4BZ **MAP: 3-J3**
020 7300 0300 — **www**.eneko.london
Temple

Menu £22 (lunch and early dinner) - Carte £26/89

FRENCHIE

Modern cuisine • Bistro

A well-run modern-day bistro - younger sister to the Paris original, which shares the name given to chef-owner Greg Marchand when he was head chef at Fifteen. The adventurous, ambitious cooking is informed by his extensive travels.

16 Henrietta St ✉ WC2E 8QH **MAP: 3-J3**
020 7836 4422 — **www**.frenchiecoventgarden.com
Covent Garden

Menu £27 (lunch) - Carte £45/60
Closed 25-26 December and 1 January

Ⓝ FROG BY ADAM HANDLING

Modern cuisine • Fashionable

The chef put his name in the title to signify that this is the flagship of his bourgeoning group. His dishes, which change regularly, are attractive creations and quite detailed in their composition. The well-run room is not without some understated elegance.

34-35 Southampton St ✉ WC2E 7HG **MAP: 3-J3**
✆ 020 7199 8370 — **www**.frogbyadamhandling.com
⊖ Charing Cross
Menu £35 (lunch and early dinner) - Carte £48/61
Closed Sunday

THE IVY

Traditional British • Fashionable

This landmark restaurant has had a facelift and while the glamorous clientele remain, it now has an oval bar as its focal point. The menu offers international dishes alongside the old favourites and personable staff anticipate your every need.

9 West St ✉ WC2H 9NE **MAP: 3-I3**
✆ 020 7836 4751 — **www**.the-ivy.co.uk
⊖ Leicester Square
Menu £24 (weekday lunch) - Carte £32/74
Closed 25 December

J.SHEEKEY

Seafood • Fashionable

Festooned with photographs of actors and linked to the theatrical world since opening in 1890. Wood panels and alcove tables add famed intimacy. Accomplished seafood cooking.

28-32 St Martin's Ct ✉ WC2N 4AL **MAP: 3-I3**
✆ 020 7240 2565 — **www**.j-sheekey.co.uk
⊖ Leicester Square
Carte £40/72
Closed 25-26 December - booking essential

J.SHEEKEY ATLANTIC BAR ꟾO

Seafood • Intimate

An addendum to J. Sheekey restaurant. Sit at the bar to watch the chefs prepare the same quality seafood as next door but at slightly lower prices; fish pie and fruits de mer are the popular choices. Open all day.

33-34 St Martin's Ct. ✉ WC2 4AL — **MAP: 3-I3**
✆ 020 7240 2565 — **www**.jsheekeyatlanticbar.co.uk
⊖ Leicester Square
Carte £22/49
Closed 25-26 December

Ⓝ OYSTERMEN ꟾO

Seafood • Rustic

Covent Garden isn't an area usually associated with independent restaurants but this bustling and modestly decorated little spot is thriving. From its tiny open kitchen come oysters, crabs and expertly cooked fish.

32 Henrietta St ✉ WC2E 8NA — **MAP: 3-J3**
✆ 020 7240 4417 — **www**.oystermen.co.uk
⊖ Covent Garden
Carte £28/48
Closed 25 December-1 January

Ⓝ PETERSHAM ꟾO

Mediterranean cuisine • Elegant

Along with a deli, shop and florist is this elegant restaurant with contemporary art, Murano glass and an abundance of fresh flowers. The Italian-based menu uses produce from their Richmond nursery and Devon farm. The lovely terrace is shared with La Goccia, their more informal spot for sharing plates.

2 Floral Court ✉ WC2E 9FB — **MAP: 3-I3**
✆ 020 7305 7676 — **www**.petershamnurseries.com
⊖ Covent Garden
Carte £42/73

RULES

Traditional British • Traditional décor

London's oldest restaurant boasts a fine collection of antique cartoons, drawings and paintings. Tradition continues in the menu, specialising in game from its own estate.

35 Maiden Ln ✉ WC2E 7LB **MAP: 3-J3**
020 7836 5314 — **www**.rules.co.uk
⊖ Leicester Square
Carte £39/70
Closed 25-26 December - booking essential

SPRING

Italian • Fashionable

Spring occupies the 'new wing' of Somerset House that for many years was inhabited by the Inland Revenue. It's a bright, feminine space under the aegis of chef Skye Gyngell. Her cooking is Italian-influenced and ingredient-led.

New Wing, Somerset House, Strand (Entrance on Lancaster Pl) ✉ WC2R 1LA **MAP: 3-J3**
020 3011 0115 — **www**.springrestaurant.co.uk
⊖ Temple
Menu £32 (lunch) - Carte £41/63
Closed Sunday

TREDWELLS

Modern British • Brasserie

Chef-owner Chantelle Nicholson's contemporary cooking makes good use of British ingredients and also displays the occasional Asian twist. It's set over three floors, with a subtle art deco feel. A good choice for a Sunday roast.

4a Upper St Martin's Ln ✉ WC2H 9EF **MAP: 3-I3**
020 3764 0840 — **www**.tredwells.com
⊖ Leicester Square
Menu £30 (lunch and early dinner) - Carte £29/57
Closed 24-26 December and 1 January

BELGRAVIA · VICTORIA

The well-worn cliché 'an area of contrasts' certainly applies to these ill-matched neighbours. To the west, Belgravia equates to fashionable status and elegant, residential calm; to the east, Victoria is a chaotic jumble of backpackers, milling commuters and cheap-and-not-always-so-cheerful hotels. At first sight, you might think there's little to no common ground, but the umbilical cord that unites them is, strange to say, diplomacy and politics. Belgravia's embassies are dotted all around the environs of **Belgrave Square,** while at the furthest end of bustling Victoria Street stands **Parliament Square.**

Belgravia – named after 'beautiful grove' in French - was developed during the nineteenth century by Richard Grosvenor, the second Marquess of Westminster, who employed top architect Thomas Cubitt to come up with something rather fetching for the upper echelons of society. The grandeur of the classical designs has survived for the best part of two centuries, evident in the broad streets and elegant squares, where the rich rub shoulders with the uber-rich beneath the stylish balconies of a consulate or outside a high-end antiques emporium. You can still sample an atmosphere of the village it once was, as long as your idea of a village includes exclusive designer boutiques and even more exclusive mews cottages.

By any stretch of the imagination you'd have trouble thinking of **Victoria** as a village. Its local railway station is one of London's major hubs and its coach station brings in visitors from not only all corners of Britain, but Europe too. Its main 'church', concealed behind office blocks, could hardly be described as humble, either: **Westminster Cathedral** is a grand concoction based on Istanbul's Hagia Sophia, with a view from the top of the bell tower which is breathtaking. From there you can pick out other hidden charms of the area: the dramatic headquarters of Channel 4 TV, the revolving sign famously leading into New Scotland Yard, and the neat little Christchurch Gardens, burial site of Colonel Blood, last man to try and steal the Crown Jewels. Slightly easier for the eye to locate are the grand designs of **Westminster Abbey,** crowning glory and resting place of most of England's kings and queens, and the neo-gothic pile of the **Houses of Parliament.** Victoria may be an eclectic mix of people and architectural styles, but its handy position as a kind of epicentre of the Westminster Village makes it a great place for political chit-chat. And the place to go for that is The Speaker, a pub in Great Peter Street, named after the Commons' centuries-old peacekeeper and 'referee'. It's a backstreet gem, where it's not unknown for a big cheese from the House to be filmed over a pint.

Winston Churchill is someone who would have been quite at home holding forth at The Speaker, and half a mile away in King Charles Street, based within the **Cabinet War Rooms** – the secret underground HQ of the war effort - is the Churchill Museum, stuffed full of all things Churchillian. However, if your passion is more the easel and the brush, then head down to the river where another great institution of the area, **Tate Britain,** gazes out over the Thames. Standing where the grizzly Millbank Penitentiary once festered, it offers, after the National Gallery, the best collection of historical art in London. There's loads of space for the likes of Turner and Constable, while Hogarth, Gainsborough and Blake are well represented, too. Artists from the modern era are also here, with Freud and Hockney on show, and there are regular installations showcasing upwardly mobile British talent. All of which may give you the taste for a trip east along the river to Tate Modern; this can be done every forty minutes courtesy of the Tate to Tate boat service.

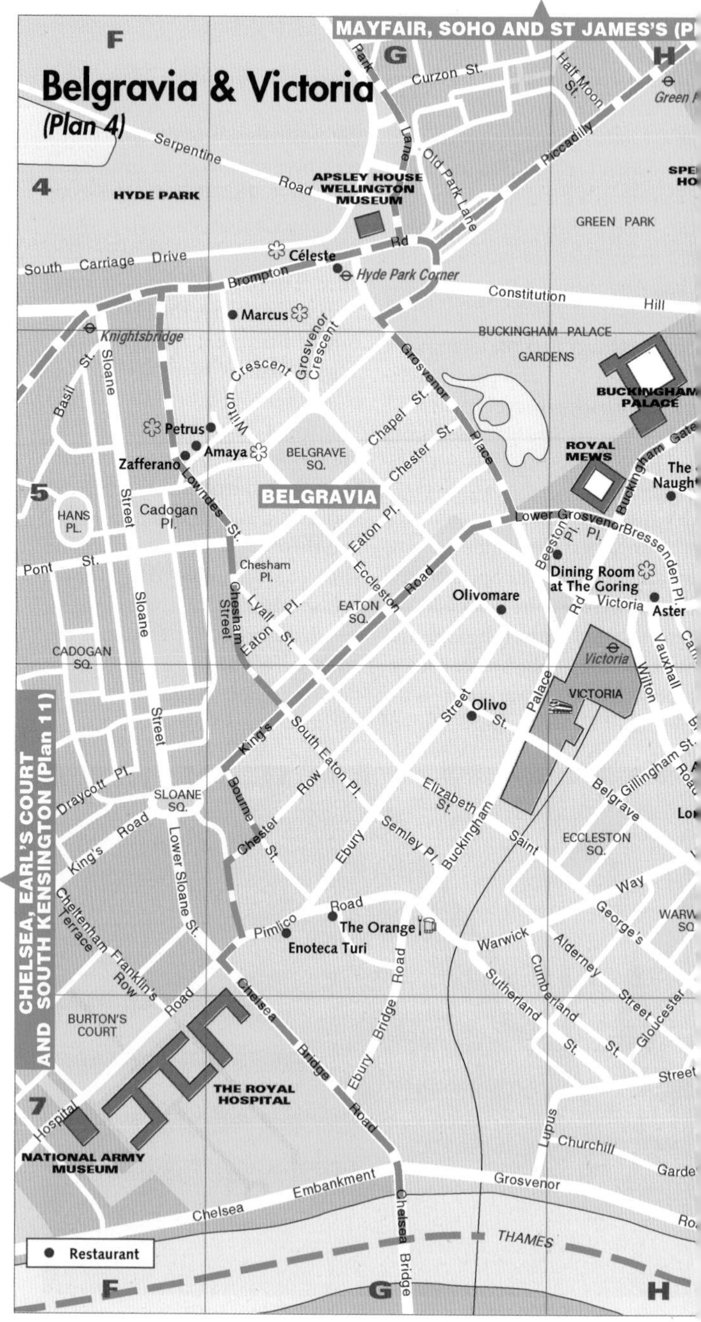

Belgravia & Victoria
(Plan 4)
MAYFAIR, SOHO AND ST JAMES'S
CHELSEA, EARL'S COURT AND SOUTH KENSINGTON (Plan 11)
HYDE PARK
APSLEY HOUSE WELLINGTON MUSEUM
GREEN PARK
Céleste
Hyde Park Corner
Marcus
Knightsbridge
BUCKINGHAM PALACE GARDENS
BUCKINGHAM PALACE
ROYAL MEWS
Petrus
Amaya
Zafferano
BELGRAVE SQ.
BELGRAVIA
HANS PL.
Cadogan Pl.
Chesham Pl.
EATON SQ.
Dining Room at The Goring
Olivomare
Aster
CADOGAN SQ.
Victoria
VICTORIA
Olivo
SLOANE SQ.
ECCLESTON SQ.
The Orange
Enoteca Turi
BURTON'S COURT
THE ROYAL HOSPITAL
NATIONAL ARMY MUSEUM
THAMES
Restaurant

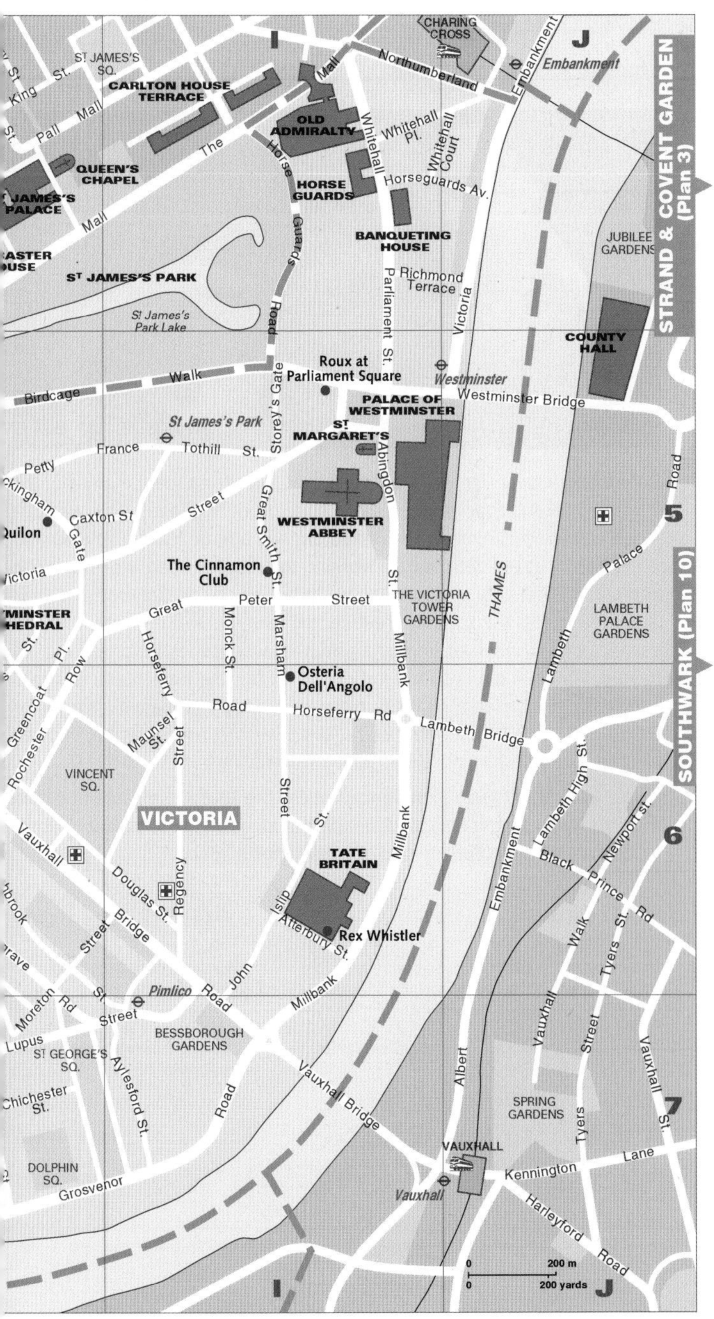

CHARING CROSS
Embankment
STRAND & COVENT GARDEN (Plan 3)
CARLTON HOUSE TERRACE
OLD ADMIRALTY
QUEEN'S CHAPEL
HORSE GUARDS
BANQUETING HOUSE
JUBILEE GARDENS
ST JAMES'S PARK
St James's Park Lake
COUNTY HALL
Roux at Parliament Square
Westminster
PALACE OF WESTMINSTER
St James's Park
ST MARGARET'S
WESTMINSTER ABBEY
Quilon
The Cinnamon Club
THE VICTORIA TOWER GARDENS
LAMBETH PALACE GARDENS
THAMES
SOUTHWARK (Plan 10)
Osteria Dell'Angolo
VINCENT SQ.
VICTORIA
TATE BRITAIN
Rex Whistler
Pimlico
BESSBOROUGH GARDENS
ST GEORGE'S SQ.
SPRING GARDENS
VAUXHALL
Vauxhall
DOLPHIN SQ.
200 m
200 yards

A. WONG ✿

Chinese • Neighbourhood

Before taking over the family business, Andrew Wong spent many months travelling through the provinces of China, garnering ideas. This was obviously time well spent as the restaurant has a huge local following and is regularly packed with people wanting to taste his fresh, well-balanced and stimulating cooking. His skill lies in taking classic Cantonese dishes and reinventing them using creative, modern techniques; retaining the essence of a dish whilst adding an impressive lightness and intensity of flavour. Lunchtime dim sum is very popular, but the main menu is where you really see the chef's skill, in dishes like 'Moo shu' pancake wraps or crispy chilli, caramelised beef and pickled carrots, as well as fun choices like the disconcertingly lifelike 'goldfish' dumplings.

If you want the full-on experience opt for the 10-course Taste of China menu; a 3 hour journey around China, with a focus on the 14 border regions. Sit at the counter if you want to see the chefs in action.

FIRST COURSE	MAIN COURSE	DESSERT
Crab claw and cured scallop with wasabi mayonnaise. • Dong Po slow-braised Ibérico pork belly.	Roasted char sui with sausage and foie gras. • Yunnan seared beef with mint, chilli, lemongrass and pulled noodle cracker.	Poached meringue, orange sorbet, pomelo and passion fruit tofu. • Tea-smoked banana with nut crumble, slow-cooked pineapple and chocolate.

■ 70 Wilton Rd ✉ SW1V 1DE **MAP: 4-H6**
☎ 020 7828 8931 — **www**.awong.co.uk
⊖ Victoria

■ Carte £24/54
Closed 23 December-4 January, Monday lunch and Sunday - booking essential

AMAYA ✿

Indian • Design

London has many open kitchens but at this Indian restaurant the shooting flames and enticing aromas from the tawa, tandoor and sigri grills will instantly alert your tastebuds that something interesting is about to happen. Amaya loosely translates as 'without boundaries' and this is reflected in its open layout as well as its varied clientele, from families and friends to business types and couples. The service is as bright and lively as the surroundings, which helps make it feel so fresh and current.

The menu evolves with the seasons, allowing the experienced chef to try out original combinations of ingredients alongside permanent fixtures like grilled lamb chops, tandoori-cooked wild prawns and wild venison seekh kebab. Bring your appetite and order a couple of small plates from the first two sections of the menu, then a curry or a biryani and some naan; and don't ignore the excellent vegetable dishes like spinach and fig tikka or chargrilled aubergine.

FIRST COURSE	MAIN COURSE	DESSERT
Turmeric and tarragon chicken tikka. • Beetroot kebab patty.	Tandoori wild prawns. • Smoked chilli lamb chops.	Lime tart with limoncello jelly and blackberry compote. • Gulab jamun.

Halkin Arcade, 19 Motcomb St ✉ SW1X 8JT **MAP: 4-F5**
020 7823 1166 — **www**.amaya.biz
⊖ Knightsbridge

Menu £26/85 - Carte £33/82

ASTER

Modern cuisine • Contemporary décor

Aster has a deli, a café, a bar and a terrace, as well the restaurant; a stylish, airy space on the first floor. The Finnish chef brings a Nordic slant to the modern French cuisine, with dishes that are light, refined and full of flavour.

150 Victoria St SW1E 5LB **MAP: 4-H5**
020 3875 5555 — **www**.aster-restaurant.com
Victoria
Carte £36/55
Closed Sunday

THE CINNAMON CLUB

Indian • Historic

Locals and tourists, business people and politicians - this smart Indian restaurant housed in the listed former Westminster Library attracts them all. The fairly elaborate dishes arrive fully garnished and the spicing is quite subtle.

30-32 Great Smith St SW1P 3BU **MAP: 4-I5**
020 7222 2555 — **www**.cinnamonclub.com
St James's Park
Menu £28 (weekday lunch) - Carte £37/84
Closed bank holidays except 25 December

ENOTECA TURI

Italian • Neighbourhood

In 2016 Putney's loss was Pimlico's gain when, after 25 years, Giuseppe and Pamela Turi had to find a new home for their Italian restaurant. They brought their warm hospitality and superb wine list with them, and the chef has introduced a broader range of influences from across the country.

87 Pimlico Rd SW1W 8PU **MAP: 4-G6**
020 7730 3663 — **www**.enotecaturi.com
Sloane Square
Menu £25 (lunch) - Carte £39/59
Closed 25-26 December, 1 January, Sunday and bank holiday lunch

CÉLESTE ✿

Creative French • Elegant

For those who regard a shared refectory table and a jam jar wine glass as simply anathema, there is Céleste, the unapologetically formal restaurant on the ground floor of The Lanesborough hotel. With its crystal chandeliers, immaculately dressed tables, Wedgwood blue friezes and fluted columns, this is a room in which you feel truly cosseted, especially as it is one that's administered by a veritable army of staff.

The menu is overseen by Éric Fréchon, head chef of Le Bristol in Paris, so expect some of his specialities like the Heritage tomato dish. However, the kitchen is also unafraid of adding its own decidedly modern touches, like the nori crust on the Marsh lamb or the satay-spiced octopus with the rabbit. Furthermore, the ingredients are often sourced from the British Isles, such as Cornish halibut and mackerel, Yorkshire rhubarb and Scottish langoustines. A wine list of impressive stature is the ideal accompaniment.

FIRST COURSE

Fluffy organic Scotch egg. • Scottish langoustine ravioli with lemongrass-infused claw velouté.

MAIN COURSE

Lamb saddle with nori crust, kohlrabi purée and gnocchi. • Slow-cooked rainbow trout with glazed asparagus, girolles and lemon butter sauce.

DESSERT

Coffee ice cream with caramelised pecan nuts and milk chocolate Chantilly. • Yorkshire rhubarb soufflé with yoghurt sorbet.

The Lanesborough Hotel, Hyde Park Corner ✉ SW1X 7TA
✆ 020 7259 5599 — **www.**lanesborough.com
⊖ Hyde Park Corner

MAP: 4-G4

Menu £39 (lunch) - Carte £72/100

♿ A/C

DINING ROOM AT THE GORING ✿

Traditional British • Elegant

If you've ever wondered what the difference is between a restaurant and a dining room then book a table here. The Goring is a model of British style and understatement and its ground floor dining room the epitome of grace and decorum. Designed by Viscount Linley, it appeals to those who 'like things done properly' and is one of the few places in London for which everyone appears to dress up – but don't come thinking it's going to be stuffy in any way. Even those who decry tradition will be charmed by the earnestness of the well-choreographed service team.

Chef Shay Cooper's menu shows respect for the hotel's reputation for classic British food while also acknowledging that tastes and techniques move on, so there are more modern, lighter options alongside recognisable old favourites. All the dishes are prepared with equal care and equally superb ingredients, and the skilful kitchen displays an impressive understanding of balance, flavour and texture.

FIRST COURSE	MAIN COURSE	DESSERT
Orkney scallop and kedgeree with shiso and lime. • Veal tartare with smoked anchovy, crispy potatoes and seaweed salt.	Salt-marsh lamb with haggis bun, shallot purée and seaweed tapenade. • Cornish cod with Jersey Royals, asparagus, peas and cockle & bacon velouté.	Brown sugar cake with poached pear, pine caramel and ginger ice cream. • Marigold apple with sweet woodruff, buttermilk custard and green apple sorbet.

Goring Hotel, 15 Beeston Pl ✉ SW1W 0JW **MAP: 4-H5**
✆ 020 7396 9000 — **www**.thegoring.com
⊖ Victoria

Menu £52/64
Closed Saturday lunch

LORNE 🍴

Modern cuisine • Simple

A small, simply furnished restaurant down a busy side street. The experienced chef understands that less is more and the modern menu is an enticing list of unfussy, well-balanced British and European dishes. Diverse wine list.

76 Wilton Rd ✉ SW1V 1DE **MAP: 4-H6**
✆ 020 3327 0210 — **www**.lornerestaurant.co.uk
⊖ Victoria

Menu £27 (lunch and early dinner) - Carte £34/52
Closed 1 week Christmas, Sunday dinner, Monday lunch and bank holidays - booking essential

---

OLIVO 🍴

Italian • Neighbourhood

A popular, pleasant and relaxed neighbourhood Italian with rough wooden floors, intimate lighting and contemporary styling. Carefully prepared, authentic and tasty dishes, with the robust flavours of Sardinia to the fore.

21 Eccleston St ✉ SW1W 9LX **MAP: 4-G6**
✆ 020 7730 2505 — **www**.olivorestaurants.com
⊖ Victoria

Menu £27 (weekday lunch) - Carte £34/51
Closed lunch Saturday-Sunday and bank holidays - booking essential

---

OLIVOMARE 🍴

Seafood • Design

Expect understated and stylish piscatorial decoration and seafood with a Sardinian base. Fortnightly changing menu, with high quality produce, much of which is available in the deli next door.

10 Lower Belgrave St ✉ SW1W 0LJ **MAP: 4-G5**
✆ 020 7730 9022 — **www**.olivorestaurants.com
⊖ Victoria

Carte £39/51
Closed bank holidays

MARCUS ✿

Modern cuisine • Elegant

Marcus Wareing's eponymous restaurant inside the glamorous Berkeley Hotel is elegant, stylish and eminently comfortable. It also has a relaxed and easy-going feel, due in no small part to the professional yet engaging staff who, refreshingly, seem to have been hired as much for their personality as for their experience and know-how.

The kitchen is run by two of Marcus' long-serving protégés: a husband and wife team who share his philosophy and are now joint chef-patrons. There's a steadfast Britishness to the menu, with superlative produce arriving from all corners of the country, like Isle of Gigha halibut, Cornish turbot, Galloway beef and Cumbrian rose veal. The chefs eschew complication and instead let the main ingredient speak for itself. The 5 or 8 course tasting menus are paired with a choice of two differently priced wine pairings.

FIRST COURSE

Pheasant egg with short-rib ragu, wild garlic and asparagus. • Scallop with apple, verbena and roasted beef dressing.

MAIN COURSE

Middle White suckling pig with bacon broth and agnolotti. • Cornish turbot with artichoke, courgette and mint.

DESSERT

Salted milk chocolate aero with sorrel and clementine. • Lemon, meringue and iced tea.

Berkeley Hotel, Wilton Pl ✉ SW1X 7RL

MAP: 4-G4

✆ 020 7235 1200 – **www**.marcusrestaurant.com

⊖ Knightsbridge

Menu £55/120

Closed Sunday

THE ORANGE

Modern cuisine • *Friendly*

The old Orange Brewery is as charming a pub as its stucco-fronted façade suggests. Try the fun bar or book a table in the more sedate upstairs room. The menu has a Mediterranean bias; spelt or wheat-based pizzas are a speciality. Bedrooms are stylish and comfortable.

37 Pimlico Rd ✉ SW1W 8NE **MAP: 4-G6**
020 7881 9844 — **www**.theorange.co.uk
⊖ Sloane Square.
Carte £25/48

OSTERIA DELL' ANGOLO

Italian • *Neighbourhood*

At lunch, this Italian opposite the Home Office is full of bustle and men in suits; at dinner it's a little more relaxed. Staff are personable and the menu is reassuringly familiar; homemade pasta and seafood dishes are good.

47 Marsham St ✉ SW1P 3DR **MAP: 4-I6**
020 3268 1077 — **www**.osteriadellangolo.co.uk
⊖ St James's Park
Menu £19 (lunch) - Carte £26/50
Closed 1-4 January, 24-28 December, Easter, Saturday lunch, Sunday and bank holidays - booking essential at lunch

A/C

THE OTHER NAUGHTY PIGLET

Modern cuisine • *Simple*

A light, spacious restaurant with friendly staff and a relaxed atmosphere, set on the first floor of The Other Palace theatre. Eclectic modern small plates are designed for sharing and accompanied by an interesting list of natural wines.

The Other Palace, 12 Palace St ✉ SW1E 5JA **MAP: 4-H5**
020 7592 0322 — **www**.theothernaughtypiglet.co.uk
⊖ Victoria
Menu £22 (lunch) - Carte £18/35
Closed Christmas, Sunday and lunch Monday - booking essential

A/C

PÉTRUS ✿

French • Elegant

The experienced kitchen at Gordon Ramsay's sophisticated Belgravia restaurant has a clear passion for classic French cuisine but isn't afraid of adding its own touches of creativity alongside some unexpected flavours, particularly when it comes to desserts. They also know that customers in these parts like having plenty of choice so provide an extensive main menu along with tasting and vegetarian options.

For anyone who wants to see how it is all done, there's a Chef's Table downstairs in the kitchen facing the 'pass'. For the rest of us, there's a smart, sophisticated and well-dressed room, at the centre of which is a striking circular wine store. Its contents are highly prized as the wine list is quite staggering and includes, appropriately enough, Château Pétrus going back to 1928. Meanwhile, the service is undertaken by a courteous and highly professional team who make everyone feel at ease as soon as they step through the door.

FIRST COURSE

Steak tartare with crispy tendons, wasabi leaf and egg yolk. • Dorset crab with avocado, green almond and pink grapefruit.

MAIN COURSE

Fillet of Cornish brill with rouille, confit peppers and shellfish bisque. • Rack of Herdwick lamb, artichoke, pomme purée and mint.

DESSERT

'Black Forest' kirsch mousse with Amarena and Morello cherry sorbet. • Raspberry soufflé with raspberry and rosemary ice cream.

1 Kinnerton St ✉ SW1X 8EA **MAP: 4-G5**
✆ 020 7592 1609 — **www**.gordonramsayrestaurants.com/petrus
⊖ Knightsbridge

Menu £45/105
Closed 21-27 December and 1 January

QUILON ✿

Indian • Design

Anyone jaded by the generic fare found in many a local Indian restaurant could do with a visit to Quilon – the experience will remind them how fresh, vibrant, colourful and indeed healthy, Indian food can be.

This restaurant's great strength is that it focuses largely on just one region of the country, namely the southwest coast. That means lots of fish and a cooking style that eschews oil and butter – a style which, in turn, makes the dishes light and easy to eat. That's not to say they don't pack a punch as Chef Sriram Aylur and his team understand how to get the best out of their prime produce and they add their own original touches. They also put equal care into the vegetable dishes: the baby aubergines are excellent and okra, that most maligned of vegetables, is served wonderfully crisp. The set menu, rather than the à la carte, will give you the best and most rounded experience; pescatarians can go for the wholly seafood set menu.

FIRST COURSE

Lobster broth with coriander and coconut cream. • Marinated lamb with onion, chilli, and ginger.

MAIN COURSE

Venison chilli fry with onions and curry leaves. • Goan spice marinated lemon sole.

DESSERT

Baked yoghurt with palm jaggery, orange, mango and lychee. • Chai latte crème brûlée.

St James' Court Hotel, 41 Buckingham Gate ✉ SW1E 6AF
✆ 020 7821 1899 — **www**.quilon.co.uk
⊖ St James's Park

MAP: 4-H5

Menu £31/60 - Carte £42/57
Closed 25 December

REX WHISTLER

Modern cuisine • *Classic décor*

A hidden gem, tucked away on the lower ground floor of Tate Britain; its most striking element is Whistler's restored mural, 'The Expedition in Pursuit of Rare Meats', which envelops the room. The menu is stoutly British and the remarkably priced wine list has an unrivalled 'half bottle' selection.

Tate Britain, Millbank ✉ SW1P 4RG **MAP: 4-I6**
020 7887 8825 — **www**.tate.org.uk/visit/tate-britain/rex-whistler-restaurant
Pimlico

Menu £36
Closed 24-26 December - (lunch only)

ROUX AT PARLIAMENT SQUARE

Modern cuisine • *Elegant*

Light floods through the Georgian windows of this comfortable restaurant within the offices of the Royal Institute of Chartered Surveyors. Carefully crafted, elaborate and sophisticated cuisine, with some interesting flavour combinations.

Royal Institution of Chartered Surveyors, Parliament Sq. ✉ SW1P 3AD **MAP: 4-I5**
020 7334 3737 — **www**.rouxatparliamentsquare.co.uk
Westminster

Menu £42/79
Closed 2 weeks August, Christmas, New Year, Saturday, Sunday and bank holidays XXX

ZAFFERANO

Italian • *Fashionable*

The immaculately coiffured regulars continue to support this ever-expanding, long-standing and capably run Italian restaurant. They come for the reassuringly familiar, if rather steeply priced dishes from all parts of Italy.

15 Lowndes St ✉ SW1X 9EY **MAP: 4-F5**
020 7235 5800 — **www**.zafferanorestaurant.com
Knightsbridge

Menu £27 (weekday lunch) - Carte £36/85
Closed 25 December - booking essential

REGENT'S PARK · MARYLEBONE

The neighbourhood north of chaotic Oxford Street is actually a rather refined place where shoppers like to venture for the smart boutiques, and where idlers like to saunter for the graceful parkland acres full of rose gardens and quiet corners. In fact, Marylebone and Regent's Park go rather well together, a moneyed village with a wonderful park for its back garden.

Marylebone may now exude a fashionable status, but its history tells a very different tale. Thousands used to come here to watch executions at Tyburn gallows, a six hundred year spectacle that stopped in the late eighteenth century. Tyburn stream was covered over, and the area's modern name came into being as a contraction of St Mary by the Bourne, the parish church. Nowadays the people who flock here come to gaze at less ghoulish sights, though some of the inhabitants of the eternally popular Madame Tussauds deserved no better fate than the gallows. South across the busy Marylebone Road, the preponderance of swish restaurants and snazzy specialist shops announces your arrival at **Marylebone High Street.** There are patisseries, chocolatiers, cheese shops and butchers at every turn, nestling alongside smart places to eat and drink. At St Marylebone Church, each Saturday heralds a posh market called Cabbages & Frocks, where artisan food meets designer clothing in a charming garden. Further down, the century old Daunt Books has been described as London's most beautiful bookshop: it has long oak galleries beneath graceful conservatory skylights. Close by, the quaintly winding Marylebone Lane boasts some truly unique shops like tiny emporium The Button Queen, which sells original Art Deco, Victorian and Edwardian buttons. In complete contrast, just down the road from here is the mighty **Wigmore Hall,** an art nouveau gem with great acoustics and an unerringly top-notch classical agenda that can be appreciated at rock-bottom prices. Meanwhile, art lovers can indulge an eclectic fix at the **Wallace Collection** in **Manchester Square,** where paintings by the likes of Titian and Velazquez rub shoulders with Sevres porcelain and grand Louis XIV furniture.

Regent's Park – an idyllic Georgian oasis stretching off into London's northern suburbs - celebrated its two hundredth birthday in 2011. Before architect John Nash and his sponsor The Prince Regent gave it its much-loved geometric makeover, it had been farming land, and prior to that, one of Henry VIII's hunting grounds. His spirit lives on, in the sense that various activities are catered for, from tennis courts to a running track. And there are animals too, albeit not roaming free, at **London Zoo,** in the park's northerly section. Most people, though, come here to while away an hour or two around the boating lake or amble the Inner Circle which contains **Queen Mary's Gardens** and their enchanting bowers of fragrant roses. Others come for a summer sojourn to the Open Air Theatre where taking in a performance of 'A Midsummer Night's Dream' is very much *de rigueur*. The Regent's Canal provides another fascinating element to the park. You can follow its peaceful waters along a splendid walk from the **Little Venice** houseboats in the west, past the golden dome of the **London Central Mosque,** and on into the north-west confines of Regent's Park as it snakes through London Zoo, before it heads off towards Camden Lock. On the other side of Prince Albert Road, across from the zoo, the scenic glory takes on another dimension with a climb up Primrose Hill. Named after the grassy promontory that sets it apart from its surrounds, to visitors this is a hill with one of the best panoramas in the whole of London; to locals (ie, actors, pop stars, media darlings and the city set) it's an ultra fashionable place to live with pretty Victorian terraces and accordingly sky-high prices. Either way you look at it (or from it), it's a great place to be on a sunny day with the breeze in your hair.

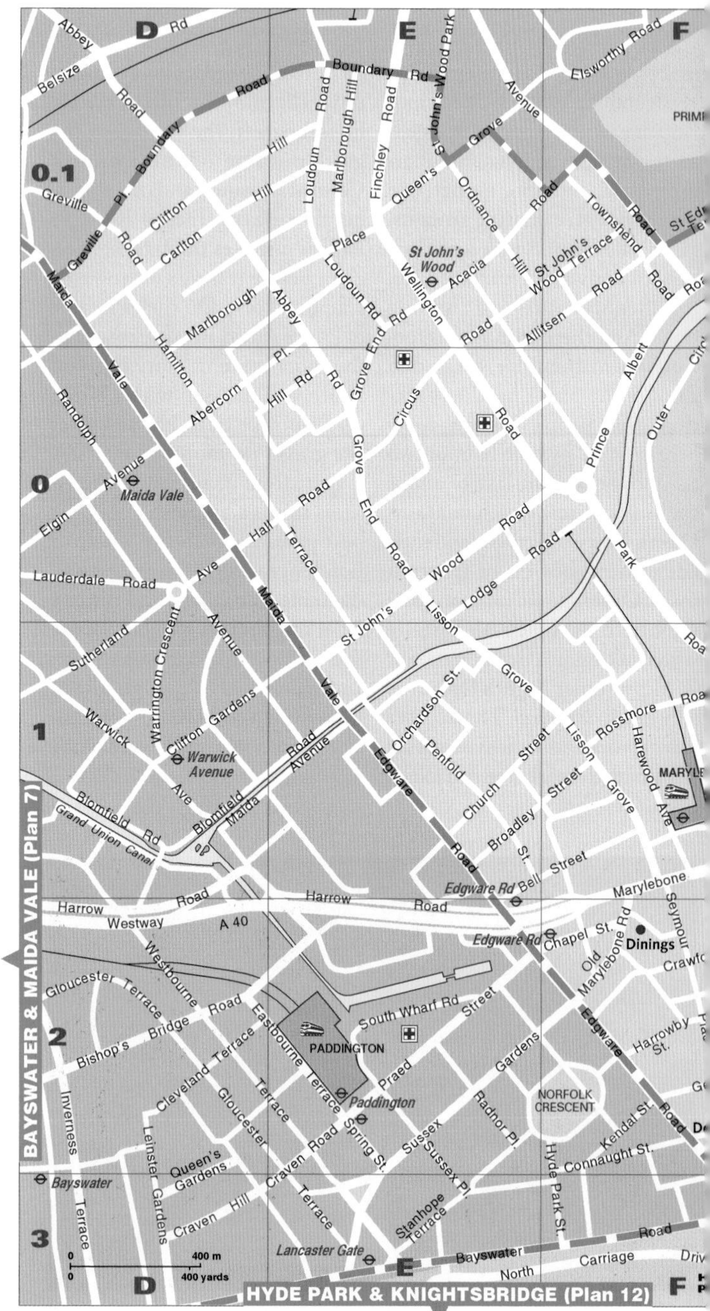

BAYSWATER & MAIDA VALE (Plan 7)
HYDE PARK & KNIGHTSBRIDGE (Plan 12)
St John's Wood
Maida Vale
Warwick Avenue
PADDINGTON
Paddington
Edgware Rd
Dinings
NORFOLK CRESCENT
Bayswater
Lancaster Gate
MARYLE
Grand Union Canal

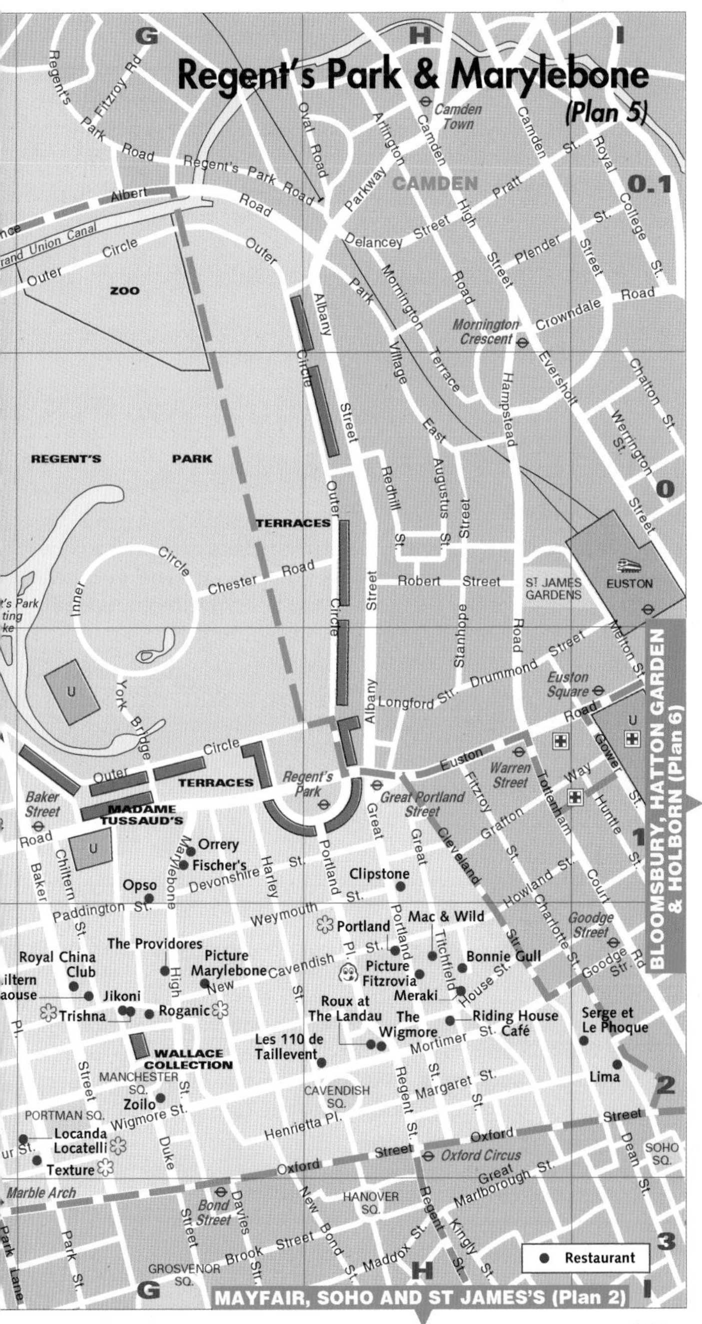
Regent's Park & Marylebone
(Plan 5)
CAMDEN
Camden Town
ZOO
REGENT'S
PARK
TERRACES
TERRACES
Mornington Crescent
ST JAMES GARDENS
EUSTON
Euston Square
Warren Street
Great Portland Street
Regent's Park
Baker Street
MADAME TUSSAUD'S
WALLACE COLLECTION
MANCHESTER SQ.
PORTMAN SQ.
CAVENDISH SQ.
HANOVER SQ.
GROSVENOR SQ.
SOHO SQ.
Goodge Street
Oxford Circus
Bond Street
Marble Arch
Orrery
Fischer's
Opso
Clipstone
Portland
Mac & Wild
Bonnie Gull
The Providores
Picture Marylebone
Picture Fitzrovia
Meraki
Royal China Club
Jikoni
Trishna
Roganic
Roux at The Landau
The Wigmore
Riding House Café
Les 110 de Taillevent
Serge et Le Phoque
Lima
Zoilo
Locanda Locatelli
Texture
Restaurant
BLOOMSBURY, HATTON GARDEN & HOLBORN (Plan 6)
MAYFAIR, SOHO AND ST JAMES'S (Plan 2)

BONNIE GULL

Seafood • Simple

Sweet Bonnie Gull calls itself a 'seafood shack' - a reference perhaps to its modest beginnings as a pop-up. Start with something from the raw bar then go for classics like Cullen skink, Devon cock crab or fish and chips. There's another branch in Soho.

21a Foley St W1W 6DS **MAP: 5-H2**
020 7436 0921 — **www**.bonniegull.com
Goodge Street

Carte £31/45
Closed 25 December-3 January - booking essential

CHILTERN FIREHOUSE

World cuisine • Fashionable

How appropriate - one of the hottest tickets in town is a converted fire station. The room positively bursts with energy but what makes this celebrity hangout unusual is that the food is rather good. Nuno Mendes' menu is full of vibrant North and South American dishes that are big on flavour.

Chiltern Firehouse Hotel, 1 Chiltern St WIU 7PA **MAP: 5-G2**
020 7073 7676 — **www**.chilternfirehouse.com
Baker Street

Carte £37/63

CLIPSTONE

Modern cuisine • Fashionable

Another wonderful neighbourhood spot from the owners of Portland, just around the corner. The sharing menu is a lesson in flavour and originality; choose one charcuterie dish, one from the seasonal vegetable-based section, one main and a dessert. Cocktails and 'on-tap' wine add to the fun.

5 Clipstone St W1W 6BB **MAP: 5-H1**
020 7637 0871 — **www**.clipstonerestaurant.co.uk
Great Portland Street

Menu £24 (lunch) - Carte £34/40
Closed Christmas, New Year and Sunday

DININGS ǁO

Japanese • Cosy

It's hard not to be charmed by this sweet little Japanese place, with its ground floor counter and basement tables. Its strengths lie with the more creative, contemporary dishes; sharing is recommended but prices can be steep.

22 Harcourt St. ✉ W1H 4HH — **MAP: 5-F2**
020 7723 0666 — **www**.dinings.co.uk
Edgware Road

Carte £25/67
Closed Christmas - booking essential

DONOSTIA ǁO

Basque • Tapas bar

The two young owners were inspired by the food of San Sebastián to open this pintxos and tapas bar. Sit at the counter for Basque classics like cod with pil-pil sauce, chorizo from the native Kintoa pig and slow-cooked pig's cheeks.

10 Seymour Pl ✉ W1H 7ND — **MAP: 5-F2**
020 3620 1845 — **www**.donostia.co.uk
Marble Arch

Menu £20 (weekday lunch) - Carte £20/43
Closed Christmas, New Year and lunch Sunday-Monday

FISCHER'S ǁO

Austrian • Brasserie

An Austrian café and konditorei that summons the spirit of old Vienna, from the owners of The Wolseley et al. Open all day; breakfast is a highlight - the viennoiserie are great. Schnitzels are also good; upgrade to a Holstein.

50 Marylebone High St ✉ W1U 5HN — **MAP: 5-G1**
020 7466 5501 — **www**.fischers.co.uk
Baker Street

Carte £23/59
Closed 25 December

A/C

JIKONI

Indian • Elegant

Indian tablecloths and colourful cushions create a homely feel at this idiosyncratic restaurant. Born in Kenya of Indian parents and brought up in London, chef Ravinder Bhogal takes culinary inspiration from these sources and more.

19-21 Blandford St W1U 3DH **MAP: 5-G2**
020 7034 1988 — **www**.jikonilondon.com
Baker Street
Menu £20 (weekday lunch) - Carte £24/48
Closed Monday and lunch Tuesday
A/C

LIMA

Peruvian • Neighbourhood

Lima is one of those restaurants that just makes you feel good about life - and that's even without the pisco sours. The Peruvian food at this informal, fun place is the ideal antidote to times of austerity: it's full of punchy, invigorating flavours and fantastically vivid colours.

31 Rathbone Pl W1T 1JH **MAP: 5-I2**
020 3002 2640 — **www**.limalondongroup.com
Goodge Street
Menu £19 (weekday lunch) - Carte £30/59
Closed 24-26 December, 1 January and bank holidays
A/C

LURRA

Basque • Design

Its name means 'land' in Basque and reflects their use of the freshest produce, cooked over a charcoal grill. Choose tasty nibbles or sharing plates like 14 year old Galician beef, whole grilled turbot or slow-cooked shoulder of lamb.

9 Seymour Pl W1H 5BA **MAP: 5-F2**
020 7724 4545 — **www**.lurra.co.uk
Marble Arch
Menu £25 (weekday lunch) - Carte £27/70
Closed Sunday dinner and Monday lunch
A/C

LOCANDA LOCATELLI ✿

Italian • Fashionable

A few minutes in the company of Giorgio Locatelli, whether face to face or through the medium of television, reveals a man who is passionate about Italian food and it is that very passion that has kept Locanda Locatelli at the top for so long. The restaurant may be into its second decade but still looks as dapper as ever and remains in the premier league of London's most fashionable addresses. The layout and style of the room were clearly designed with conviviality in mind and this is further helped along by service that is smooth but never intrusive.

The other reason for its enduring popularity is the great food and the consistency that the kitchen maintains. The hugely appealing menu covers many of the regions of Italy and provides plenty of choice for everyone including coeliacs, as the terrific pasta dishes available include gluten-free options. Unfussy presentation and superlative ingredients allow natural flavours to shine through.

FIRST COURSE	MAIN COURSE	DESSERT
Burrata with blood orange, black olive and fennel bread crisps. • Cured neck of pork with girolles, rocket and balsamic onions.	Tagliatelle with kid goat ragu, chilli and pecorino. • Fillet of John Dory with potatoes and green olives.	Liquorice semifreddo with lime jelly, caviar and Branca Menta sauce. • Tonka bean panna cotta with white chocolate crumble and raspberries.

8 Seymour St. ✉ W1H 7JZ — **MAP: 5-G2**

✆ 020 7935 9088 — **www**.locandalocatelli.com

⊖ Marble Arch

Carte £49/74

Closed 24-26 December and 1 January

♿ A/C ⛶ ✿

MAC & WILD

Scottish • Friendly

The owner of this 'Highland restaurant' is the son of an Ardgay butcher – it is all about their wild venison and top quality game and seafood from Scotland. Don't miss the 'wee plates' like the deliriously addictive haggis pops. There's also a choice of over 100 whiskies.

65 Great Titchfield St ✉ W1W 7PS **MAP: 5-H2**
020 7637 0510 — **www.**macandwild.com
Oxford Circus

Carte £21/62
Closed Sunday dinner

A/C

MERAKI

Greek • Fashionable

A lively Greek restaurant from the same owners as Roka and Zuma; its name a fitting reference to the passion put into one's work. Contemporary versions of classic Greek dishes; much of the produce is imported from Greece, including the wines.

80-82 Great Titchfield St ✉ W1W 7QT **MAP: 5-H2**
020 7305 7686 — **www.**meraki-restaurant.com
Goodge Street

Menu £20 (lunch) – Carte £25/60
Closed Christmas and Sunday dinner

A/C

LES 110 DE TAILLEVENT

French • Elegant

Ornate high ceilings and deep green banquettes create an elegant look for this French brasserie deluxe, which is more food orientated than the Paris original. It also offers 110 wines by the glass: 4 different pairings for each dish, in 4 different price brackets.

16 Cavendish Sq ✉ W1G 9DD **MAP: 5-H2**
020 3141 6016 — **www.**les-110-taillevent-london.com
Oxford Circus

Menu £28 (lunch) – Carte £38/76

A/C

OPSO

Greek • Neighbourhood

A modern Greek restaurant which has proved a good fit for the neighbourhood - and not just because it's around the corner from the Hellenic Centre. It serves small sharing plates that mix the modern with the traditional.

10 Paddington St W1U 5QL **MAP: 5-G1**
020 7487 5088 — **www**.opso.co.uk
Baker Street
Carte £14/55
Closed 23 December-3 January

ORRERY

Modern cuisine • Neighbourhood

The most recent redecoration left this comfortable restaurant, located in what were converted stables from the 19C, looking lighter and more contemporary; the bar and terrace are also smarter. Expect quite elaborate, modern European cooking, strong on presentation and with the occasional twist.

55 Marylebone High St W1U 5RB **MAP: 5-G1**
020 7616 8000 — **www**.orrery-restaurant.co.uk
Regent's Park
Menu £25/59
Booking essential

PICTURE FITZROVIA

Modern British • Simple

An ex Arbutus and Wild Honey triumvirate created this cool, great value restaurant. The look may be a little stark but the delightful staff add warmth. The small plates are vibrant and colourful, and the flavours are assured.

110 Great Portland St. W1W 6PQ **MAP: 5-H2**
020 7637 7892 — **www**.picturerestaurant.co.uk
Oxford Circus
Menu £23 (lunch) - Carte £23/33
Closed Sunday and bank holidays

PICTURE MARYLEBONE

Modern British • Design

This follow-up to Picture Fitzrovia hit the ground running. The cleverly created à la carte of flavoursome small plates lists 3 vegetable, 3 fish and 3 meat choices, followed by 3 desserts – choose one from each section.

19 New Cavendish St ✉ W1G 9TZ — **MAP: 5-G2**
020 7935 0058 — **www.**picturerestaurant.co.uk
⊖ Bond Street

Menu £23 (lunch) – Carte £27/33
Closed Sunday, Monday and bank holidays

THE PROVIDORES

Creative • Trendy

Tables and tapas are shared in the buzzing ground floor; head to the elegant, slightly more sedate upstairs room for innovative fusion cooking, with ingredients from around the world. New Zealand wine list; charming staff.

109 Marylebone High St. ✉ W1U 4RX — **MAP: 5-G2**
020 7935 6175 — **www.**theprovidores.co.uk
⊖ Bond Street

Carte £36/48
Closed Easter, dinner 24 and 31 December and 25-26 December

RIDING HOUSE CAFÉ

Modern cuisine • Rustic

It's less a café, more a large, quirkily designed, all-day New York style brasserie and cocktail bar. The small plates have more zing than the main courses. The 'unbookable' side of the restaurant is the more fun part.

43-51 Great Titchfield St ✉ W1W 7PQ — **MAP: 5-H2**
020 7927 0840 — **www.**ridinghousecafe.co.uk
⊖ Oxford Circus

Carte £25/49
Closed 25-26 December

PORTLAND ✿

Modern cuisine • Intimate

Portland has settled nicely on the street after which it is named and pitches everything just so. The open kitchen is very much a dominant feature so the chefs are on show, but the wine is as big a feature as the food. The pared-down look of the room is just the right side of austere, helped by some original art on the walls, and the service team are knowledgeable and happy to make recommendations.

The cooking respects the principles of sourcing and seasonality; in fact the menu is often reprinted after lunch as ingredients are used up and replaced by different ones. The kitchen believes in doing as little as possible to the raw ingredients to allow their natural flavours to come through. The bread, flavoured with treacle and porter, is stunning. Plates are never fussy or over crowded but neither will one leave here unsated.

FIRST COURSE	MAIN COURSE	DESSERT
Asparagus, frozen egg yolk, nettles and ricotta gnudi. • Mackerel with white asparagus and herb buttermilk.	Gloucester Old Spot loin with braised treviso and lardo with quince. • Cornish pollock with mussels, broad beans and lemon balm.	Bergamot custard with Douglas fir ice cream and burnt meringue. • 70% Grenadian chocolate cream with frozen woodruff and nutmeg.

113 Great Portland St ✉ W1W 6QQ **MAP: 5-H2**
✆ 020 7436 3261 — **www**.portlandrestaurant.co.uk
⊖ Great Portland Street

Menu £30/75 - Carte dinner £43/61
Closed 23 December-3 January and Sunday - booking essential
A/C

Ⓝ ROGANIC ✿

Creative British • Minimalist

Keen followers of London's restaurant landscape will remember Roganic as a two year pop-up a few years ago. It gave diners a taste of the style of food Simon Rogan served at his L'Enclume restaurant without having to make the journey up to the Lake District. In 2018 it opened once again in Marylebone village, with several members of the original team on board, but this time it's a few doors down in the old premises of L'Autre Pied and, more significantly, it's permanent.

It's not intended to be a copy of L'Enclume but rather to deliver elements of it, with some dishes designed to reflect the London location. Many ingredients, however, do come from their farm in Cartmel and the cuisine style – which uses plenty of techniques, including pickling and curing – is such that diners will inevitably feel closer to nature than they usually do when eating out in the capital.

FIRST COURSE	MAIN COURSE	DESSERT
Cured mackerel with radishes and sorrel sauce. • Peas with ox tongue and mint.	Cornish lamb with broad beans and courgettes. • Monkfish with mussels and seaweeds.	Caramelised apple tart with Douglas fir ice cream. • Strawberry, buttermilk and yoghurt.

5-7 Blandford St ✉ W1U 3DB **MAP: 5-G2**
020 3370 6260 — **www**.roganic.uk
⊖ Bond Street

Menu £35/95
Closed 22 December-7 January, 25 August-2 September, Sunday and Monday. - booking essential - (tasting menu only)

ROUX AT THE LANDAU

French • Elegant

There's been a change to a more informal style for this restaurant run under the aegis of the Roux organisation - it's now more akin to a modern bistro in looks and atmosphere and is all the better for it. The cooking is classical French and informed by the seasons; shellfish is a highlight.

Langham Hotel, 1c Portland Pl., Regent St. W1B 1JA **MAP: 5-H2**
020 7965 0165 — **www**.rouxatthelandau.com
Oxford Circus

Menu £25 (weekday lunch) - Carte £33/71
Closed Monday

A/C

ROYAL CHINA CLUB

Chinese • Oriental décor

Service is fast-paced and to the point, which is understandable considering how busy this restaurant always is. The large menu offers something for everyone and the lunchtime dim sum is very good; at dinner try their more unusual Cantonese dishes.

40-42 Baker St W1U 7AJ **MAP: 5-G2**
020 7486 3898 — **www**.royalchinagroup.co.uk
Baker Street

Carte £35/80
Closed 25-27 December

A/C

N SERGE ET LE PHOQUE

Modern cuisine • Design

This outpost of the Hong Kong original may be in the Mandrake hotel but decoratively it's quite subdued compared to the rest of the building. Dishes, on the other hand, are quite dramatic; from the Earth, Sea and Land come some fine ingredients partnered with flavours and spices from around the world.

Mandrake Hotel, 20-21 Newman St W1T 1PG **MAP: 5-H2**
020 3146 8880 — **www**.serge.london
Tottenham Court Road

Menu £22 (lunch) - Carte £18/41
Closed 24-27 December

A/C

TEXTURE ✿

Creative • Design

Chef-owner Agnar Sverrisson has steadily gone about creating an exceedingly good restaurant. The Champagne Bar at the front has become a destination in itself and is separated from the restaurant by a large cabinet so you never feel too detached from it. The high ceilings add a little grandeur to the place and the service is very pleasant, with staff all willing and ready with a smile.

Agnar's cooking is a little less showy than when Texture first opened over a decade ago and is all the better for that; you feel he's now cooking the food he wants to cook rather than the food he thought he should be cooking. Iceland is his country of birth so it is no surprise to find lamb, cod (whose crisp skin is served with drinks), langoustine and skyr, the dairy product that nourished the Vikings; the bread, and the olive oils are very good too. There's considerable technical skill and depth to the cooking but dishes still appear light and refreshing and, since the use of cream and butter is largely restricted to the desserts, you even feel they're doing you good.

FIRST COURSE

Salmon gravlax with Oscietra caviar, mustard and sorrel. • Anjou quail with chargrilled sweetcorn, shallot, bacon popcorn and red wine essence.

MAIN COURSE

Lightly salted cod with avocado, Jersey Royals, romanesco and wild garlic. • Pyrenean rose veal with baby artichokes, sugar snap peas and girolles.

DESSERT

Icelandic skyr with vanilla, Gariguette strawberries and rye bread crumbs. • White chocolate mousse and ice cream with dill and cucumber.

34 Portman St ✉ W1H 7BY **MAP: 5-G2**
☎ 020 7224 0028 — **www**.texture-restaurant.co.uk
⊖ Marble Arch

Menu £29/95 - Carte £70/95
Closed 2 weeks August, 1 week Easter, Christmas-New Year, Sunday, Monday and lunch Tuesday-Wednesday

TRISHNA ❀

Indian • Neighbourhood

The coast of southwest India provides the kitchen with most of its influences and the interesting menu is full of vibrant, exciting dishes, ranging from the playful – try their own mini version of 'fish and chips' as a starter – to the original: the succulent guinea fowl comes with lentils, fennel seed and star anise. However, the undoubted star of the show is a version of the dish made famous by the original Trishna in Mumbai: brown crab, in this case from Dorset, comes with lots of butter and a little kick of wild garlic; it is so wondrously rich no man alone can finish a bowl, and you'll be licking your lips for days afterwards. The various tasting menus often provide the most rounded experience but all the dishes are as fresh tasting and beautifully spiced as they are colourful. Much thought has also gone into matching wines with specific dishes.

The restaurant is dressed in an elegant, understated style and its charming staff exude a sense of calm.

FIRST COURSE	MAIN COURSE	DESSERT
Aloo tokri chaat. • Shahi salmon tikka with smoked tomato kachumber.	Dorset brown crab with butter, pepper, chilli and garlic. • Corn-fed chicken with curry leaf, coconut and baby shallots.	Baked yoghurt with apricot chutney. • Pistachio and fig kheer.

15-17 Blandford St. ✉ W1U 3DG — **MAP: 5-G2**
020 7935 5624 — **www.**trishnalondon.com
⊖ Baker Street

Menu £28/65 - Carte £32/59
Closed 25-27 December and 1-3 January

Ⓝ THE WIGMORE

Traditional British • Pub

The impressively high ceiling can only mean one thing - this was once a bank. Booths, high tables, a sizeable bar and bold emerald green tones lend a clubby feel to this addendum to The Langham. Classic, hearty British dishes are given an update.

Langham Hotel, 15 Langham Place, Upper Regent St ✉ W1B 1JA — **MAP: 5-H2**
020 7965 0198 — **www**.the-wigmore.co.uk
Oxford Circus
Carte £26/40

ZOILO

Argentinian • Friendly

It's all about sharing so plonk yourself at the counter and discover Argentina's regional specialities. Typical dishes include braised pig head croquettes or grilled scallops with pork belly, and there's an appealing all-Argentinian wine list.

9 Duke St. ✉ W1U 3EG — **MAP: 5-G2**
020 7486 9699 — **www**.zoilo.co.uk
Bond Street
Menu £19 (lunch) - Carte £29/53
Closed Sunday

Look for our symbol
spotlighting restaurants
with a notable wine list.

BLOOMSBURY · HATTON GARDEN · HOLBORN

A real sense of history pervades this central chunk of London. From the great collection of antiquities in the British Museum to the barristers who swarm around the Royal Courts of Justice and Lincoln's Inn; from the haunts of Charles Dickens to the oldest Catholic church in Britain, the streets here are dotted with rich reminders of the past. Hatton Garden's fame as the city's diamond and jewellery centre goes back to Elizabethan times while, of a more recent vintage, Bloomsbury was home to the notorious Group (or Set) who, championed by Virginia Woolf, took on the world of art and literature in the 1920s.

A full-on encounter with **Holborn** is, initially, a shock to the system. Coming up from the tube, you'll find this is where main traffic arteries collide and a rugby scrum regularly ensues. Fear not, though; the relative calm of London's largest square, part-flanked by two quirky and intriguing museums, is just round the corner. The square is **Lincoln's Inn Fields,** which boasts a canopy of characterful oak trees and a set of tennis courts. On its north side is **Sir John Soane's Museum,** a gloriously eccentric place with over forty thousand exhibits where the walls open out like cabinets to reveal paintings by Turner and Canaletto. On its south side, the Hunterian Museum, is a fascinating repository of medical bits and pieces. Visitors with a Damien Hirst take on life will revel in the likes of animal digestive systems in formaldehyde, or perhaps the sight of half of mathematician Charles Babbage's brain. Others not so fascinated by the gory might flee to the haunting silence of **St Etheldreda's church** in Ely Place, the only surviving example of thirteenth-century Gothic architecture in London. It survived the Great Fire of 1666, and Latin is still the language of choice.

Contemplation of a different kind takes centre stage in the adjacent **Hatton Garden.** This involves eager-eyed couples gazing at the glittering displays of rings and jewellery that have been lighting up the shop fronts here for many generations, ever since the leafy lane and its smart garden environs took the fancy of Sir Christopher Hatton, a favourite of Elizabeth I.

After gawping at the baubles, there's liquid refreshment on hand at one of London's most atmospheric old pubs, the tiny Ye Old Mitre hidden down a narrow passageway. The preserved trunk of a cherry tree stands in the front bar, and, by all accounts, Elizabeth I danced the maypole round it (a legend that always seems more believable after the second pint).

Bloomsbury has intellectual connotations, and not just because of the writers and artists who frequented its townhouses in the twenties. This is where the University of London has its headquarters, and it's also home to the **British Museum,** the vast treasure trove of international artefacts that attracts visitors in even vaster numbers. As if the exhibits themselves weren't lure enough, there's also the fantastic glass-roofed Great Court, opened to much fanfare at the start of the Millennium, which lays claim to being the largest covered public square in Europe. To the north of here by the Euston Road is the **British Library,** a rather stark red brick building that holds over 150 million items and is one of the greatest centres of knowledge in the world. Meanwhile, Dickens fans should make for the north east corner of Bloomsbury for the great man's museum in **Doughty Street:** this is one of many London houses in which he lived, but it's the only one still standing. He lived here for three years, and it proved a fruitful base, resulting in Nicholas Nickleby and Oliver Twist. The museum holds manuscripts, letters and Dickens' writing desk. If your appetite for the written word has been truly whetted, then a good tip is to head back west half a mile to immerse yourself in the bookshops of Great Russell Street.

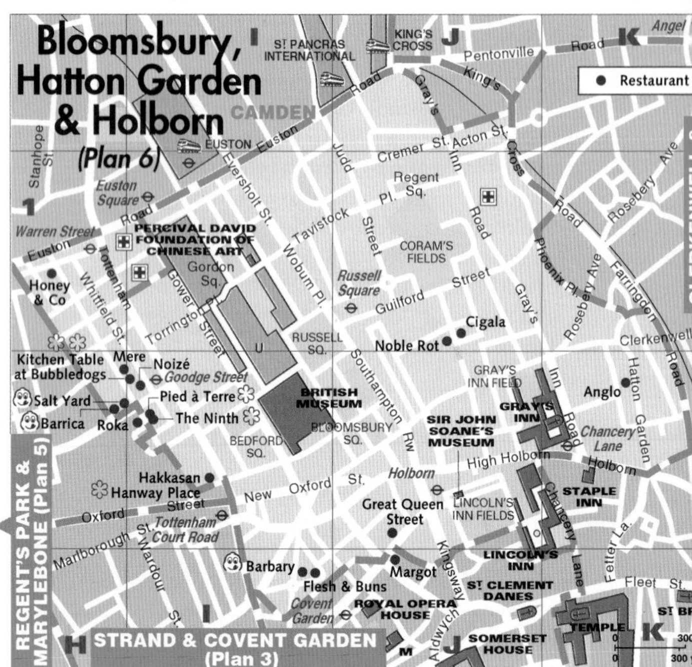
Bloomsbury, Hatton Garden & Holborn
(Plan 6)
Restaurant
Honey & Co
Kitchen Table at Bubbledogs
Mere
Noizé
Salt Yard
Barrica
Roka
Pied à Terre
The Ninth
Hakkasan
Hanway Place
Cigala
Noble Rot
Anglo
Great Queen Street
Barbary
Margot
Flesh & Buns
BRITISH MUSEUM
SIR JOHN SOANE'S MUSEUM
PERCIVAL DAVID FOUNDATION OF CHINESE ART
GRAY'S INN
STAPLE INN
LINCOLN'S INN
ST CLEMENT DANES
ROYAL OPERA HOUSE
SOMERSET HOUSE
TEMPLE
ST PANCRAS INTERNATIONAL
KING'S CROSS
EUSTON
CAMDEN
REGENT'S PARK & MARYLEBONE (Plan 5)
STRAND & COVENT GARDEN (Plan 3)

ANGLO

Creative British • Rustic

As its name suggests, British produce is the mainstay of the menu at this pared-down, personally run restaurant, with 'home-grown' ingredients often served in creative ways. Cooking is well-executed with assured flavours.

30 St Cross St ✉ ECIN 8UH **MAP: 6-K2**
020 7430 1503 – **www**.anglorestaurant.com
Farringdon
Menu £42/60 - Carte lunch £34/53
Closed 22 December-4 January, Sunday and lunch Monday

BARBARY

World cuisine • Tapas bar

A sultry, atmospheric restaurant from the team behind Palomar: a tiny place with 24 non-bookable seats squeezed around a horseshoe-shaped, zinc-topped counter. The menu of small sharing plates lists dishes from the former Barbary Coast. Service is keen, as are the prices.

16 Neal's Yard ✉ WC2H 9DP **MAP: 6-I3**
www.thebarbary.co.uk
Covent Garden
Carte £16/36
Closed dinner 24-26 December - bookings not accepted

BARRICA

Spanish • Tapas bar

All the staff at this lively little tapas bar are Spanish, so perhaps it's national pride that makes them run it with a passion lacking in many of their competitors. When it comes to the food, authenticity is high on the agenda. Dishes pack a punch and are fairly priced.

62 Goodge St ✉ W1T 4NE **MAP: 6-H2**
020 7436 9448 – **www**.barrica.co.uk
Goodge Street
Carte £22/38
Closed 25-31 December, 1 January, Easter, Sunday and bank holidays - booking essential

CIGALA

Spanish • Neighbourhood

Longstanding Spanish restaurant, with a lively and convivial atmosphere, friendly and helpful service and an appealing and extensive menu of classics. The dried hams are a must and it's well worth waiting the 30 minutes for a paella.

54 Lamb's Conduit St. WC1N 3LW **MAP: 6-J1**
020 7405 1717 — **www**.cigala.co.uk
Russell Square
Menu £24 (weekday lunch) - Carte £34/46
Closed 24-26 December and 1 January - booking essential

GREAT QUEEN STREET

Modern British • Rustic

The menu is a model of British understatement and is dictated by the seasons; the cooking, confident and satisfying and served in generous portions. Lively atmosphere and enthusiastic service. Highlights include the shared dishes like the suet-crusted steak and ale pie for two.

32 Great Queen St WC2B 5AA **MAP: 6-J2**
020 7242 0622 — **www**.greatqueenstreetrestaurant.co.uk
Holborn
Menu £18 (weekday lunch) - Carte £22/42
Closed Christmas-New Year, Sunday dinner and bank holidays - booking essential

A/C

HONEY & CO

World cuisine • Simple

The husband and wife team at this sweet little café were both Ottolenghi head chefs so expect cooking full of freshness and colour. Influences stretch beyond Israel to the wider Middle East. Open from 8am; packed at night.

25a Warren St W1T 5LZ **MAP: 6-H1**
020 7388 6175 — **www**.honeyandco.co.uk
Warren Street
Menu £35
Closed 24-26, 31 December, 1-3 January and Sunday - booking essential

A/C

HAKKASAN HANWAY PLACE ✿

Chinese • *Trendy*

Over recent years Hakkasans have opened in several cities around the world but it all started here in 2001 in this unexceptional alleyway just off Tottenham Court Road. Thanks to its sensual looks, air of exclusivity and glamorous atmosphere – characteristics now synonymous with the brand – the original Hakkasan wowed London back then and, judging by the crowds, continues to do so today. The restaurant has always managed the art of coping equally well with all types of customers, from large parties out to celebrate to couples on a date, and the well-organised and helpful staff are a fundamental part of that success.

Lunchtime dim sum here is a memorable, relaxed experience; at dinner try the Signature menus which represent better value than the à la carte. Thanks to the huge brigade in the kitchen, the Cantonese specialities are prepared with care and consistency; dishes are exquisitely presented and while there are moments of inventiveness, they never come at the expense of flavour.

FIRST COURSE

Dim sum platter. • Smoked beef ribs with jasmine tea.

MAIN COURSE

Grilled Chilean sea bass in honey. • Slow-cooked Szechuan pork belly with lily bulb and dry chilli.

DESSERT

Chocolate and olive oil ganache. • Apple and sesame croustillant.

8 Hanway Pl. ✉ W1T 1HD **MAP: 6-12**
✆ 020 7927 7000 — **www.**hakkasan.com
⊖ Tottenham Court Road

Carte £35/135
Closed 24-25 December

KITCHEN TABLE AT BUBBLEDOGS ✿✿

Modern cuisine • Fashionable

Ignore the throngs enjoying the curious combination of hotdogs with champagne and head for the curtain – behind it you'll find a horseshoe-shaped counter and a look of expectation on the faces of your fellow diners. Chef-owner James Knappett and his team prepare a no-choice menu of around 12 dishes; each one is described on the blackboard in a single noun so you have to place your trust in them. The produce is some of the best you can find and the small dishes come with a clever creative edge, without being overly complicated. The cooking has developed considerably over the years and now displays admirable poise.

With seating for just 19, the atmosphere is very convivial, especially if you're a fully paid-up member of the foodie community. The chefs interact with their customers over the counter and offer comprehensive explanations of each dish; they are helped out by James' wife Sandia, who is charm personified.

FIRST COURSE	MAIN COURSE	DESSERT
Orkney scallops with warm charcoal cream and Exmouth caviar. • Crispy chicken skin with rosemary mascarpone and bacon jam.	Duck with black garlic, blood orange purée, turnip and shiso. • Cornish lobster with wild garlic, shellfish sauce and tomatoes.	Milk ice cream with rhubarb and charred black pepper meringue. • Cherry blossom panna cotta.

70 Charlotte St ✉ W1T 4QG **MAP: 6-H2**
✆ 020 7637 7770 — **www**.kitchentablelondon.co.uk
⊖ Goodge Street

Menu £125
Closed first 2 weeks January, 2 weeks September, 23-27 December and Sunday-Tuesday – booking essential – (dinner only) – (tasting menu only)
A/C

MARGOT

Italian • Elegant

Bucking the trend of casual eateries is this glamourous, elegant Italian, where a doorman greets you, staff sport tuxedos and the surroundings are sleek and stylish. The seasonal, regional Italian cooking has bags of flavour and a rustic edge.

45 Great Queen St ✉ WC2 5AA — **MAP: 6-J3**
020 3409 4777 — **www**.margotrestaurant.com
Holborn
Menu £25 (lunch and early dinner) - Carte £30/61
Closed 25 December

MERE

Modern cuisine • Fashionable

Monica Galetti's first collaboration with her husband, David, is an understatedly elegant basement restaurant flooded with natural light. Global, ingredient-led cooking features French influences with a nod to the South Pacific.

74 Charlotte St ✉ W1T 4QH — **MAP: 6-H2**
020 7268 6565 — **www**.mere-restaurant.com
Goodge Street
Menu £35 (weekday lunch) - Carte £46/64
Closed Sunday and bank holidays

NOBLE ROT

Traditional British • Rustic

A wine bar and restaurant from the people behind the wine magazine of the same name. Unfussy cooking comes with bold, gutsy flavours; expect fish from the Kent coast as well as classics like terrines, rillettes and home-cured meats.

51 Lamb's Conduit St ✉ WC1N 3NB — **MAP: 6-J1**
020 7242 8963 — **www**.noblerot.co.uk
Russell Square
Menu £16 (weekday lunch) - Carte £33/49
Closed 25-26 December and Sunday

THE NINTH ✿

Mediterranean cuisine • *Brasserie*

Jun Tanaka's career began in the early '90s and this – the ninth restaurant in which he has worked – is also the first he has owned. Although situated on foodie Charlotte Street, it's very much a neighbourhood spot, and both the lively downstairs with its counter for walk-ins and the more intimate first floor have a great feel to them.

The on-trend menu has sections including 'snacks', 'salads' and 'raw and cured', as well as 'meat' and 'fish'; staff suggest 3 starters, 2 mains and 2 vegetable dishes for two, although you're equally welcome to come in for a couple of plates and a glass of wine. Skilful cooking uses classical French techniques with a spotlight on the Mediterranean; dishes arrive at a good pace and certainly look the part – but the focus here is firmly on flavour. Vegetables are much more than just an accompaniment, with dishes such as Savoy cabbage with hazelnut pesto or charcoal-roasted celeriac with smoked almonds and wild garlic a highlight.

FIRST COURSE

Salted beef cheek, oxtail consommé and sauce ravigote. • Langoustine ravioli with consommé and kale.

MAIN COURSE

Chargrilled sea bream, lemon confit and miso. • Roe deer in salt crust with cavolo nero, hazelnuts and beetroot.

DESSERT

Pain perdu with vanilla ice cream. • Caramel panna cotta with clementine sauce.

22 Charlotte St ✉ W1T 2NB **MAP: 6-12**
✆ 020 3019 0880 — **www**.theninthlondon.com
⊖ Goodge Street

Menu £27 (lunch) - Carte £39/66
Closed Christmas-New Year, Sunday and bank holidays
A/C

NOIZÉ

Modern French • Neighbourhood

A softly spoken Frenchman, an alumnus of Pied à Terre, took over the former Dabbous site and created a delightfully relaxed, modern bistro. The unfussy French food is served at fair prices; sauces are a great strength. The wine list, with plenty of depth and fair mark-ups, is another highlight.

39 Whitfield St W1T 2SF **MAP: 6-H1**
020 7323 1310 — **www**.noize-restaurant.co.uk
Goodge Street
Carte £34/56
Closed 2 weeks August, 23 December-3 January, Easter, Saturday lunch, Sunday and Monday

---

ROKA

Japanese • Fashionable

The original Roka, where people come for the lively atmosphere as much as the cooking. The kitchen takes the flavours of Japanese food and adds its own contemporary touches; try specialities from the on-view Robata grill.

37 Charlotte St W1T 1RR **MAP: 6-I2**
020 7636 5228 — **www**.rokarestaurant.com
Goodge Street
Carte £42/75
Closed 25 December

SALT YARD

Mediterranean cuisine • Tapas bar

A ground floor bar and buzzy basement restaurant specialising in good value plates of tasty Italian and Spanish dishes, ideal for sharing. Ingredients are top-notch; charcuterie is a speciality. Super wine list and sincere, enthusiastic staff.

54 Goodge St. W1T 4NA **MAP: 6-H2**
020 7637 0657 — **www**.saltyard.co.uk
Goodge Street
Carte £20/28
Closed 31 December-1 January and dinner 24-25 December

PIED À TERRE ✿

Creative • Elegant

Over the last quarter of a century few London streets have seen more restaurants come and go than Charlotte Street, but one constant over that period has been David Moore's Pied à Terre. One of the reasons for its longevity has been its subtle reinventions: nothing ever too grandiose – just a little freshening up with some new art or clever lighting to keep the place looking relevant and vibrant. The room is undeniably intimate and the professional, thoughtful service goes a long way in ensuring the atmosphere remains serene and welcoming.

Of course, the restaurant's success is also due to the consistent standard of the cooking. The current chef continues to produce dishes based on classical French techniques but he also puts in a few nods to his own Greek background and this has given the cooking a bolder, more muscular edge than has been seen here for a while.

FIRST COURSE	MAIN COURSE	DESSERT
Smoked quail spelt risotto with coral mushrooms and watercress. • BBQ suckling pig with smoked eel and cabbage.	Poached turbot with langoustine and spinach. • Veal cutlet with trompettes and pommes soufflées.	Pink and red pavlova with raspberries, kaffir lime and a lavender custard. • Citrus crémeux with hazelnuts and meringue.

34 Charlotte St ✉ W1T 2NH **MAP: 6-12**
✆ 020 7636 1178 — **www**.pied-a-terre.co.uk
⊖ Goodge Street

Menu £38/80

Closed 23 December-9 January, Saturday lunch, Sunday and bank holidays - booking essential

BAYSWATER · MAIDA VALE

There may not appear to be an obvious link between Maida Vale and Italy, but the name of this smart area to the west of central London is derived from a battle fought over two hundred years ago in Southern Italy, and the most appealing visitor attraction in the neighbourhood is the charming canalside **Little Venice.** To stroll around here on a summer's day brings to mind promenading in a more distant European clime; it's hard to believe that the ear-shattering roar of the Westway is just a short walk away. South of this iconic elevated roadway – a snaking route out from Marylebone to the western suburbs – is Bayswater, a busy area of imposing nineteenth century buildings that's the epicentre of London's Middle Eastern community.

During its Victorian heyday, **Bayswater** was a grand and glamorous address for affluent and elegant types who wanted a giant green space (Hyde Park) on their doorstep. The whole area had been laid out in the mid 1800s, when grand squares and cream stuccoed terraces started to fill the acres between Brunel's curvy Paddington station and the park. But during the twentieth century Bayswater's cachet nose-dived, stigmatised as 'the wrong side of the park' by the arrivistes of Knightsbridge and Kensington. Today it's still a backpacker's paradise: home to a bewildering number of tourist hotels, flatshares and B&Bs, converted from the grand houses. But this tells only a fraction of the modern story, because the area has undergone a massive facelift. The hub of this makeover was the **Paddington Basin,** a gigantic reclamation of the old Grand Union Canal basin in the shadow of the rail terminus. From a ramshackle wasteground, it's now a shimmering zone of metal, steel and glass, a phantasmagoria of blue chip HQs, homes, shops and leisure facilities. Even the barges have been turned into permanently moored 'business barges'. Tree-lined towpaths along the perimeter complete the picture of a totally modern waterscape.

Lovers of the old Bayswater can still relish what made it famous in the first place: radiating out from **Lancaster Gate,** away from Hyde Park, is a web of streets with handsome squares and tucked-away mews, and it still retains pockets of close-knit communities, such as Porchester Square, west of Paddington station. Meanwhile, the 'cathedral' of the area, Whiteleys shopping centre in **Queensway**, remains a pivotal landmark, as it has been for more than a century. Just beyond Whiteleys heading away from central London, **Westbourne Grove** is still reassuringly expensive, or at least the bit that heads determinedly towards Notting Hill. But the wind of change has rustled other parts of the neighbourhood: Connaught Street has evolved into a villagey quarter of boutiques, galleries and restaurants, while, further west, Craven Hill Gardens is the height of chic.

Little Venice pretty much acts as a dividing line between Bayswater and Maida Vale. Technically, it's the point where the Paddington arm of the Grand Union Canal meets the **Regent's Canal,** but the name, coined by poet Robert Browning who lived close by, has come to encompass the whole area just to the north of the soaring Westway. Narrow boat moorings vie for attention alongside the cafés and pubs that mercifully lack the frantic high street buzz so typical of their kind away from the water's edge. The permanently moored boats were here a long time before those upstarts at Paddington Basin. This is where you can find old-time favourites including a floating art gallery and a puppet theatre barge. A wander round the residential streets of Maida Vale is also very pleasant, dominated by the impressive Edwardian blocks of flats that conjure up a distinctive well-to-do scene.

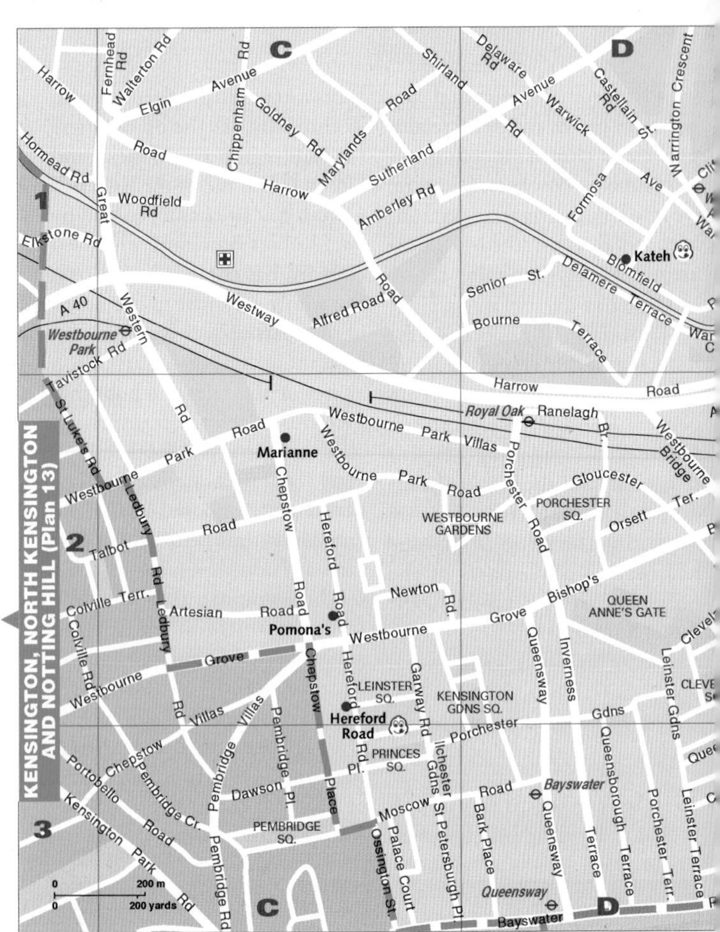
KENSINGTON, NORTH KENSINGTON AND NOTTING HILL (Plan 13)
Kateh
Marianne
Pomona's
Hereford Road
Westway
Harrow Road
Westbourne Grove
Chepstow Place
Queensway
Bayswater
Royal Oak
Westbourne Park
200 m
200 yards

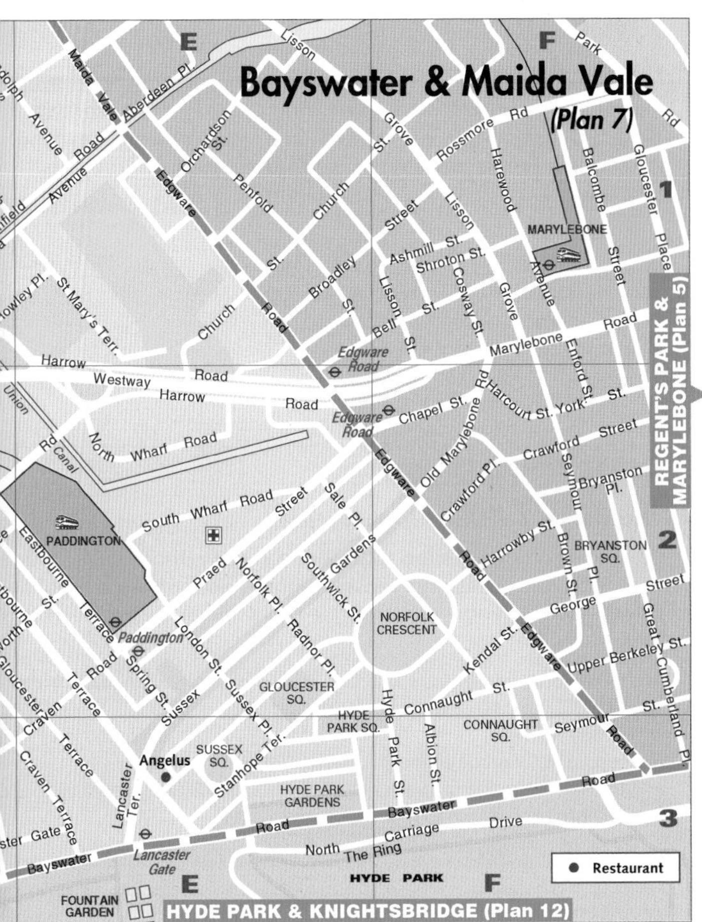
Bayswater & Maida Vale
(Plan 7)
E
F
1
2
3
MARYLEBONE
PADDINGTON
NORFOLK CRESCENT
BRYANSTON SQ.
GLOUCESTER SQ.
HYDE PARK SQ.
CONNAUGHT SQ.
SUSSEX SQ.
HYDE PARK GARDENS
HYDE PARK
FOUNTAIN GARDEN
Angelus
Restaurant
Edgware Road
Paddington
Lancaster Gate
Maida Vale
Edgware Road
Aberdeen Pl.
Lisson Grove
Park Rd
Rossmore Rd
Orchardson St.
Penfold St.
Church St.
Broadley St.
Ashmill St.
Shroton St.
Cosway St.
Bell St.
Harewood Avenue
Balcombe Street
Gloucester Place
Marylebone Road
Harrow Road
Westway
North Wharf Road
South Wharf Road
Chapel St.
Old Marylebone Rd
Harcourt St.
York St.
Crawford Street
Crawford Pl.
Bryanston Pl.
Seymour Pl.
Enford St.
Harrowby St.
Brown St.
George Street
Great Cumberland Pl.
Upper Berkeley St.
Kendal St.
Connaught St.
Seymour St.
Praed Street
Sale Pl.
Norfolk Pl.
Southwick St.
Sussex Gardens
Radnor Pl.
London St.
Sussex Pl.
Spring St.
Stanhope Ter.
Hyde Park St.
Albion St.
Lancaster Ter.
Bayswater Road
North Carriage Drive
The Ring
Eastbourne Terrace
Craven Road
Craven Terrace
Gloucester Terrace
St Mary's Terr.
Union Canal
Avenue Road
REGENT'S PARK & MARYLEBONE (Plan 5)
HYDE PARK & KNIGHTSBRIDGE (Plan 12)

ANGELUS

French • Brasserie

Hospitable owner has created an attractive French brasserie within a 19C former pub, with a warm and inclusive feel. Satisfying and honest French cooking uses seasonal British ingredients.

4 Bathurst St ✉ W2 2SD **MAP: 7-E3**
020 7402 0083 — **www**.angelusrestaurant.co.uk
Lancaster Gate
Menu £28/41 - Carte £39/54
Closed 24-25 December and 1 January

HEREFORD ROAD

Traditional British • Neighbourhood

Converted butcher's shop specialising in tasty British dishes without frills, using first-rate, seasonal ingredients; offal a highlight. Booths for six people are the prized seats. Friendly and relaxed feel.

3 Hereford Rd ✉ W2 4AB **MAP: 7-C2**
020 7727 1144 — **www**.herefordroad.org
Bayswater
Menu £16 (weekday lunch) - Carte £25/32
Closed 24 December-3 January and August bank holiday - booking essential

---

KATEH

Mediterranean cuisine • Neighbourhood

Booking is imperative if you want to join the locals who have already discovered what a little jewel they have in the form of this buzzy, busy Persian restaurant. Authentic stews, expert chargrilling and lovely pastries and teas.

5 Warwick Pl ✉ W9 2PX **MAP: 7-D1**
020 7289 3393 — **www**.katehrestaurant.co.uk
Warwick Avenue
Carte £21/38
Closed 25-26 December - booking essential - (dinner only and lunch Saturday-Sunday)

MARIANNE

French • Cosy

With just six tables, there are few more intimate restaurants that this one, set up by Marianne Lumb, a former finalist on MasterChef. The menus are changed daily and while the cooking is classically based, it also keeps things quite light.

104a Chepstow Rd W2 5QS **MAP: 7-C2**
020 3675 7750 — **www**.mariannerestaurant.com
Westbourne Park

Menu £48/75
Closed 22 December-7 January, 19 August-2 September, Monday and bank holidays - booking essential - (dinner only and lunch Friday-Sunday) - (tasting menu only)

POMONA'S

World cuisine • Neighbourhood

A large neighbourhood restaurant with bright décor, an airy, open feel and a fun, laid-back Californian vibe. All-day menus offer soulful, colourful cooking with breakfast, smoothies, salads, house specials and small plates.

47 Hereford Rd W2 5AH **MAP: 7-C2**
020 7229 1503 — **www**.pomonas.co.uk
Bayswater

Carte £23/51
Closed 25-26 December

Look for our symbol spotlighting restaurants with a notable wine list.

CITY OF LONDON · CLERKENWELL FINSBURY · SOUTHWARK

Say what you like about London, **The City** is the place where it all started. The Romans developed this small area – this square mile – nearly two thousand years ago, and today it stands as the economic heartbeat of not only the capital, but the country as a whole. Each morning it's besieged with an army of bankers, lawyers and traders, and each evening it's abandoned to an eerie ghost-like fate. Of course, this mass exodus is offset by the two perennial crowd-pullers, **St Paul's** and the **Tower of London**, but these are both on the periphery of the area, away from the frenetic commercial zone within. The casual visitor tends to steer clear of the City, but for those willing to mix it with the daytime swarm of office workers, there are many historical nuggets hidden away, waiting to be mined. You can find here, amongst the skyscrapers, a tempting array of Roman ruins, medieval landmarks and brooding churches designed by Wren and Hawksmoor. One of the best ways of encapsulating everything that's happened here down the centuries is to visit the Museum of London, on London Wall, which tells the story of the city from the very start, and the very start means 300,000 BC.

For those seeking the hip corners of this part of London, the best advice is to head slightly north-west, using the brutalist space of the **Barbican Arts Centre** as your marker. You're now entering **Clerkenwell**. Sliding north/south through here - and ending up at the historic Smithfield Meat Market - is the bustling and buzzy St John Street, home to the original St John restaurant, pioneer of nose-to-tail eating. Further West, Exmouth Market teems with trendy bars and restaurants, popular with those on their way to the perennially excellent dance concerts at Sadler's Wells Theatre. Clerkenwell's revivalist vibe has seen the steady reclamation of old warehouse space: during the Industrial Revolution, the area boomed with the introduction of breweries, print works and the manufacture of clocks and watches. After World War II, decline set in, but these days city professionals and loft-dwellers are drawn to the area's zeitgeist-leading galleries and clubs, not to mention the wonderful floor-to-ceiling delicatessens.

The area was once a religious centre, frequented by monks and nuns; its name derives from the parish clerks who performed Biblical mystery plays around the Clerk's Well set in a nunnery wall. This can be found in **Farringdon Lane** complete with an exhibition explaining all. Close by in St John's Lane is the 16C gatehouse which is home to the Museum of the Order of St John (famous today for its ambulance services), and chock full of fascinating objects related to the Order's medieval history.

Not too long ago, a trip over London Bridge to **Southwark** was for locals only, its trademark grimness ensuring it was well off the tourist map. These days, visitors treat it as a place of pilgrimage as three of London's modern success stories reside here in the shadow of The Shard. **Tate Modern** has become the city's most visited attraction, a huge former power station that generates a blistering show of modern art from 1900 to the present day, its massive turbine hall a must-see feature in itself. Practically next door but a million miles away architecturally is Shakespeare's **Globe,** a wonderful evocation of medieval showtime. Half a mile east is tourists' favourite, **Borough Market**. Foodies can't resist the organic, feel-good nature of the place, with, its mind-boggling number of stalls selling produce ranging from every kind of fruit and veg to rare-breed meats, oils, preserves, chocolates and breads. And that's just for hors-d'œuvres...

I. Dimitrov/age fotostock

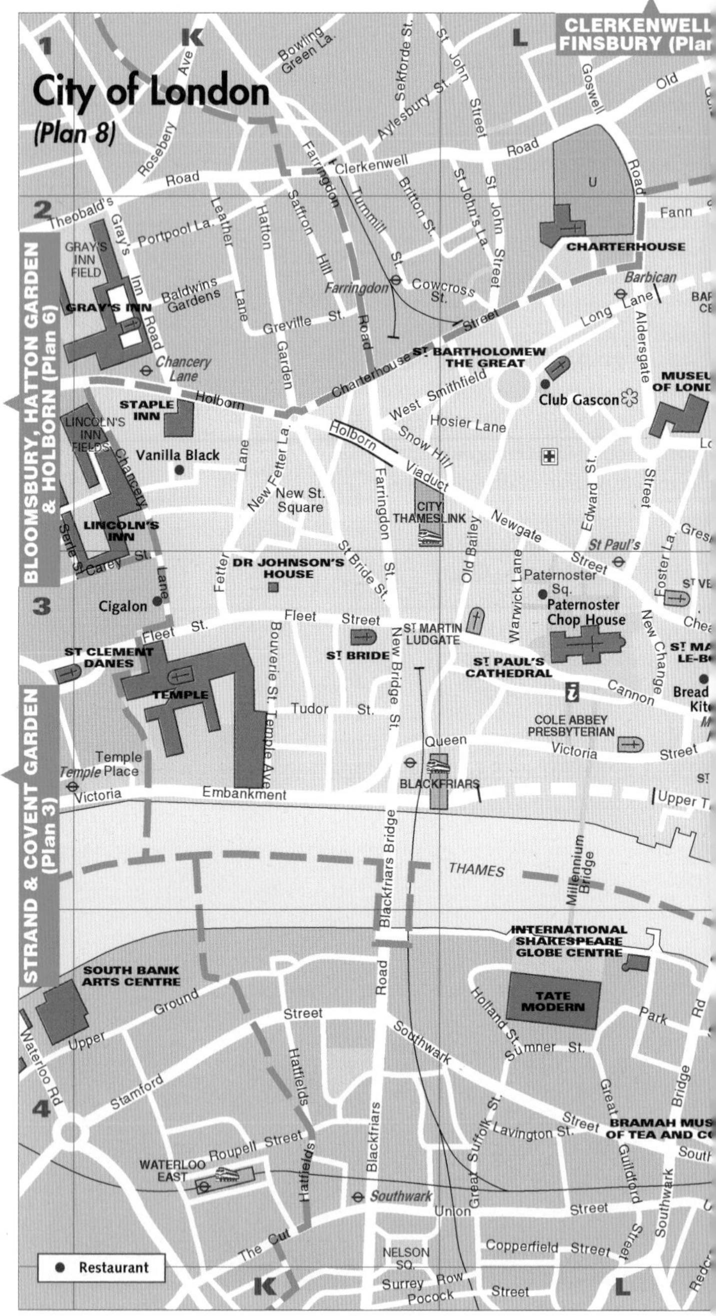
City of London
(Plan 8)
CLERKENWELL FINSBURY (Plan
BLOOMSBURY, HATTON GARDEN & HOLBORN (Plan 6)
STRAND & COVENT GARDEN (Plan 3)
CHARTERHOUSE
ST BARTHOLOMEW THE GREAT
Club Gascon
STAPLE INN
Vanilla Black
LINCOLN'S INN
DR JOHNSON'S HOUSE
Cigalon
ST CLEMENT DANES
TEMPLE
ST BRIDE
ST MARTIN LUDGATE
ST PAUL'S CATHEDRAL
Paternoster Chop House
COLE ABBEY PRESBYTERIAN
CITY THAMESLINK
BLACKFRIARS
THAMES
INTERNATIONAL SHAKESPEARE GLOBE CENTRE
TATE MODERN
SOUTH BANK ARTS CENTRE
BRAMAH MUS OF TEA AND C
WATERLOO EAST
Southwark
Restaurant

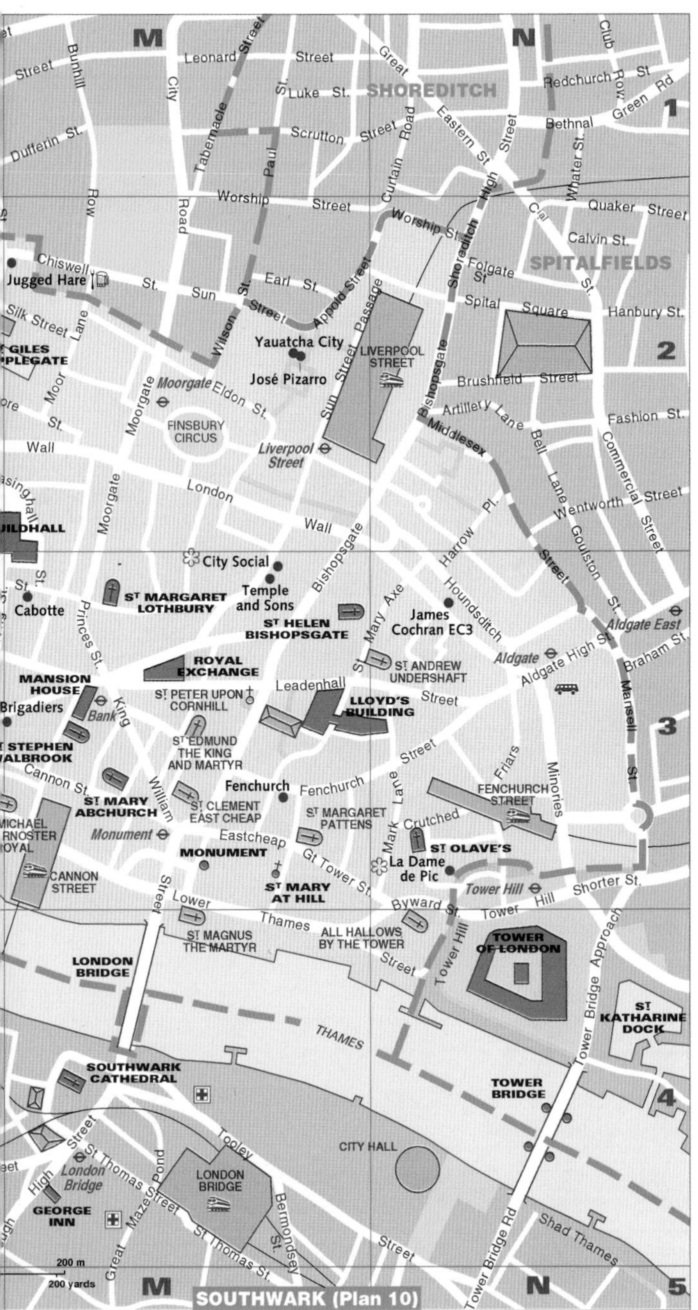

M
N
SHOREDITCH
SPITALFIELDS
1
2
3
4
5
Jugged Hare
Yauatcha City
José Pizarro
LIVERPOOL STREET
Moorgate
FINSBURY CIRCUS
Liverpool Street
City Social
Temple and Sons
Cabotte
ST MARGARET LOTHBURY
ST HELEN BISHOPSGATE
James Cochran EC3
ROYAL EXCHANGE
MANSION HOUSE
Brigadiers
Bank
ST PETER UPON CORNHILL
LLOYD'S BUILDING
ST ANDREW UNDERSHAFT
Aldgate
Aldgate East
ST EDMUND THE KING AND MARTYR
ST MARY ABCHURCH
ST CLEMENT EAST CHEAP
Fenchurch
ST MARGARET PATTENS
FENCHURCH STREET
Monument
MONUMENT
ST OLAVE'S
La Dame de Pic
CANNON STREET
ST MARY AT HILL
Tower Hill
TOWER OF LONDON
ST MAGNUS THE MARTYR
ALL HALLOWS BY THE TOWER
LONDON BRIDGE
THAMES
ST KATHARINE DOCK
SOUTHWARK CATHEDRAL
TOWER BRIDGE
CITY HALL
London Bridge
LONDON BRIDGE
GEORGE INN
200 m
200 yards
SOUTHWARK (Plan 10)

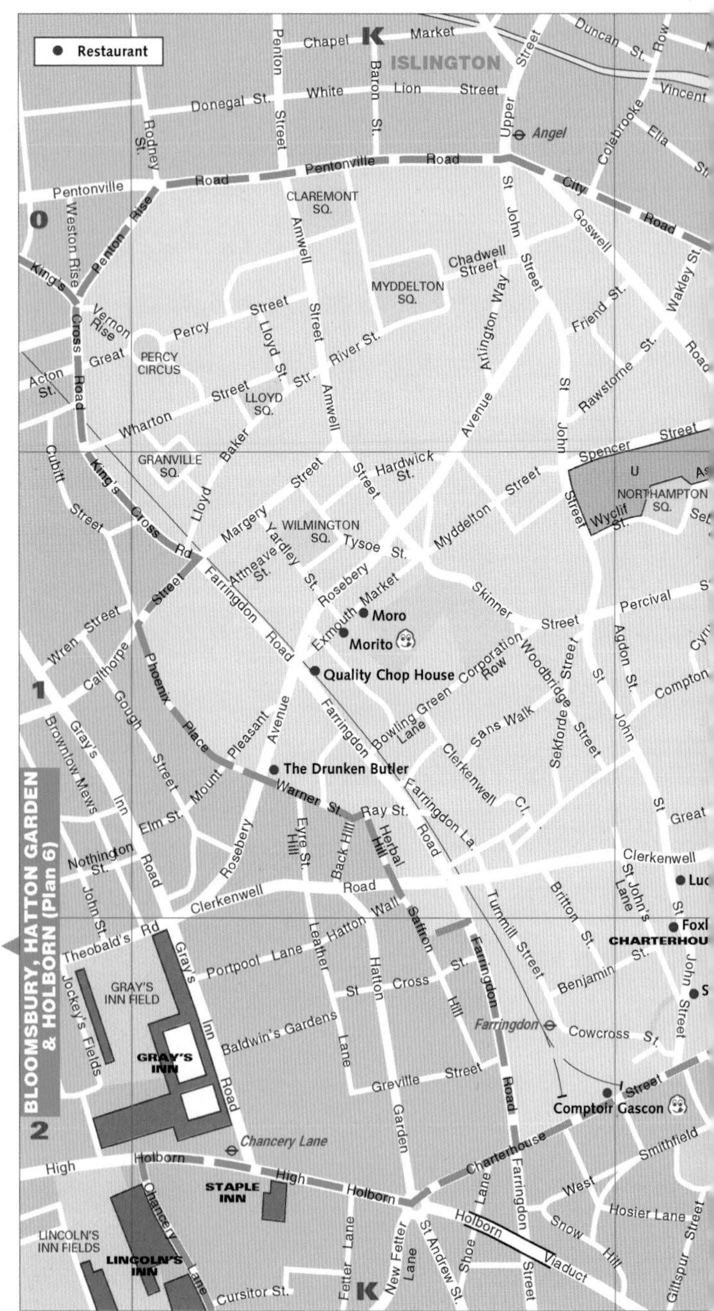
Restaurant
ISLINGTON
BLOOMSBURY, HATTON GARDEN & HOLBORN (Plan 6)
Moro
Morito
Quality Chop House
The Drunken Butler
Comptoir Gascon
CLAREMONT SQ.
MYDDELTON SQ.
PERCY CIRCUS
LLOYD SQ.
GRANVILLE SQ.
WILMINGTON SQ.
NORTHAMPTON SQ.
GRAY'S INN FIELD
GRAY'S INN
STAPLE INN
LINCOLN'S INN FIELDS
LINCOLN'S INN
CHARTERHOU
Angel
Farringdon
Chancery Lane
Pentonville Road
City Road
King's Cross Road
Farringdon Road
Clerkenwell Road
Rosebery Avenue
High Holborn
Holborn Viaduct
Charterhouse Street
Hatton Garden
Exmouth Market

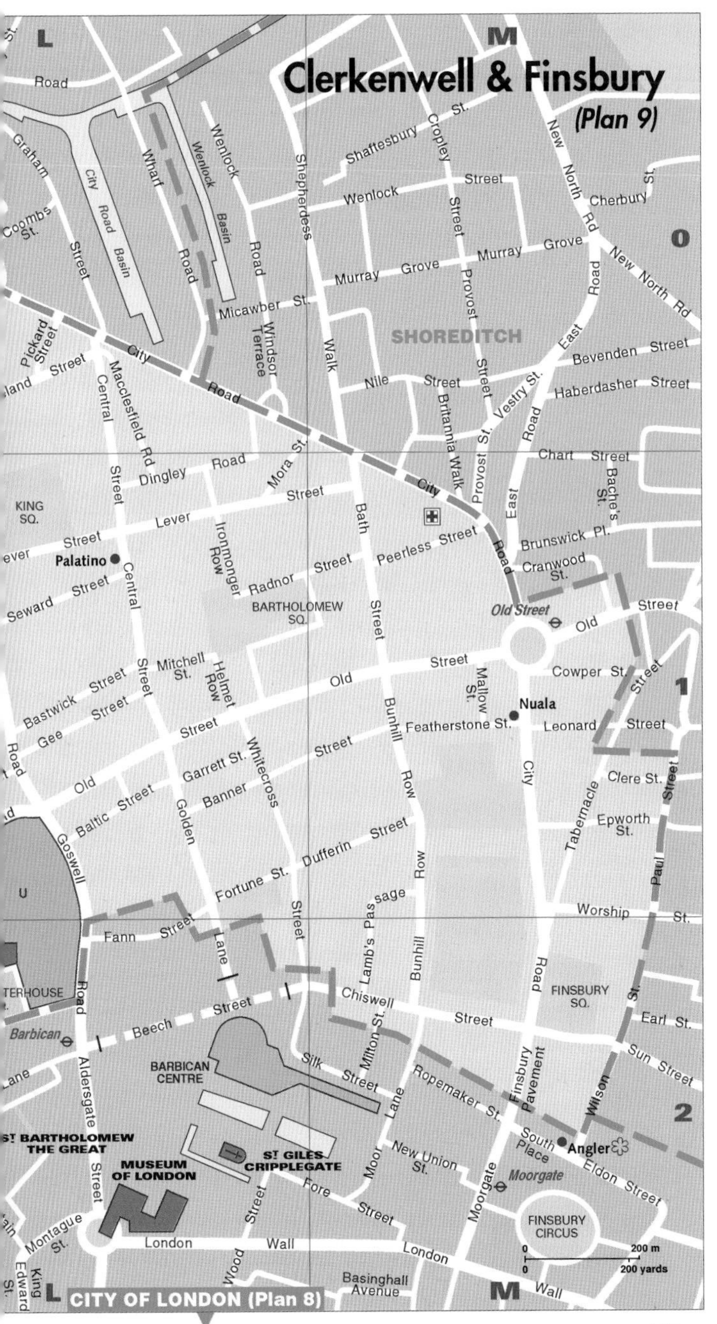
Clerkenwell & Finsbury
(Plan 9)
SHOREDITCH
KING SQ.
BARTHOLOMEW SQ.
FINSBURY SQ.
FINSBURY CIRCUS
BARBICAN CENTRE
MUSEUM OF LONDON
ST GILES CRIPPLEGATE
ST BARTHOLOMEW THE GREAT
Palatino
Nuala
Angler
Old Street
Barbican
Moorgate
City Road
Old Street
Goswell Road
Aldersgate Street
Whitecross Street
Bunhill Row
Chiswell Street
Moorgate
London Wall
CITY OF LONDON (Plan 8)
200 m
200 yards

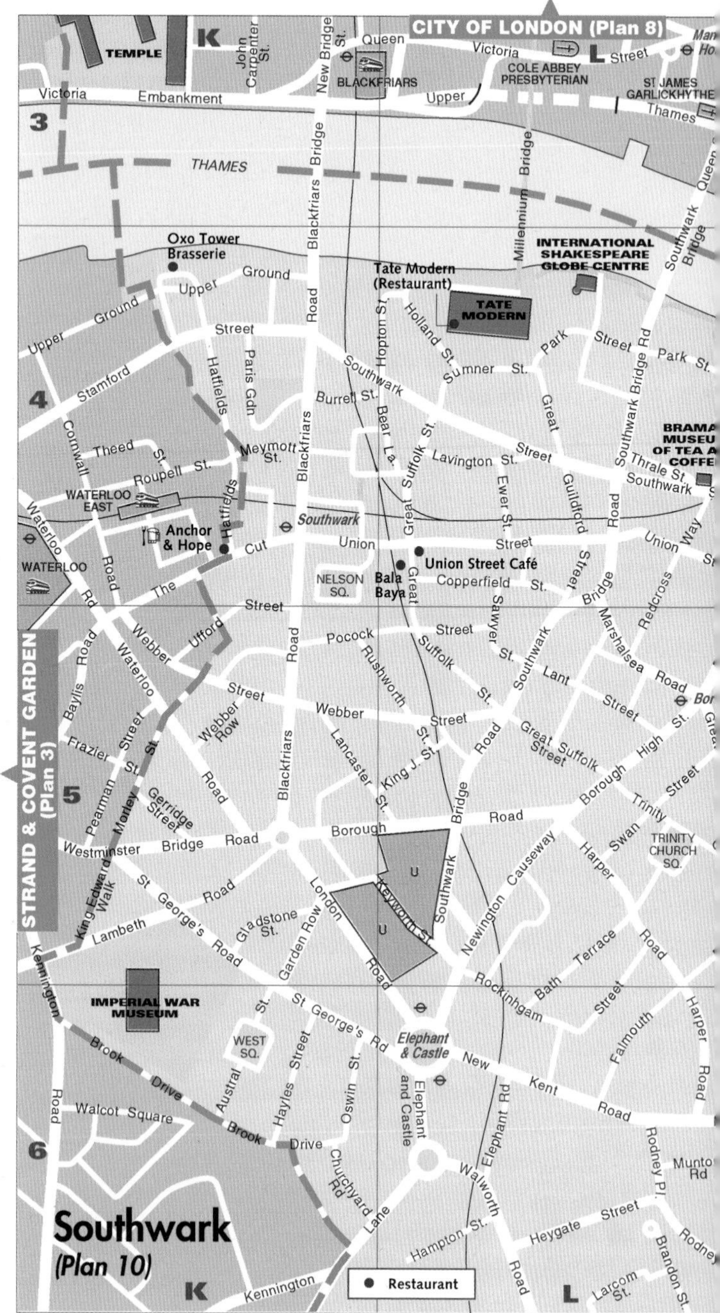
CITY OF LONDON (Plan 8)
TEMPLE
BLACKFRIARS
COLE ABBEY PRESBYTERIAN
ST JAMES GARLICKHYTHE
THAMES
Oxo Tower Brasserie
Tate Modern (Restaurant)
TATE MODERN
INTERNATIONAL SHAKESPEARE GLOBE CENTRE
WATERLOO EAST
WATERLOO
Anchor & Hope
Southwark
NELSON SQ.
Bala Baya
Union Street Café
TRINITY CHURCH SQ.
IMPERIAL WAR MUSEUM
WEST SQ.
Elephant & Castle
STRAND & COVENT GARDEN (Plan 3)
Southwark
(Plan 10)
Restaurant

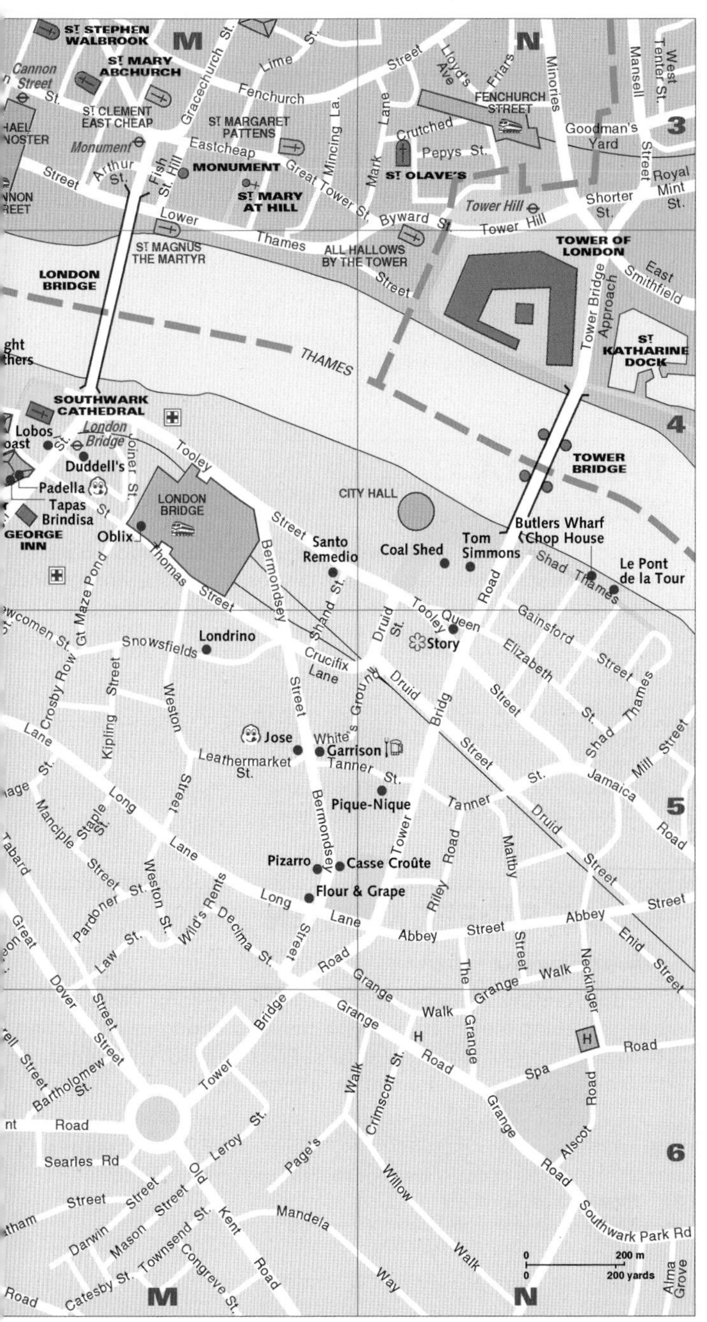

Southwark Cathedral
London Bridge
Lobos
Duddell's
Padella
Tapas Brindisa
George Inn
Oblix
Santo Remedio
Coal Shed
Tom Simmons
Butlers Wharf Chop House
Le Pont de la Tour
Story
Londrino
Jose
Garrison
Pique-Nique
Pizarro
Casse Croûte
Flour & Grape
Tower of London
Tower Bridge
St Katharine Dock
City Hall
Thames
Monument
St Mary at Hill
St Olave's
All Hallows by the Tower
St Magnus the Martyr
Fenchurch Street
Tower Hill

ANCHOR & HOPE

Modern British • *Pub*

As popular as ever thanks to its congenial feel and lived-in looks but mostly because of the appealingly seasonal menu and the gutsy, bold cooking that delivers on flavour. No reservations so be prepared to wait at the bar.

36 The Cut ✉ SE1 8LP — **MAP: 10-K4**
020 7928 9898 — **www**.anchorandhopepub.co.uk
Southwark.

Menu £17 (weekday lunch) - Carte £19/46
Closed Christmas-New Year, Sunday dinner, Monday lunch and bank holidays - bookings not accepted

---

BALA BAYA

Middle Eastern • *Design*

A friendly, lively restaurant which celebrates the Middle Eastern heritage of its passionate owner. Dishes are fresh, vibrant and designed for sharing and the bright, modern interior is inspired by the Bauhaus architecture of Tel Aviv.

Arch 25, Old Union Yard Arches, 229 Union St ✉ SE1 0LR — **MAP: 10-L4**
020 8001 7015 — **www**.balabaya.co.uk
Southwark

Menu £19 (lunch) - Carte £31/45
Closed 25-26 December and Sunday dinner

BREAD STREET KITCHEN

Modern cuisine • *Trendy*

Gordon Ramsay's take on NY loft-style dining comes with a large bar, thumping music, an open kitchen and enough zinc ducting to kit out a small industrial estate. For the food, think modern bistro dishes with an element of refinement.

10 Bread St ✉ EC4M 9AJ — **MAP: 8-L3**
020 3030 4050 — **www**.gordonramsayrestaurants.com/bread-street-kitchen
St Paul's

Carte £32/62

ANGLER ✿

Seafood • Elegant

As the restaurant's name suggests, fish is the mainstay of the menu – the majority of it from Cornwall and Scotland – and the kitchen has the confidence to know that when it is of this quality, it needs little in the way of adornment. That's not to say there isn't a certain vibrancy to the cooking, and the satisfying dishes display plenty of colour, balance and poise. Much thought has also gone into the white wine orientated wine list, with its commendable number of keenly priced labels.

The restaurant itself may be on the top floor of the South Place hotel but feels very much like a separate, stand-alone restaurant with its own personality. The first thing you notice is the ornate mirrored ceiling and the brightness of the room. It also feels very intimate and comes with its own terrace where, on a warm evening, you'll see the cocktails go flying out.

FIRST COURSE

Roast octopus with taramasalata, potatoes and red wine bagna càuda. • Dorset crab and Orkney scallop ravioli with roasted seaweed broth.

MAIN COURSE

Cod with garlic, morels and squid. • Cornish red mullet with Jersey Royal cream, smoked bacon and parsley.

DESSERT

Rhubarb, Brillat-Savarin cream and stem ginger ice cream. • Apricot soufflé with camomile ice cream and almond biscotti.

South Place Hotel, 3 South Pl ✉ EC2M 2AF **MAP: 9-M2**
✆ 020 3215 1260 — **www**.anglerrestaurant.com
⊖ Moorgate

Menu £34 (weekday lunch) - Carte £50/72
Closed 26-30 December, Saturday lunch and Sunday

Ⓝ BRIGADIERS

Indian • *Exotic décor*

The army mess clubs of India provide the theme for this large restaurant on the ground floor of the Bloomberg building. BBQ and street food from around India is the focus; with 'Feast' menus for larger parties. Beer and whisky are also a feature. The atmosphere is predictably loud and lively.

1-5 Bloomberg Arcade ✉ EC4N 8AR **MAP: 8-M3**
020 3319 8140 — **www**.brigadierslondon.com
⊖ Bank

Menu £25 (lunch) - Carte £27/45
Closed Christmas - booking essential

BUTLERS WHARF CHOP HOUSE

Traditional British • *Brasserie*

Grab a table on the terrace in summer and dine in the shadow of Tower Bridge. Rustic feel to the interior; noisy and fun. The menu focuses on traditional English ingredients and dishes; grilled meats a speciality.

36e Shad Thames, Butlers Wharf ✉ SE1 2YE **MAP: 10-N4**
020 7403 3403 — **www**.chophouse-restaurant.co.uk
⊖ London Bridge

Menu £30 - Carte £29/58
Closed 1 January

CABOTTE

French • *Wine bar*

A bistro de luxe with a stunning wine list - owned by two master sommeliers who share a passion for the wines of Burgundy. Cooking comes with the same regional bias and the accomplished classics are simple in style and rich in flavour.

48 Gresham St ✉ EC2V 7AY **MAP: 8-M3**
020 7600 1616 — **www**.cabotte.co.uk
⊖ Bank

Carte £35/51
Closed Saturday, Sunday and bank holidays - booking essential

CASSE CROÛTE

French • Bistro

Squeeze into this tiny bistro and you'll find yourself transported to rural France. A blackboard menu offers three choices for each course but new dishes are added as others run out. The cooking is rustic, authentic and heartening.

109 Bermondsey St ✉ SE1 3XB **MAP: 10-M5**
020 7407 2140 — **www**.cassecroute.co.uk
London Bridge

Carte £31/37
Closed Sunday dinner - booking essential

CIGALON

French • Elegant

Hidden away among the lawyers offices on Chancery Lane, this bright, high-ceilinged restaurant pays homage to the food and wine of Provence. Expect flavoursome French classics like salade niçoise and bouillabaisse.

115 Chancery Ln ✉ WC2A 1PP **MAP: 8-K3**
020 7242 8373 — **www**.cigalon.co.uk
Chancery Lane

Menu £23/37 - Carte lunch £31/46
Closed Christmas, New Year, Saturday, Sunday and bank holidays
A/C

N COAL SHED

Meats and grills • Design

Coal Shed was established in Brighton before opening here in this modern development by Tower Bridge. It's set over two floors and specialises in steaks but there's also plenty of seafood on offer. Desserts are good too; try the various 'sweets'.

Unit 3.1, One Tower Bridge, 4 Crown Sq ✉ SE1 2SE **MAP: 10-N4**
020 3384 7272 — **www**.coalshed-restaurant.co.uk
London Bridge

Menu £20 (lunch and early dinner) - Carte £27/54
Closed 25-26 December
A/C

CITY SOCIAL ✿

Modern cuisine • *Elegant*

The buzz from the bar is the first thing you notice at Jason Atherton's handsome, well-run restaurant on the 24th floor of Tower 42. Dark and moody with a subtle art deco twist, it boasts impressive views of the City's ever-changing skyline – especially if you're sitting at one of the coveted window tables. Large parties should request one of the comfortable circular booths; those with bigger plans should ask for table 10, the proposal table.

The menu is the same at lunch and dinner, but has some flexibility built in. Influences are largely European and dishes like côte de boeuf for two, lobster and chips and black olive potato gnocchi are not only incredibly tasty but also good value. The kitchen has a deft touch but wisely acknowledges its customer base by making dishes quite robust in flavour and generous in size – this is elegant, refined but satisfying cooking. The wine list is also noteworthy, with a good mix of styles and prices.

FIRST COURSE

Brixham crab with pickled kohlrabi, nashi pear and pink grapefruit. • Pig's trotter and ham hock with black pudding, apple and Madeira.

MAIN COURSE

Isle of Gigha halibut with Wye Valley asparagus and tomato consommé. • Saddle of rabbit with girolles, spelt, lovage emulsion and black garlic.

DESSERT

Hazelnut plaisir sucré, chocolate syrup, biscuit, milk ice cream. • Raspberry soufflé with chocolate ice cream.

Tower 42 (24th floor), 25 Old Broad St **MAP: 8-M3**
EC2N 1HQ
020 7877 7703 — **www.**citysociallondon.com
Liverpool Street

Carte £47/90
Closed Sunday and bank holidays

CLUB GASCON ✿

French • Elegant

Those living in Gascony enjoy a diet with the highest fat content in France yet they tend to live longer than their compatriots. This 'Gascony Paradox' is surely reason enough to explore further this most indulgent of cuisines. Chef-owner Pascal Aussignac is passionate about all things south western: get him started on the quality of the produce and he'll talk the hind legs off an âne.

Head to the 'Gascon' section of the menu for the signature dishes, 'Season' for the ones celebrating the time of year and 'Garden' for vegetarian dishes. Alternatively, the tasting menu is a good way to sample a variety of the robustly flavoured but refined dishes. Service these days has a little more personality and the bar has been removed to open up the place and give diners a little more elbow room. What hasn't changed is the beautiful vintage marble walls and the vast signature floral display.

FIRST COURSE	MAIN COURSE	DESSERT
Venison carpaccio with sea urchin jus, cauliflower and sansho pepper. • King scallop and white asparagus with black pudding and argan oil.	Veal sweetbreads with lobster and cuttlefish tagliatelle. • Turbot with ox sauce, rhubarb and dill vinaigrette.	Pineapple and ginger soufflé with lemongrass sorbet. • Roquefort pebble with sugarcane and walnut.

■ 57 West Smithfield ✉ EC1A 9DS — **MAP: 8-L2**
✆ 020 7600 6144 — **www**.clubgascon.com
⊖ Barbican

■ Menu £40/84 - Carte £46/76
Closed 22 December-7 January, Saturday lunch, Monday lunch, Sunday and bank holidays - booking essential

A/C 🍇

COMPTOIR GASCON

French • Bistro

A buzzy, well-priced restaurant; sister to Club Gascon. Rustic and satisfying specialities from the SW of France include wine, bread, cheese and plenty of duck, with cassoulet and duck rillettes perennial favourites and the duck burger popular at lunch. There's also produce on display to take home.

61-63 Charterhouse St. ✉ EC1M 6HJ **MAP: 9-K2**
✆ 020 7608 0851 — **www**.comptoirgascon.com
⊖ Farringdon

Carte £18/34
Closed Christmas-New Year, Saturday lunch, Sunday, Monday and bank holidays - booking essential
A/C

N THE DRUNKEN BUTLER

French • Regional décor

The chef-owner's quiet enthusiasm pervades every aspect of this small but bright restaurant. The cooking is classical French at heart but also informed by his travels and Persian heritage; dishes provide plenty of colour, texture and flavour.

20 Rosebery Ave ✉ EC1R 4SX **MAP: 9-K1**
✆ 020 7101 4020 — **www**.thedrunkenbutler.com
⊖ Farringdon

Menu £24/49
Closed 1 week August, Saturday lunch, Sunday and Monday - booking essential
A/C

N DUDDELL'S

Chinese • Historic

A former church, dating from 1703, seems an unlikely setting for a Cantonese restaurant but this striking conversion is the London branch of the Hong Kong original. Lunchtime dim sum is a highlight but be sure to order the Peking duck which comes with 8 condiments in two servings.

9A St. Thomas St ✉ SE1 9RY **MAP: 10-M4**
✆ 020 3957 9932 — **www**.duddells.co/london
⊖ London Bridge

Menu £25 (weekday lunch) - Carte £36/69
Closed 25 December and 1 January

LA DAME DE PIC ✿

Modern French • Design

You'd expect a famous chef bringing her brand from Paris to London to seek out a grand space for her restaurant. And while this high-ceilinged, columned room, situated in the impressive Beaux-Arts style Four Seasons Hotel, is certainly striking; the restaurant is not so much a formal temple of gastronomy as a charming brasserie deluxe – stylish, spacious and contemporary, with lots of white, plenty of light and some attractive modern art.

Anne-Sophie Pic's cuisine is refined, colourful and original; it's rooted in classic French techniques yet delivered in a modern manner, relying on exciting flavour combinations of top quality ingredients. Signature dishes include Berlingots (pasta parcels of smoked Pélardon cheese), wild sea bass with caviar and champagne sauce, and the arresting 'white millefeuille' for dessert. The well-structured wine list highlights wines from the Rhône Valley – home of restaurant Maison Pic, the Valence institution owned by the Pic family.

FIRST COURSE	MAIN COURSE	DESSERT
Berlingots with smoked Brillat-Savarin, asparagus, bergamot and mint. • Steamed crab with lovage mayonnaise and blackcurrant & elderflower jelly.	Challans chicken with tonka bean tea, pumpkin parcels, chestnut and yuzu. • Honey-marinated salmon with cardamom, marigold and asparagus.	The white millefeuille. • Pic chocolate with cinnamon leaf ice cream, chocolate mousse and confit lemon.

■ Four Seasons Hotel London at Ten Trinity Square, 10 Trinity Sq ✉ EC3N 4AJ **MAP: 8-N3**
☎ 020 3297 3799 — **www.**ladamedepiclondon.co.uk
⊖ Tower Hill

■ Menu £39 (lunch) - Carte £69/91
Closed Sunday

EL PASTÓR

Mexican • Trendy

A lively, informal restaurant under the railway arches at London Bridge; inspired by the taquerias of Mexico City. Flavours are beautifully fresh, fragrant and spicy; don't miss the Taco Al Pastór after which the restaurant is named.

7a Stoney St, Borough Market ✉ SE1 9AA **MAP: 10-M4**
020 7440 1461 — **www**.tacoselpastor.co.uk
London Bridge

Carte £14/32
Closed 25-26 December, 1 January, Sunday dinner and bank holidays - bookings not accepted

A/C

ELLIOT'S

Modern cuisine • Rustic

A lively, unpretentious café which sources its ingredients from Borough Market, in which it stands. The appealing menu is concise and the cooking is earthy, pleasingly uncomplicated and very satisfying. Try one of the sharing dishes.

12 Stoney St, Borough Market ✉ SE1 9AD **MAP: 10-M4**
020 7403 7436 — **www**.elliotscafe.com
London Bridge

Carte £21/41
Closed Sunday and bank holidays

FENCHURCH

Modern cuisine • Design

Arrive at the 'Walkie Talkie' early so you can first wander round the Sky Garden and take in the views. The smartly dressed restaurant is housed in a glass box within the atrium. Dishes are largely British and the accomplished cooking uses modern techniques.

Level 37, Sky Garden, 20 Fenchurch St ✉ EC3M 3BY **MAP: 8-M3**
0333 772 0020 — **www**.skygarden.london
Monument

Menu £35 (weekday lunch) - Carte £53/68
Closed 25-27 December

A/C

Ⓝ FLOUR & GRAPE

Italian • Simple

The clue's in the name - pasta and wine. A choice of 7 or 8 antipasti are followed by the same number of homemade pasta dishes, with a dessert menu largely centred around gelato. Add in a well-chosen wine list with some pretty low mark-ups and it's no wonder this place is busy.

214 Bermondsey St ✉ SE1 3TQ **MAP: 10-M5**
020 7407 4682 — **www**.flourandgrape.com
⊖ London Bridge
Carte £15/28
Closed Christmas and Monday lunch - bookings not accepted

FOXLOW

Meats and grills • Neighbourhood

From the clever Hawksmoor people comes this fun and funky place where the staff ensure everyone's having a good time. There are steaks available but plenty of other choices too, with influences from Italy, Asia and the Middle East.

69-73 St John St ✉ EC1M 4AN **MAP: 9-L2**
020 7680 2702 — **www**.foxlow.co.uk
⊖ Farringdon
Menu £18 (weekdays) - Carte £22/39
Closed 24 December-1 January and bank holidays

GARRISON

Mediterranean cuisine • Pub

Known for its charming vintage look, booths and sweet-natured service, The Garrison boasts a warm, relaxed vibe. Open from breakfast until dinner, when a Mediterranean-led menu pulls in the crowds.

99-101 Bermondsey St ✉ SE1 3XB **MAP: 10-M5**
020 7089 9355 — **www**.thegarrison.co.uk
⊖ London Bridge.
Carte £26/40
Closed 25 December - booking essential at dinner

JAMES COCHRAN EC3

Modern cuisine • *Simple*

A spacious, simply furnished restaurant where the eponymous chef offers original combinations of interesting ingredients in an array of gutsy, good value small plates. The 6 course evening tasting menu is available with matching wines.

19 Bevis Marks ✉ EC3A 7JA **MAP: 8-N3**
020 3302 0310 — **www**.jcochran.restaurant
Liverpool Street
Carte £40/45
Closed Christmas, Saturday lunch, Sunday and bank holidays - booking essential at lunch

---

JOSÉ

Spanish • *Minimalist*

Standing up while eating tapas feels so right, especially at this snug, lively bar that packs 'em in like boquerones. The vibrant dishes are intensely flavoured - five per person should suffice; go for the daily fish dishes from the blackboard. There's a great list of sherries too.

104 Bermondsey St ✉ SE1 3UB **MAP: 10-M5**
020 7403 4902 — **www**.josepizarro.com
London Bridge
Carte £16/34
Closed 25-27 December and 1-2 January - bookings not accepted

---

JOSÉ PIZARRO

Spanish • *Tapas bar*

The eponymous chef's third operation is a good fit here: it's well run, flexible and fairly priced - and that includes the wine list. The Spanish menu is nicely balanced, with the seafood dishes being the standouts.

36 Broadgate Circle ✉ EC2M 1QS **MAP: 8-M2**
020 7256 5333 — **www**.josepizarro.com
Liverpool Street
Carte £17/56
Closed Sunday

JUGGED HARE

Traditional British • Pub

Vegetarians may feel ill at ease - and not just because of the taxidermy. The atmospheric dining room, with its open kitchen down one side, specialises in stout British dishes, with meats from the rotisserie a highlight.

42 Chiswell St ✉ EC1Y 4SA — **MAP: 8-M2**
020 7614 0134 — **www**.thejuggedhare.com
⊖ Barbican.
Menu £25 (early dinner) - Carte £27/58
Closed 25-26 December - booking essential

LOBOS

Spanish • Tapas bar

A dimly lit, decidedly compact tapas bar under the railway arches - sit upstairs to enjoy the theatre of the open kitchen. Go for one of the speciality meat dishes like the leg of slow-roasted Castilian milk-fed lamb.

14 Borough High St ✉ SE1 9QG — **MAP: 10-M4**
020 7407 5361 — **www**.lobostapas.co.uk
⊖ London Bridge
Carte £15/48
Closed 25-26 December and 1 January

Ⓝ LONDRINO

Portuguese • Design

The chef-owner takes his influences from his home country of Portugal, from the various London restaurants in which he has worked and from his own extensive travels. The modern dishes are meant for sharing and the bright, open space has an easy-going feel.

36 Snowsfields ✉ SE1 3SU — **MAP: 10-M5**
020 3911 4949 — **www**.londrino.co.uk
⊖ London Bridge
Menu £22 (weekday lunch) - Carte £29/58
Closed Christmas-New Year, Sunday dinner and Monday

LUCA

Italian • Design

Owned by the people behind The Clove Club, but less a little sister, more a distant cousin. There's a cheery atmosphere, a bar for small plates and a frequently changing menu of Italian dishes made with quality British ingredients.

88 St. John St ✉ EC1M 4EH — MAP: 9-L1
020 3859 3000 — **www**.luca.restaurant
Farringdon

Menu £19 (lunch and early dinner) - Carte £35/79
Closed Sunday - booking essential

MORITO

Spanish • Tapas bar

From the owners of next door Moro comes this authentic and appealingly down to earth little tapas bar. Seven or eight dishes between two should suffice but over-ordering is easy and won't break the bank.

32 Exmouth Mkt ✉ EC1R 4QE — MAP: 9-K1
020 7278 7007 — **www**.morito.co.uk
Farringdon

Carte £14/29
Closed 24 December-2 January

MORO

Mediterranean cuisine • Friendly

It's the stuff of dreams - pack up your worldly goods, drive through Spain, Portugal, Morocco and the Sahara, and then back in London, open a restaurant and share your love of Moorish cuisine. The wood-fired oven and chargrill fill the air with wonderful aromas and food is vibrant and colourful.

34-36 Exmouth Mkt ✉ EC1R 4QE — MAP: 9-K1
020 7833 8336 — **www**.moro.co.uk
Farringdon

Carte £33/45
Closed 24 December-2 January - booking essential

NUALA

Modern British • Rustic

The infectiously enthusiastic Northern Irish chef-owner trained as a butcher and much of the produce comes from the family farm. The main ingredients are cooked over an open flame with a mix of oak, apple, birch, ash and beech. The open kitchen allows the aromas to whet the appetite.

70-74 City Rd ✉ EC1Y 2BJ **MAP: 9-M1**
020 3904 0462 — **www**.nualalondon.com
Old Street

Menu £20 (lunch) - Carte £20/44
Closed Christmas-New Year, Sunday and Monday

A/C

OBLIX

Meats and grills • Trendy

A New York grill restaurant on the 32nd floor of The Shard; window tables for two are highly prized. Meats and fish from the rotisserie, grill and Josper oven are the stars of the show; brunch in the lounge bar at weekends.

Level 32, The Shard, 31 St Thomas St. ✉ SE1 9RY **MAP: 10-M4**
020 7268 6700 — **www**.oblixrestaurant.com
London Bridge

Menu £38 (weekday lunch) - Carte £33/111

A/C

OXO TOWER BRASSERIE

Modern cuisine • Design

Less formal but more fun than the next-door restaurant. The open-plan kitchen produces modern, colourful and easy-to-eat dishes with influences from the Med. Great views too from the bar.

Oxo Tower Wharf (8th floor), Barge House St ✉ SE1 9PH **MAP: 10-K4**
020 7803 3888 — **www**.oxotower.co.uk
Southwark

Menu £30 (lunch) - Carte £27/49
Closed 25 December

A/C

PADELLA

Italian • Bistro

This lively little sister to Trullo offers a short, seasonal menu where hand-rolled pasta is the star of the show. Sauces and fillings are inspired by the owners' trips to Italy and prices are extremely pleasing to the pocket. Sit at the ground floor counter overlooking the open kitchen.

6 Southwark St, Borough Market ✉ SE1 1TQ **MAP: 10-M4**
www.padella.co
⊖ London Bridge

Carte £12/22
Closed 25-26 December and bank holidays – bookings not accepted
A/C

PALATINO

Italian • Design

Stevie Parle's airy, canteen-like, all-day restaurant has an open kitchen, yellow booths and an industrial feel. The seasonal Italian menu has a strong emphasis on Rome, with dishes like rigatoni with veal pajata.

71 Central St ✉ EC1V 8AB **MAP: 9-L1**
020 3481 5300 — **www**.palatino.london
⊖ Old Street

Menu £16 (lunch and early dinner) - Carte £16/38
Closed 23 December-3 January, Sunday and bank holidays
A/C

PATERNOSTER CHOP HOUSE

Traditional British • Brasserie

Appropriately British menu in a restaurant lying in the shadow of St Paul's Cathedral. Large, open room with full-length windows; busy bar attached. Kitchen uses thoughtfully sourced produce.

Warwick Ct., Paternoster Sq. ✉ EC4M 7DX **MAP: 8-L3**
020 7029 9400 — **www**.paternosterchophouse.co.uk
⊖ St Paul's

Menu £24 (lunch and early dinner) - Carte £29/58
Closed 26-30 December, 1 January and dinner Sunday
A/C

PIQUE-NIQUE

French • *Bistro*

Set in a converted 1920s park shelter is this fun French restaurant with a focus on rotisserie-cooked Bresse chicken. Concise menu of French classics; go for the 6 course 'Menu autour du poulet de Bresse' which uses every part of the bird.

Tanner St. Park ✉ SE1 3LD **MAP: 10-N5**
☎ 020 7403 9549 – **www.**pique-nique.co.uk
London Bridge
Carte £24/44
Closed Sunday dinner - booking essential

PIZARRO

Mediterranean cuisine • *Neighbourhood*

José Pizarro has a refreshingly simple way of naming his establishments: after José, his tapas bar, comes Pizarro, a larger restaurant a few doors down. Go for the small plates, like prawns with piquillo peppers and jamón.

194 Bermondsey St ✉ SE1 3TQ **MAP: 10-M5**
☎ 020 7378 9455 – **www.**josepizarro.com
London Bridge
Carte £19/50
Closed 25-27 December and 1-2 January

LE PONT DE LA TOUR

French • *Elegant*

Few restaurants can beat the setting, especially when you're on the terrace with its breathtaking views of Tower Bridge. For its 25th birthday it got a top-to-toe refurbishment, resulting in a warmer looking room in which to enjoy the French-influenced cooking.

36d Shad Thames, Butlers Wharf ✉ SE1 2YE **MAP: 10-N4**
☎ 020 7403 8403 – **www.**lepontdelatour.co.uk
London Bridge
Menu £30 - Carte £35/75
Closed 1 January

QUALITY CHOP HOUSE

Traditional British • Cosy

In the hands of owners who respect its history, this 'progressive working class caterer' does a fine job of championing gutsy British grub; game is best but steaks from the butcher next door are also worth ordering. The terrific little wine list has lots of gems. The Grade II listed room, with its trademark booths, has been an eating house since 1869.

- 92-94 Farringdon Rd EC1R 3EA **MAP: 9-K1**
  020 7278 1452 — **www**.thequalitychophouse.com
  Farringdon
- Menu £25 (weekday lunch) - Carte £23/51
  Closed 24-31 December, Sunday dinner and bank holidays - booking essential

ROAST

Modern British • Friendly

Known for its British food and for promoting UK producers - not surprising considering the restaurant's in the heart of Borough Market. The 'dish of the day' is often a highlight; service is affable and there's live music at night.

- The Floral Hall, Borough Market SE1 1TL **MAP: 10-M4**
  020 3006 6111 — **www**.roast-restaurant.com
  London Bridge
- Carte £35/63
  Closed 25-26 December, 1 January and Sunday dinner - booking essential

N SANTO REMEDIO

Mexican • Colourful

The cooking inspiration comes from the owner's time spent in Mexico City, the Yucatan and Oaxaca. Ingredients are a mix of imported - like grasshoppers to liven up the guacamole - and home-grown like Hertfordshire pork. Spread over two floors, the rooms are as colourful as the food.

- 152 Tooley St SE1 2TU **MAP: 10-M4**
  020 7403 3021 — **www**.santoremedio.co.uk
  London Bridge
- Menu £20 (weekday lunch) - Carte £23/35
  Closed Christmas and Sunday dinner

ST JOHN ✿

Traditional British • Simple

There's no standing on ceremony here at St John; indeed, very little ceremony at all, and that makes eating here such a joyful experience as one's focus is directed entirely at the food. There's little distraction from the surroundings either, which come in a shade of detention centre white.

You can play it safe and go for some crab and then roast beef but this is the place to try new flavours, whether that's cuttlefish or ox tongue. Game is a favourite and the only gravy will be the blood of the bird – this is natural, 'proper' food. Seasonality is at its core – the menu is rewritten for each service – and nothing sums up the philosophy more than the potatoes and greens: they are always on the menu but the varieties and types change regularly. The waiters spend time in the kitchen so they know what they're talking about and are worth listening to. There are dishes for two as well as magnums of wine for real trenchermen – and be sure to order a dozen warm madeleines to take home.

FIRST COURSE

Roast bone marrow with parsley salad. • Brown shrimps with white cabbage.

MAIN COURSE

Grilled ox heart with beetroot, red cabbage and pickled walnut. • Dover sole with mayonnaise and tomatoes.

DESSERT

Ginger loaf with butterscotch sauce. • Honey and brandy parfait.

26 St John St ✉ EC1M 4AY — **MAP: 9-L2**
☎ 020 7251 0848 — **www**.stjohnrestaurant.com
⊖ Farringdon

Carte £26/63
Closed 25-26 December, 1 January, Saturday lunch and Sunday dinner – booking essential

SKYLON

Modern cuisine • Design

Ask for a window table here at the Royal Festival Hall. Informal grill-style operation on one side, a more formal and expensive restaurant on the other, with a busy cocktail bar in the middle.

1 Southbank Centre, Belvedere Rd SE1 8XX — MAP: 3-J4
020 7654 7800 — **www**.skylon-restaurant.co.uk
Waterloo

Menu £30 (weekdays) - Carte £38/52
Closed 25 December

TAPAS BRINDISA

Spanish • Tapas bar

A blueprint for many of the tapas bars that subsequently sprung up over London. It has an infectious energy and the well-priced, robust dishes include Galician-style octopus and black rice with squid; try the hand-carved Ibérico hams.

18-20 Southwark St, Borough Market SE1 1TJ — MAP: 10-M4
020 7357 8880 — **www**.brindisatapaskitchens.com
London Bridge

Carte £14/38
Bookings not accepted

TATE MODERN (RESTAURANT)

Modern British • Design

A contemporary, faux-industrial style restaurant on the ninth floor of the striking Switch House extension. Modern menus champion British ingredients; desserts are a highlight and the wine list interesting and well-priced.

Switch House (9th floor), Tate Modern, Bankside SE1 9TG — MAP: 10-L4
020 7401 5621 — **www**.tate.org.uk
Southwark

Menu £25 - Carte £26/36
Closed 24-26 December - (lunch only and dinner Friday-Saturday)

STORY ✿

Modern cuisine • Design

Brace yourself if you don't like surprises because here at Restaurant Story you aren't offered a menu when you sit down. Instead, chef Tom Sellers and his kitchen present a mixture of their classic dishes along with others informed by the seasons and the produce provided by their suppliers. There are playful elements to the food, which are often inspired by Tom's childhood memories – along with the imaginative snacks which kick things of, you can expect a 'candle' made of beef dripping for your bread and maybe a 'sandwich' inspired by Paddington Bear. But this is also cooking with real depth and substance.

In 2018 the restaurant underwent more than just a major refit – it felt more like a rebirth. The huge picture window is still the dominant feature, allowing light to flood in during the day, but the room now offers a greater level of comfort and feels more intimate. The number of tables was also reduced to improve diners' overall experience.

FIRST COURSE

Bread and 'dripping'. • Fairground onions.

MAIN COURSE

Chicken, morels and truffle. • Turbot, champagne and sea herbs.

DESSERT

Almond and dill. • Lemon sherbet.

199 Tooley St ✉ SE1 2JX **MAP: 10-N5**
✆ 020 7183 2117 — **www.**restaurantstory.co.uk
⊖ London Bridge

Menu £80 (weekday lunch)/145
Closed 2 weeks Christmas-New Year, Sunday dinner and Monday lunch – booking essential – (surprise menu only)

TEMPLE AND SONS

Traditional British • Bistro

In a glass cube next to Tower 42 is this relaxed restaurant styled on a Victorian grocer's shop, with a bar serving home-canned cocktails, and a menu of traditional British dishes like sausage and mash and sticky toffee pudding.

22 Old Broad St ✉ EC2N 1HQ — **MAP: 8-M3**
020 7877 7710 — **www**.templeandsons.co.uk
Liverpool Street
Carte £22/52
Closed Sunday

TOM SIMMONS

Modern cuisine • Simple

The eponymous chef went from being a contestant on 'MasterChef: The Professionals' to having his name above the door of his own restaurant here in this modern development near Tower Bridge. His Welsh heritage comes through on the modern menu, with its use of Welsh lamb and beef.

2 Still Walk ✉ SE1 2RA — **MAP: 10-N4**
020 3848 2100 — **www**.tom-simmons.co.uk
London Bridge
Menu £24/27 - Carte £29/54
Closed Monday

UNION STREET CAFÉ

Italian • Trendy

Occupying a former warehouse, this Gordon Ramsay restaurant has been busy since day one and comes with a New York feel, a faux industrial look and a basement bar. The Italian menu keeps things simple and stays true to the classics.

47-51 Great Suffolk St ✉ SE1 0BS — **MAP: 10-L4**
020 7592 7977 — **www**.gordonramsayrestaurants.com
London Bridge
Menu £26 - Carte £22/49

VANILLA BLACK

Vegetarian • Intimate

A vegetarian restaurant where real thought has gone into the creation of dishes, which deliver an array of interesting texture and flavour contrasts. Modern techniques are subtly incorporated and while there are some original combinations, they are well-judged.

17-18 Tooks Ct. ✉ EC4A 1LB **MAP: 8-K2**
020 7242 2622 — **www**.vanillablack.co.uk
⊖ Chancery Lane
Menu £22 (weekday lunch)/55
Closed 2 weeks Christmas and bank holidays - booking essential

---

WRIGHT BROTHERS

Seafood • Cosy

Originally an oyster wholesaler; now offers a wide range of oysters along with porter, as well as fruits de mer, daily specials and assorted pies. It fills quickly and an air of contentment reigns.

11 Stoney St, Borough Market ✉ SE1 9AD **MAP: 10-M4**
020 7403 9554 — **www**.thewrightbrothers.co.uk
⊖ London Bridge
Carte £29/40
Closed 25-26 December and 1 January

YAUATCHA CITY

Chinese • Fashionable

A more corporate version of the stylish Soho original, with a couple of bars and a terrace at both ends. All the dim sum greatest hits are on the menu but the chefs have some work to match the high standard found in Broadwick Street.

Broadgate Circle ✉ EC2M 2QS **MAP: 8-M2**
020 3817 9880 — **www**.yauatcha.com
⊖ Liverpool Street
Menu £35/48 - Carte £32/77
Closed 24 December-3 January and bank holidays

CHELSEA · EARL'S COURT · HYDE PARK · KNIGHTSBRIDGE · SOUTH KENSINGTON

Though its days of unbridled hedonism are long gone - and its 'alternative' tag is more closely aligned to property prices than counter-culture - there's still a hip feel to **Chelsea.** The place that put the Swinging into London has grown grey, distinguished and rather placid over the years, but tourists still throng to the **King's Road,** albeit to shop at the chain stores which have steadily muscled out SW3's chi-chi boutiques. It's not so easy now to imagine the heady mix of clans that used to sashay along here, from Sixties mods and models to Seventies punks, but for practically a quarter of a century, from the moment in 1955 when Mary Quant opened her trend-setting Bazaar, this was the pavement to parade down.

Chelsea's most cutting-edge destination these days is probably the gallery of modern art that bears the name of Margaret Thatcher's former favourite, Charles Saatchi. Which isn't the only irony, as Saatchi's outlandishly modish exhibits are housed in a one-time military barracks, the Duke of York's headquarters. Nearby, the traffic careers round **Sloane Square,** but it's almost possible to distance yourself from the fumes by sitting amongst the shady bowers in the centre of the square, or watching the world go by from a prime position in one of many cafés. Having said that, *the* place to get away from it all, and yet still be within striking distance of the King's Road, is the delightful **Physic Garden,** down by the river. Famous for its healing herbs for over 300 years, it's England's second oldest botanic garden.

Mind you, if the size of a green space is more important to you than its medicinal qualities, then you need to head up to **Hyde Park,** the city's biggest. Expansive enough to accommodate trotting horses on Rotten Row, swimmers and rowers in the Serpentine, up-to-the-minute art exhibitions at the Serpentine Gallery, and ranting individualists at Speakers' Corner, the park has also held within its borders thousands of rock fans for concerts by the likes of the Rolling Stones, Simon and Garfunkel and Pink Floyd.

Just across from its southern border stands one of London's most imperious sights, The **Royal Albert Hall,** gateway to the cultural hotspot that is South Kensington. Given its wings after the 1851 Great Exhibition, the area round **Cromwell Road** invested heavily in culture and learning, in the shape of three world famous museums and three heavyweight colleges. But one of its most intriguing museums is little known to visitors, even though it's only a few metres east of the Albert Hall: the Sikorski is, by turns, a moving and spectacular showpiece for all things Polish.

No one would claim to be moved by the exhibits on show in nearby **Knightsbridge,** but there are certainly spectacular credit card transactions made here. The twin retail shrines of Harvey Nichols and Harrods are the proverbial honey-pots to the tourist bee, where a 'credit crunch' means you've accidentally trodden on your visa. Between them, in **Sloane Street,** the world's most famous retail names line up like an A-lister's who's who. At the western end of Knightsbridge is the rich person's Catholic church of choice, the Brompton Oratory, an unerringly lavish concoction in a baroque Italianate style. Behind it is the enchanting Ennismore Gardens Mews, a lovely thoroughfare that dovetails rather well with the Oratory.

Further west along Old Brompton Road is **Earl's Court,** an area of grand old houses turned into bedsits and spartan hotels. An oddly bewitching contrast sits side by side here, the old resting alongside the new. The old in this case is Brompton Cemetery, an enchanting wilderness of monuments wherein lie the likes of Samuel Cunard and Emmeline Pankhurst. At its southwest corner, incongruously, sits the new, insomuch as it's the home of a regular influx of newcomers from abroad, who are young, gifted and possessed of vast incomes: the players of Chelsea FC.

xelpe/iStock

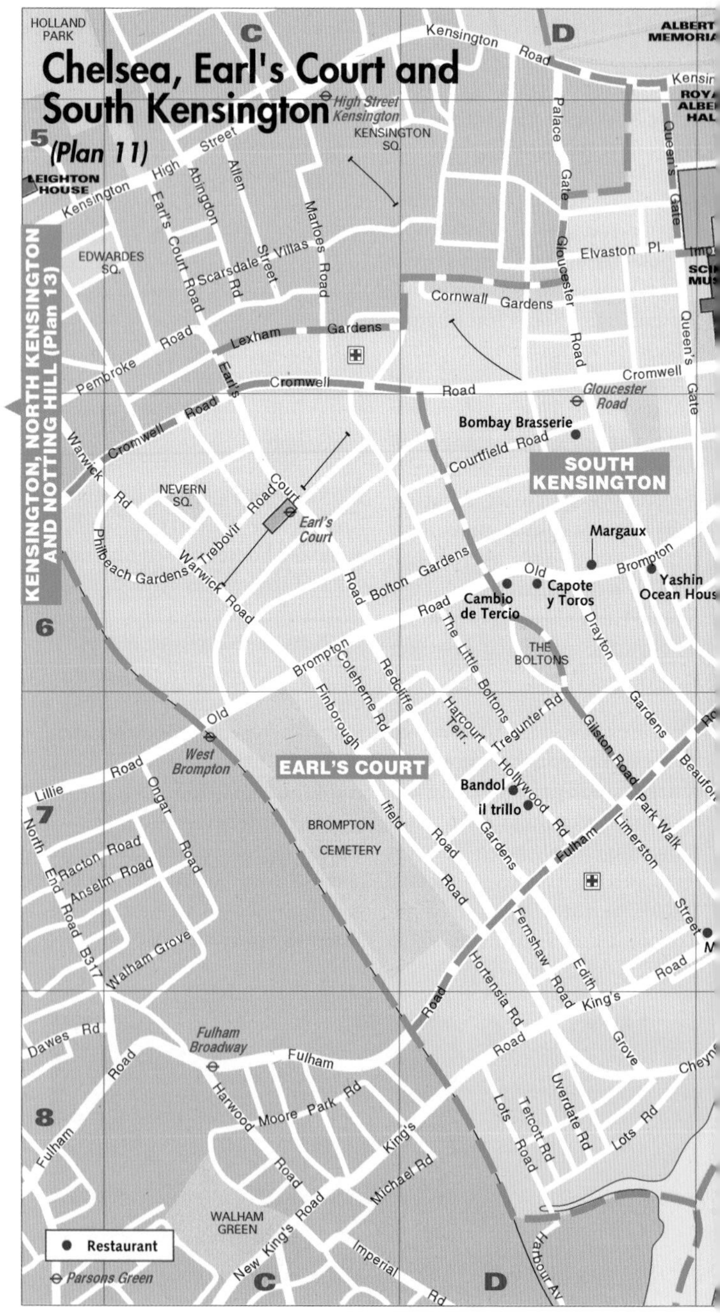
Chelsea, Earl's Court and South Kensington
(Plan 11)
KENSINGTON, NORTH KENSINGTON AND NOTTING HILL (Plan 13)
Restaurant
Parsons Green
Bombay Brasserie
Margaux
Capote y Toros
Cambio de Tercio
Yashin Ocean House
Bandol
il trillo
SOUTH KENSINGTON
EARL'S COURT
HOLLAND PARK
LEIGHTON HOUSE
EDWARDES SQ.
KENSINGTON SQ.
NEVERN SQ.
THE BOLTONS
BROMPTON CEMETERY
WALHAM GREEN
ALBERT MEMORIAL
High Street Kensington
Gloucester Road
Earl's Court
West Brompton
Fulham Broadway
Kensington Road
Kensington High Street
Cromwell Road
Old Brompton Road
Fulham Road
King's Road
Lillie Road
North End Road B317
Warwick Road
Earl's Court Road
Gloucester Road
Palace Gate
Queen's Gate
Elvaston Pl.
Cornwall Gardens
Lexham Gardens
Pembroke Road
Courtfield Road
Bolton Gardens
Drayton Gardens
Gilston Road
Park Walk
Limerston Street
Redcliffe Road
Finborough Road
Ifield Road
Hollywood Rd
Harcourt Terr.
Tregunter Rd
The Little Boltons
Coleherne Rd
Philbeach Gardens
Trebovir Road
Scarsdale Villas
Abingdon Rd
Allen Street
Marloes Road
Ongar Road
Racton Road
Anselm Road
Walham Grove
Dawes Rd
Harwood Road
Moore Park Rd
Michael Rd
New King's Road
Imperial Rd
Harbour Av
Lots Road
Tetcott Rd
Uverdate Rd
Hortensia Rd
Fernshaw Road
Edith Grove
Beaufort
Cheyne
C
D
5
6
7
8

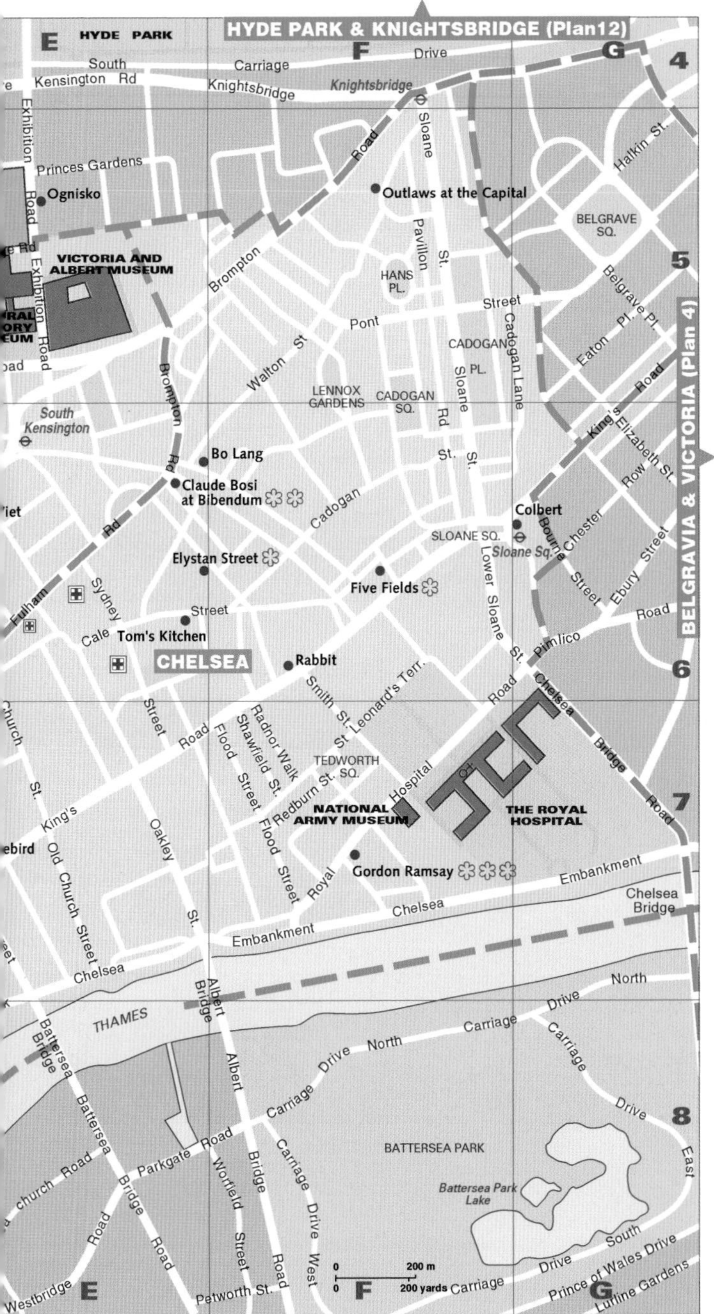
HYDE PARK & KNIGHTSBRIDGE (Plan12)
BELGRAVIA & VICTORIA (Plan 4)
HYDE PARK
South Carriage Drive
Kensington Rd
Knightsbridge
Exhibition Road
Princes Gardens
Ognisko
Outlaws at the Capital
Sloane St.
Halkin St.
BELGRAVE SQ.
VICTORIA AND ALBERT MUSEUM
Brompton Road
Pavillon
HANS PL.
Pont Street
Belgrave Pl.
Eaton Pl.
CADOGAN PL.
Cadogan Lane
Walton St
LENNOX GARDENS
CADOGAN SQ.
South Kensington
King's Road
Elizabeth St.
Bo Lang
Claude Bosi at Bibendum
Cadogan St.
Colbert
SLOANE SQ.
Sloane Sq.
Bourne Street
Chester Row
Ebury Street
Elystan Street
Five Fields
Lower Sloane St.
Pimlico Road
Fulham Rd
Sydney Street
Cale Street
Tom's Kitchen
CHELSEA
Rabbit
Smith St.
St Leonard's Terr.
Chelsea Bridge Road
Radnor Walk
Shawfield St.
Flood Street
TEDWORTH SQ.
Redburn St.
Hospital Road
NATIONAL ARMY MUSEUM
THE ROYAL HOSPITAL
Oakley St.
Old Church Street
Gordon Ramsay
Royal
Chelsea Embankment
Chelsea Bridge
THAMES
Albert Bridge
Battersea Bridge
North Carriage Drive
East Carriage Drive
BATTERSEA PARK
Battersea Park Lake
Parkgate Road
Battersea Bridge Road
Worfield Street
Albert Bridge Road
Carriage Drive West
South Carriage Drive
Prince of Wales Drive
Lurline Gardens
Westbridge Road
Petworth St.
200 m
200 yards
E
F
G
4
5
6
7
8

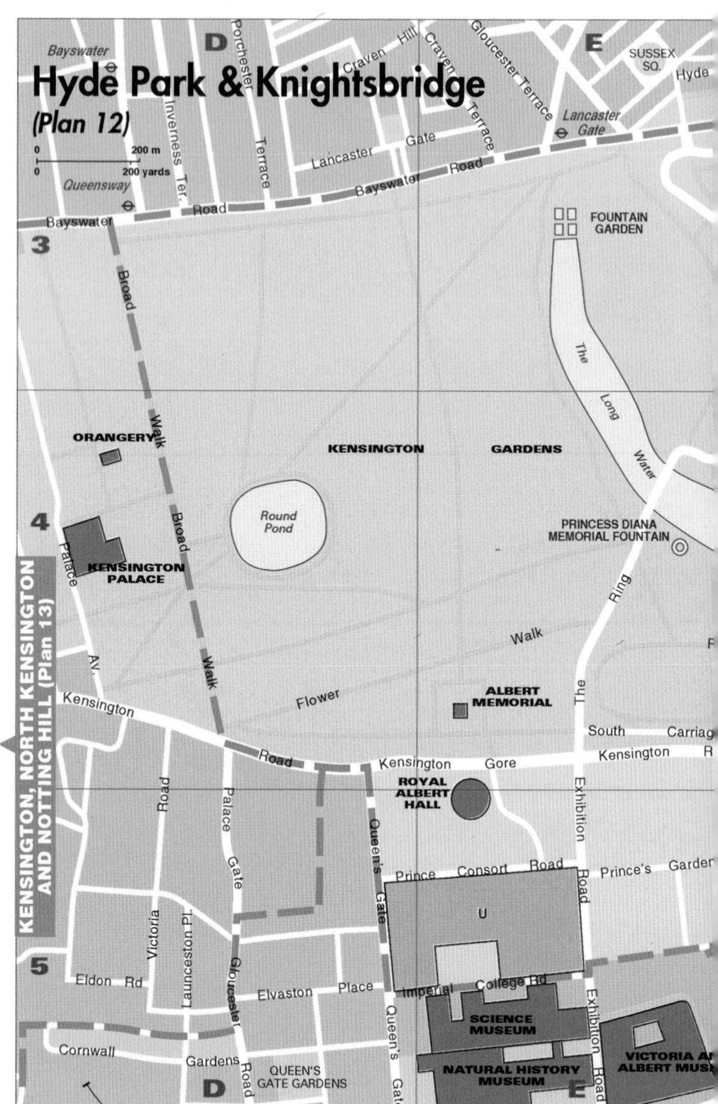

Hyde Park & Knightsbridge
(Plan 12)
0 200 m
0 200 yards
Bayswater
Queensway
Porchester Terrace
Inverness Ter.
Craven Hill
Craven Terrace
Gloucester Terrace
Lancaster Gate
Lancaster Gate
Bayswater Road
SUSSEX SQ.
Hyde
FOUNTAIN GARDEN
Broad Walk
The Long Water
ORANGERY
KENSINGTON GARDENS
Round Pond
KENSINGTON PALACE
Palace Av.
PRINCESS DIANA MEMORIAL FOUNTAIN
The Ring
Flower Walk
ALBERT MEMORIAL
Kensington Road
South Carriag
Kensington Gore
Kensington R
ROYAL ALBERT HALL
Exhibition Road
Prince Consort Road
Prince's Garden
KENSINGTON, NORTH KENSINGTON AND NOTTING HILL (Plan 13)
Victoria Road
Palace Gate
Queen's Gate
Launceston Pl.
Gloucester Road
Eldon Rd
Elvaston Place
Imperial College Rd
SCIENCE MUSEUM
NATURAL HISTORY MUSEUM
VICTORIA A ALBERT MUS
Cornwall Gardens
QUEEN'S GATE GARDENS
U
D
E
3
4
5

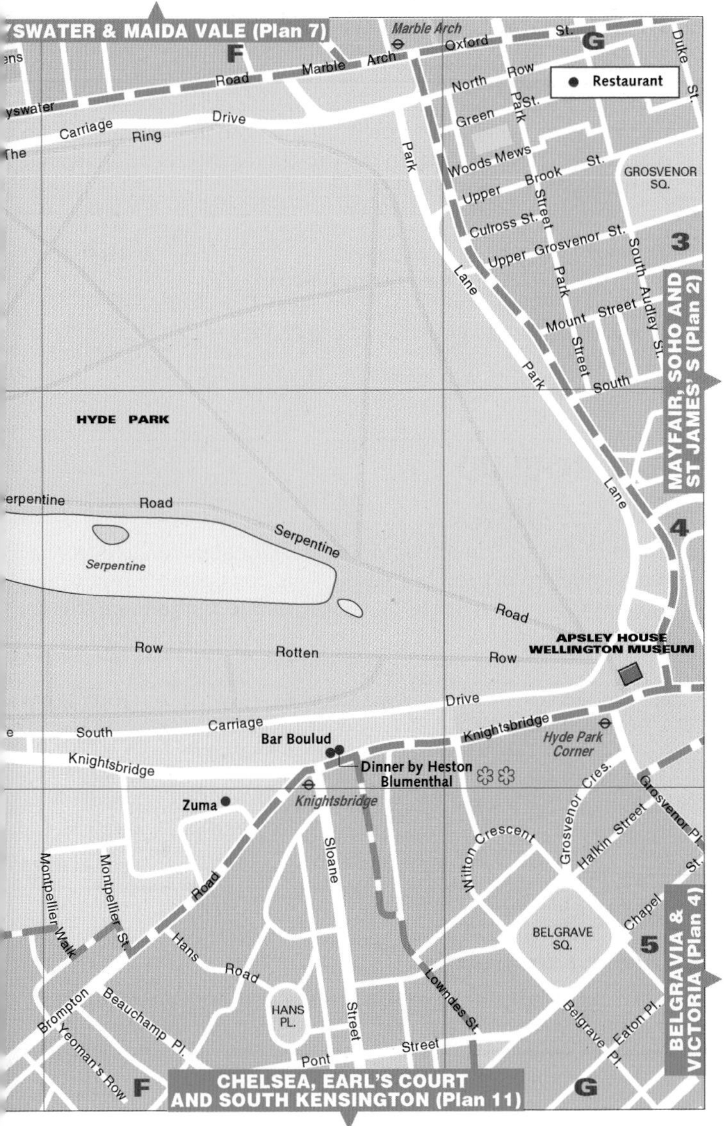

YSWATER & MAIDA VALE (Plan 7)
Marble Arch
Restaurant
Oxford St.
North Row
Green St.
Park St.
Marble Arch
Bayswater Road
The Ring
Carriage Drive
Park Lane
Woods Mews
Upper Brook St.
GROSVENOR SQ.
Culross St.
Upper Grosvenor St.
South Audley St.
Park Street
Mount Street
South St.
MAYFAIR, SOHO AND ST JAMES'S (Plan 2)
HYDE PARK
Serpentine Road
Serpentine
Rotten Row
APSLEY HOUSE WELLINGTON MUSEUM
South Carriage Drive
Knightsbridge
Hyde Park Corner
Bar Boulud
Dinner by Heston Blumenthal
Zuma
Knightsbridge
Grosvenor Cres.
Grosvenor Pl.
Halkin Street
Wilton Crescent
Sloane Street
Montpellier Walk
Montpellier St.
Brompton Road
Hans Road
HANS PL.
Chapel St.
BELGRAVE SQ.
Lowndes St.
Belgrave Pl.
Eaton Pl.
BELGRAVIA & VICTORIA (Plan 4)
Beauchamp Pl.
Yeoman's Row
Pont Street
CHELSEA, EARL'S COURT AND SOUTH KENSINGTON (Plan 11)
F
G
3
4
5

BANDOL

Provençal • Design

Stylishly dressed restaurant with a 100 year old olive tree evoking memories of sunny days spent on the French Riviera. Sharing plates take centre stage on the Provençal and Niçoise inspired menu; seafood is a highlight.

6 Hollywood Rd ✉ SW10 9HY **MAP: 11-D7**
020 7351 1322 — **www**.barbandol.co.uk
⊖ Earl's Court
Menu £15 (weekday lunch) - Carte £30/59

BAR BOULUD

French • Brasserie

Daniel Boulud's London outpost is fashionable, fun and frantic. His hometown is Lyon but he built his considerable reputation in New York, so charcuterie, sausages and burgers are the highlights.

Mandarin Oriental Hyde Park Hotel, 66 Knightsbridge ✉ SW1X 7LA **MAP: 12-F4**
020 7201 3899 — **www**.mandarinoriental.com
⊖ Knightsbridge
Menu £19 (weekday lunch) - Carte £26/57

BLUEBIRD

Modern British • Design

It boasts an épicerie, a café, a terrace and even a clothes shop, but the highlight is the first floor restaurant with its marble-topped horseshoe bar, bold print banquettes and abundance of foliage. A Mediterranean menu and super cocktails.

350 King's Rd. ✉ SW3 5UU **MAP: 11-E7**
020 7559 1000 — **www**.bluebird-restaurant.co.uk
⊖ South Kensington
Menu £30 - Carte £32/70

BO LANG

Chinese • Trendy

Come with friends for the cocktails and the dim sum at this diminutive and intimate spot, whose decorative style owes something to Hakkasan. The kitchen uses good quality ingredients and has a deft touch; the more traditional combinations often prove to be the best.

100 Draycott Ave SW3 3AD **MAP: 11-E6**
020 7823 7887 — **www**.bolangrestaurant.co.uk
South Kensington
Menu £15 (lunch) - Carte £27/47

BOMBAY BRASSERIE

Indian • Exotic décor

A well-run, well-established and comfortable Indian restaurant, featuring a very smart bar and conservatory. Creative dishes sit alongside more traditional choices on the various menus and vegetarians are well-catered for.

Courtfield Rd. SW7 4QH **MAP: 11-D6**
020 7370 4040 — **www**.bombayb.co.uk
Gloucester Road
Menu £27 (weekday lunch) - Carte £32/53
Closed 25 December

CAMBIO DE TERCIO

Spanish • Cosy

A long-standing, ever-improving Spanish restaurant. Start with small dishes like the excellent El Bulli inspired omelette, then have the popular Pluma Iberica. There are super sherries and a wine list to prove there is life beyond Rioja.

163 Old Brompton Rd. SW5 0LJ **MAP: 11-D6**
020 7244 8970 — **www**.cambiodetercio.co.uk
Gloucester Road
Menu £24 (weekday lunch) - Carte £33/55 **s**
Closed 2 weeks December and 2 weeks August

CAPOTE Y TOROS

Spanish • Tapas bar

Expect to queue at this compact and vividly coloured spot which celebrates sherry, tapas, ham... and bullfighting. Sherry is the star; those as yet unmoved by this most underappreciated of wines will be dazzled by the variety.

157 Old Brompton Road ✉ SW5 0LJ **MAP: 11-D6**
020 7373 0567 – **www**.cambiodetercio.co.uk
Gloucester Road
Carte £23/61
Closed 2 weeks Christmas, Sunday and Monday - (dinner only)

COLBERT

French • Brasserie

With its posters, chessboard tiles and red leather seats, Colbert bears more than a passing resemblance to a Parisian pavement café. It's an all-day, every day operation with French classics from croque monsieur to steak Diane.

50-52 Sloane Sq ✉ SW1W 8AX **MAP: 11-G6**
020 7730 2804 – **www**.colbertchelsea.com
Sloane Square
Carte £23/63
Closed 25 December

GO-VIET

Vietnamese • Contemporary décor

A Vietnamese restaurant from experienced chef Jeff Tan. Lunch concentrates on classics like pho and bun, while dinner provides a more sophisticated experience, offering interesting flavourful dishes with a distinct modern edge.

53 Old Brompton Rd ✉ SW7 3JS **MAP: 11-E6**
020 7589 6432 – **www**.vietnamfood.co.uk
South Kensington
Carte £22/51
Closed 24-26 December

CLAUDE BOSI AT BIBENDUM ✿✿

French • Elegant

Bibendum – on the first floor of the historic art deco building which was built as Michelin's London HQ in 1911 – now sports a clean, contemporary look, and its handsome interior cannot fail to impress. The iconic stained glass windows allow light to flood in – a fact best appreciated at lunch when the Michelin Man can be seen in all his glory; in fact, his presence is everywhere, from the butter dish to the salt and pepper pots. Service is smooth, well-paced and discreet; it's also not without humour.

Claude Bosi's cooking shows a man proud of his French heritage and confident of his abilities. His dishes are poised and well-balanced with bold, assured flavours. Choose the à la carte menu for classics like Brittany rabbit with langoustine and artichoke barigoule or turbot à la Grenobloise – and don't miss the soufflé for dessert, particularly if it's chocolate.

FIRST COURSE

Duck jelly, Oscietra caviar, spring onion and smoked sturgeon. • Cornish cock crab with apple and lime.

MAIN COURSE

'My mum's' tripe and cuttlefish gratin with pig's ear and ham cake. • Venison with quince, Jerusalem artichoke and pommes soufflées.

DESSERT

Cep vacherin, banana and crème fraîche. • Bibendum chocolate soufflé with basil ice cream.

Michelin House, 81 Fulham Rd ✉ SW3 6RD **MAP: 11-E6**
✆ 020 7581 5817 — **www**.bibendum.co.uk
⊖ South Kensington

Menu £110 (dinner)/130. Carte lunch £53/109
Closed 24-26 December, 31 December-7 January, 26 August-5 September, Monday, lunch Tuesday-Wednesday and bank holidays

A/C

DINNER BY HESTON BLUMENTHAL ✿✿

Traditional British • Design

Heston Blumenthal's international reputation was built on the multi-sensory alchemy performed at his Fat Duck restaurant in Bray but his restaurant at the Mandarin Oriental hotel is a different beast. Here, the menu celebrates British culinary triumphs through the ages, with the date of origin given to each dish along with information about its provenance.

An impressively well-manned kitchen works with obvious intelligence, calm efficiency and attention to detail to produce dishes that look deceptively simple but taste sublime. Many of them have already achieved near legendary status and so enjoy a permanent presence on the menu, like 'Meat Fruit' (c.1500) which is a thing of beauty, and 'Rice & Flesh' (c.1390) – a variation of risotto alla Milanese with oxtail.

The large, light room has quirky touches, like wall sconces shaped as jelly moulds, but the main focus is on the open kitchen, with its oversized watch mechanics powering the spit to roast the pineapple that goes with the Tipsy Cake (c.1810).

FIRST COURSE

Mandarin, chicken liver parfait and grilled bread (c.1500). • Lobster and cucumber soup (c.1730).

MAIN COURSE

Hereford rib-eye with mushroom ketchup and triple cooked chips (c.1830). • Roast sea bass and green sauce (c.1440).

DESSERT

Tipsy cake with spit-roast pineapple (c.1810). • Eggs in Verjuice (1730).

Mandarin Oriental Hyde Park Hotel, 66 Knightsbridge, ✉ SW1X 7LA
020 7201 3833 — **www**.dinnerbyheston.com
⊖ Knightsbridge

MAP: 12-F4

Menu £45 (weekday lunch) - Carte £58/121
Closed 17-31 October

ELYSTAN STREET ✿

Modern British • Elegant

Elystan Street is a joint venture between Philip Howard, for many years head chef of The Square, and experienced restaurateur Rebecca Mascarenhas. They've both put their stamp on the place, with Rebecca supplying the contemporary artwork and Philip overseeing the cooking. The look is elegant and understated with a blonde wood floor, oak and polished concrete tables, and large windows which let in plenty of light. Chairs come in air force blue and soft salmon, although the teal banquettes around the edges of the room are the best place to sit; this is a charming lunchtime spot which transmogrifies into an intimate dinner venue.

Cooking is relaxed and unfussy, yet there's a vigour and an energy to it which suggests that it comes from the heart. Dishes have a classical base but there's a lightness of touch, as well as a focus on vegetables and salads. Many dishes have Mediterranean influences and flavours are well-defined and eminently satisfying. Desserts are a highlight.

FIRST COURSE

Ravioli of Orkney scallops and Cornish crab with spring onions, radish and chives. • Tartare of veal with burrata, white peach, artichoke and olive oil.

MAIN COURSE

Fillet of cod with parmesan gnocchi, garlic leaf pesto and morels. • Duck breast with caramelised endive tarte, crushed turnip and cherries.

DESSERT

Lemon tart with yoghurt ice cream. • Apricot soufflé with camomile ripple ice cream.

43 Elystan St ✉ SW3 3NT **MAP: 11-E6**
✆ 020 7628 5005 — **www**.elystanstreet.com
⊖ South Kensington

Menu £43 (lunch) - Carte dinner £57/88
Closed 25-26 December and 1 January - booking essential

♿ A/C

FIVE FIELDS ✿

Modern cuisine • Neighbourhood

Its name comes from that given to the neighbourhood by the 18C cartographer John Rocque, and over the years this charming Chelsea restaurant has certainly built up a loyal local following. It is a formally run yet intimate place, with a discreet atmosphere and a warm, comfortable feel. The room is luxuriously decorated in crisp creams and the smart, suited staff are professional and engaging.

The chef-owner – blessed with the great name of Taylor Bonnyman – has worked in some illustrious kitchens around the world. His dishes are skilfully conceived, quite elaborate constructions; attractively presented and packed with flavour. Produce is top-notch and includes the occasional Asian ingredient, and many of the herbs and vegetables come from the restaurant's own kitchen garden in East Sussex. Alongside the classic burgundies and bordeaux, the extensive wine list also offers some more esoteric bottles from Eastern Europe and the Middle East.

FIRST COURSE

Foie gras with shimeji mushrooms and beetroot. • 'Early Spring'- greens, potatoes and roots.

MAIN COURSE

Roe deer, morels, celeriac and sorrel. • Scallops with asparagus and turmeric.

DESSERT

Apple with green shiso and jasmine. • Rhubarb with lime and Timut pepper.

8-9 Blacklands Terr ✉ SW3 2SP **MAP: 11-F6**
020 7838 1082 — **www**.fivefieldsrestaurant.com
⊖ Sloane Square

Menu £65/90
Closed Christmas-mid-January, 2 weeks August, Saturday, Sunday and bank holidays – booking essential – (dinner only)

GORDON RAMSAY ✿✿✿

French • Elegant

He may be one of the most famous chefs on the planet but Gordon Ramsay remains fiercely committed to maintaining the highest standards in his flagship restaurant. The charming Jean-Claude, who has run the restaurant since day one, oversees a team who get the service just right: yes, it's polished and professional, but it also has personality. This is the reason why every diner feels at ease and calmness rules.

Matt Abé, an Aussie who's spent over a decade working with Gordon Ramsay, is the chef. In 2018 he oversaw a kitchen redesign that resulted in a more ergonomic space and gave further proof that this restaurant never rests on its laurels. His large team create dishes that are classical in make-up but never backward-looking. The component parts marry perfectly, whether that's Isle of Skye scallops paired with apples, walnuts and cider, or Cornish turbot with celeriac and black truffle. The dishes are executed with great confidence yet also with an extraordinary lightness of touch.

FIRST COURSE

Ravioli of lobster, langoustine and salmon with oxalis and sorrel. • Brown crab with lovage, lemon thyme and English muffins.

MAIN COURSE

Herdwick lamb with spring vegetable 'navarin' • Cornish turbot with celeriac, hazelnuts, black truffle and sherry.

DESSERT

Lemonade parfait with honey, bergamot and sheep's milk yoghurt. • Cherry soufflé with pistachio ice cream.

68-69 Royal Hospital Rd. ✉ SW3 4HP **MAP: 11-F7**

020 7352 4441 – **www**.gordonramsayrestaurants.com

⊖ Sloane Square

Menu £70/120

Closed 21-28 December, Sunday and Monday - booking essential

IL TRILLO

Italian • Friendly

The Bertuccelli family have been making wine and running a restaurant in the Tuscan Hills for over 30 years. Two of the brothers now run this smart local which showcases the produce and wine from their region. Delightful courtyard.

4 Hollywood Rd ✉ SW10 9HY **MAP: 11-D7**
020 3602 1759 — **www**.iltrillo.net
Earl's Court
Menu £33 - Carte £35/58
Closed Monday - (dinner only and lunch Saturday-Sunday)

MARGAUX

Mediterranean cuisine • Neighbourhood

An earnestly run modern bistro with an ersatz industrial look. The classically trained kitchen looks to France and Italy for its primary influences and dishes are flavoursome and satisfying. The accompanying wine list has been thoughtfully compiled.

152 Old Brompton Rd ✉ SW5 0BE **MAP: 11-D6**
020 7373 5753 — **www**.barmargaux.co.uk
Gloucester Road
Menu £15 (weekday lunch) - Carte £28/58
Closed 24-26 December, 1 January and lunch August

MEDLAR

Modern cuisine • Neighbourhood

A charming, comfortable and very popular restaurant with a real neighbourhood feel, from two alumni of Chez Bruce. The service is engaging and unobtrusive; the kitchen uses good ingredients in dishes that deliver distinct flavours in classic combinations.

438 King's Rd ✉ SW10 0LJ **MAP: 11-E7**
020 7349 1900 — **www**.medlarrestaurant.co.uk
South Kensington
Menu £35/53
Closed 24-26 December, 1 January and Monday

OGNISKO

Polish • Elegant

Ognisko Polskie - The Polish Hearth Club - was founded in 1940 in this magnificent townhouse; its elegant restaurant serves traditional dishes from across Eastern Europe and the cooking is without pretence and truly from the heart.

55 Prince's Gate, Exhibition Rd ✉ SW7 2PN **MAP: 11-E5**
020 7589 0101 — **www**.ogniskorestaurant.co.uk
South Kensington
Menu £22 (lunch and early dinner) - Carte £27/37
Closed 24-26 December and 1 January

OUTLAW'S AT THE CAPITAL

Seafood • Intimate

An elegant yet informal restaurant in a personally run hotel. The seasonal menus are all about sustainable seafood, with fish shipped up from Cornwall on a daily basis. The modern cooking is delicately flavoured, with the spotlight on the freshness of the produce.

The Capital Hotel, 22-24 Basil St. ✉ SW3 1AT **MAP: 11-F5**
020 7591 1202 — **www**.capitalhotel.co.uk
Knightsbridge
Menu £33/69
Closed 25-26 December, 1 January and Sunday - booking essential

A/C

RABBIT

Modern British • Rustic

The Gladwin brothers have followed the success of The Shed with another similarly rustic and warmly run restaurant. Share satisfying, robustly flavoured plates; game is a real highlight, particularly the rabbit dishes.

172 King's Rd ✉ SW3 4UP **MAP: 11-F6**
020 3750 0172 — **www**.rabbit-restaurant.com
Sloane Square
Menu £15 (weekday lunch)/42 - Carte £26/40
Closed 22 December-2 January - pre-book at weekends

YASHIN OCEAN HOUSE

Japanese • Chic

The USP of this chic Japanese restaurant is 'head to tail' eating, although, as there's nothing for carnivores, 'fin to scale' would be more precise. Stick with specialities like the whole dry-aged sea bream for the full umami hit.

117-119 Old Brompton Rd ✉ SW7 3RN **MAP: 11-D6**
020 7373 3990 – **www.**yashinocean.com
Gloucester Road
Carte £20/55
Closed Christmas

ZUMA

Japanese • Fashionable

Now a global brand but this was the original. The glamorous clientele come for the striking surroundings, bustling atmosphere and easy-to-share food. Go for the more modern dishes and those cooked on the robata grill.

5 Raphael St ✉ SW7 1DL **MAP: 12-F5**
020 7584 1010 – **www.**zumarestaurant.com
Knightsbridge
Carte £31/150
Closed 25 December – booking essential

Look for our symbol
spotlighting restaurants
with a serious cocktail list.

THE FIRST STONE OF THE HALL

KENSINGTON · NORTH KENSINGTON · NOTTING HILL

It was the choking air of 17C London that helped put **Kensington** on the map: the little village lying to the west of the city became the favoured retreat of the asthmatic King William III who had Sir Christopher Wren build **Kensington Palace** for him. Where the king leads, the titled follow, and the area soon became a fashionable location for the rich. For over 300 years, it's had no problem holding onto its cachet, though a stroll down Kensington High Street is these days a more egalitarian odyssey than some more upmarket residents might approve of.

The shops here mix the everyday with the flamboyant, but for a real taste of the exotic you have to take the lift to the top of the Art Deco Barkers building and arrive at the Kensington Roof Gardens, which are open to all as long as they're not in use for a corporate bash. The gardens are now over seventy-five years old, yet still remain a 'charming secret'. Those who do make it up to the sixth floor discover a delightful woodland garden and gurgling stream, complete with pools, bridges and trees. There are flamingos, too, adding a dash of vibrant colour.

Back down on earth, Kensington boasts another hidden attraction in **Leighton House** on its western boundaries. The Victorian redbrick façade looks a bit forbidding as you make your approach, but step inside and things take a dramatic turn, courtesy of the extraordinary Arab Hall, with its oriental mosaics and tinkling fountain creating a scene like something from *The Arabian Knights.* Elsewhere in the building, the Pre-Raphaelite paintings of Lord Leighton, Burne-Jones and Alma-Tadema are much to the fore. Mind you, famous names have always had a hankering for W8, with a particular preponderance to dally in enchanting **Kensington Square,** where there are almost as many blue plaques as buildings upon which to secure them. William Thackeray, John Stuart Mill and Edward Burne-Jones were all residents.

One of the London's most enjoyable green retreats is **Holland Park,** just north of the High Street. It boasts the 400 year-old Holland House, which is a fashionable focal point for summertime al fresco theatre and opera. Holland Walk runs along the eastern fringe of the park, and provides a lovely sojourn down to the shops; at the Kyoto Garden, koi carp reach hungrily for the surface of their pool, while elsewhere peacocks strut around as if they own the place.

Another world beckons just north of here – the seedy-cum-glitzy environs of **Notting Hill.** The main drag itself, Notting Hill Gate, is little more than a one-dimensional thoroughfare, but to its south are charming cottages with pastel shades in leafy streets, while to the north the appealing **Pembridge Road** evolves into the boutiques of Westbourne Grove. Most people heading in this direction are making for the legendary Portobello Road market – particularly on Saturdays, which are manic. The market stretches on for more than a mile, with a chameleon-like ability to change colour and character on the way: there are antiques at the Notting Hill end, followed further up by food stalls, and then designer and vintage clothes as you reach the Westway. Those who don't fancy the madding crowds of the market can nip into the Electric Cinema and watch a movie in supreme comfort: it boasts two-seater sofas and leather armchairs. Nearby there are another two film-houses putting the hip into the Hill – the Gate, and the Coronet, widely recognised as one of London's most charming 'locals'.

Hidden in a mews just north of **Westbourne Grove** is a fascinating destination: the Museum of Brands, Packaging and Advertising, which does pretty much what it says on the label. It's both nostalgic and evocative, featuring thousands of items like childhood toys, teenage magazines… and HP sauce bottles.

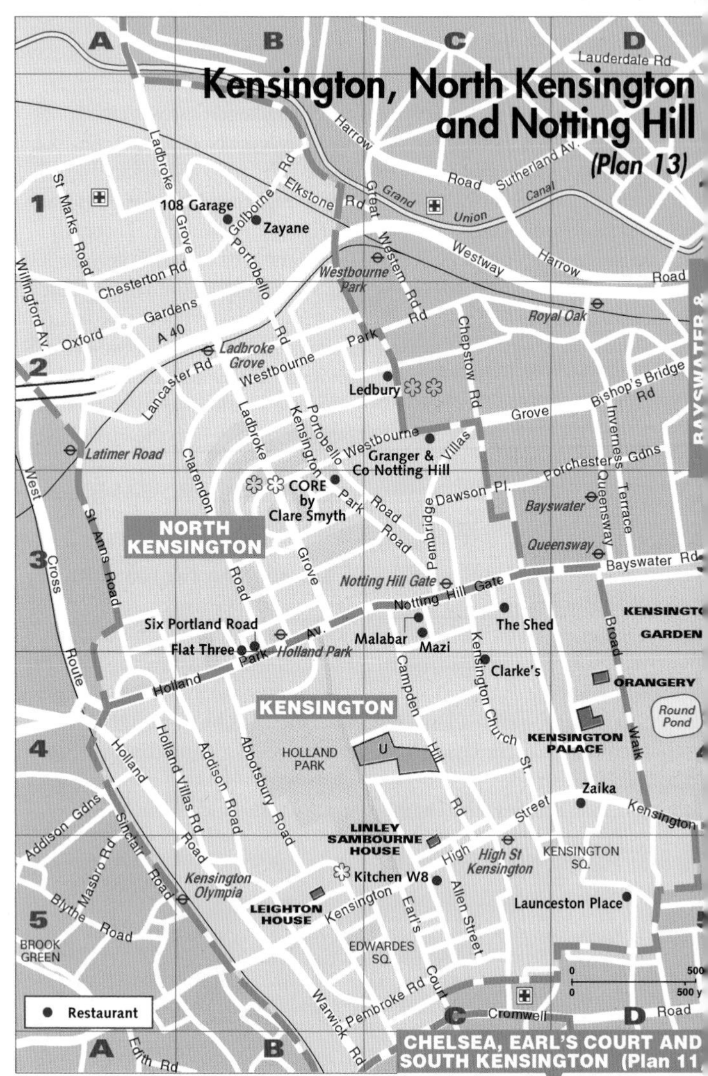
Kensington, North Kensington and Notting Hill
(Plan 13)
108 Garage
Zayane
Ledbury
Granger & Co Notting Hill
CORE by Clare Smyth
Six Portland Road
Flat Three
Malabar
Mazi
The Shed
Clarke's
Zaika
Kitchen W8
Launceston Place
NORTH KENSINGTON
KENSINGTON
HOLLAND PARK
KENSINGTON PALACE
ORANGERY
Round Pond
LINLEY SAMBOURNE HOUSE
LEIGHTON HOUSE
EDWARDES SQ.
KENSINGTON SQ.
BROOK GREEN
Westbourne Park
Royal Oak
Ladbroke Grove
Latimer Road
Bayswater
Queensway
Notting Hill Gate
Holland Park
High St Kensington
Kensington Olympia
Restaurant
CHELSEA, EARL'S COURT AND SOUTH KENSINGTON (Plan 11

CLARKE'S

Modern cuisine • Neighbourhood

Its unhurried atmosphere, enthusiastic service and dedication to its regulars are just a few reasons why Sally Clarke's eponymous restaurant has instilled such unwavering loyalty for over 30 years. Her kitchen has a light touch and understands the less-is-more principle.

124 Kensington Church St W8 4BH **MAP: 13-C4**
020 7221 9225 — **www**.sallyclarke.com
Notting Hill Gate
Menu £33/39 - Carte £42/64
Closed 1 week August, Christmas-New Year and bank holidays

FLAT THREE

Creative • Design

The open kitchen is the main feature of this roomy, basement restaurant. The flavours of Korea and Japan feature heavily in the elaborately constructed, original and creative dishes which deliver plenty of flavour. Service can be rather formal.

120-122 Holland Park Ave W11 4UA **MAP: 13-B3/4**
020 7792 8987 — **www**.flatthree.london
Holland Park
Menu £35/59
Closed 24 December-7 January, 20 August-3 September, Sunday and Monday - (dinner only and lunch Friday-Saturday)

GRANGER AND CO. NOTTING HILL

Modern cuisine • Friendly

When Bill Granger moved from sunny Sydney to cool Notting Hill he opened a local restaurant too. He brought with him that delightful 'matey' service that only Aussies do, his breakfast time ricotta hotcakes and a fresh, zesty menu.

175 Westbourne Grove W11 2SB **MAP: 13-C2**
020 7229 9111 — **www**.grangerandco.com
Bayswater
Carte £20/42
Closed August bank holiday weekend and 25 December - bookings not accepted

Ⓝ CORE BY CLARE SMYTH ✿✿

Modern British • Contemporary décor

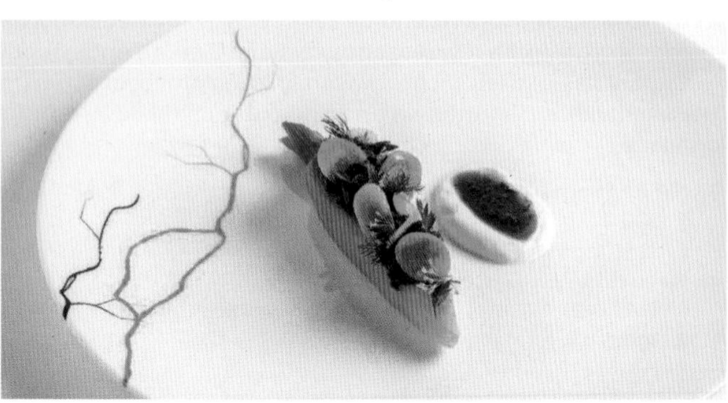

Clare Smyth – for many years Gordon Ramsay's head chef in his flagship restaurant – has realised her ambition to open her own place. It comes with an understated elegance and includes a comfortable cocktail bar and a chef's table separated from the kitchen by a glass wall. Proof of her graduation from chef to consummate restaurateur is there to see in the service, which is highly professional but also warm and engaging.

All her staff are encouraged to develop relationships with the growers of the produce they prepare, and this passion for ingredients is evident in dishes that allow their natural flavours, subtly enhanced by carefully judged accompaniments, to shine. A dish like Charlotte potato with dulse beurre blanc, a nod to her Northern Ireland upbringing, illustrates how a seemingly simple ingredient can be elevated to something extraordinary and shows the real depth that her cooking delivers.

FIRST COURSE	MAIN COURSE	DESSERT
Isle of Mull scallop tartare, sea vegetables and consommé. • 'Potato and roe', dulse beurre blanc, herring and trout roe.	Scottish venison, smoked bacon, pearl barley and whisky. • Skate with Morecambe Bay shrimps, Swiss chard and brown butter.	'Core apple'. • Warm chocolate tart, Sauternes and Banyuls.

92 Kensington Park Rd ✉ W11 2PN **MAP: 13-B3**
✆ 020 3937 5086 – **www.**coreby claresmyth.com
⊖ Notting Hill Gate

Menu £65/105
Closed 24-26 December, 1 January, Sunday, Monday and lunch Tuesday-Wednesday - booking essential

KITCHEN W8 ✿

Modern cuisine • Neighbourhood

Kitchen W8 is the sort of restaurant every neighbourhood should have because it succeeds on so many levels. Whether you're here for a special occasion on a Saturday night or a quick bite for lunch during the week, the staff will get the tone of the service just right and the food will be meticulously prepared yet very easy to eat. The restaurant is a joint venture between experienced restaurateurs Rebecca Mascarenhas and Philip Howard and their influence is clear to see.

Head Chef Mark Kempson puts as much care into the great value lunch and early evening menu as he does the main à la carte. His confident cooking delivers great flavours and subtle degrees of originality so that the dishes have personality and depth. The restaurant may not be quite as informal as the name suggests but it is certainly free of pomp or pomposity. On Sunday the restaurant entices even more locals in by making it a corkage free night which encourages them to open up their own cellars.

FIRST COURSE

Smoked eel with grilled mackerel, golden beetroot and sweet mustard. • Grilled autumn roots with BBQ onion cream, shallots and black rice.

MAIN COURSE

Caramelised lamb shoulder with Pink Fir potatoes, pickles, Calçot onions and thyme. • Roast monkfish with pumpkin, chanterelles and truffle emulsion.

DESSERT

Poached Comice pear with spiced financier and honey ice cream. • Glazed black fig with hazelnut cream, caramelised wafers, buttermilk and nettles.

11-13 Abingdon Rd ✉ W8 6AH **MAP: 13-C5**
✆ 020 7937 0120 — **www.**kitchenw8.com
⊖ High Street Kensington

Menu £28/30 (early weekday dinner) - Carte £41/54
Closed 24-26 December and bank holidays

A/C

LAUNCESTON PLACE

Modern cuisine • Neighbourhood

A favourite of many thanks to its palpable sense of neighbourhood, pretty façade and its nooks and crannies which make it ideal for trysts or tête-à-têtes. The menu is fashionably terse and the cooking is quite elaborate, with dishes big on originality and artfully presented.

1a Launceston Pl ✉ W8 5RL **MAP: 13-D5**
020 7937 6912 — **www**.launcestonplace-restaurant.co.uk
Gloucester Road

Menu £28/60
Closed 25-26 December, Monday and lunch Tuesday

MALABAR

Indian • Neighbourhood

Still going strong in this smart residential Notting Hill street, having opened back in 1983. Refreshingly, the menu is a single page - order a curry and something charcoal-grilled. The buffet lunch on Sunday is a veritable institution in these parts.

27 Uxbridge St. ✉ W8 7TQ **MAP: 13-C3**
020 7727 8800 — **www**.malabar-restaurant.co.uk
Notting Hill Gate

Carte £18/38
Closed 1 week Christmas – (dinner only and lunch Saturday-Sunday)

MAZI

Greek • Friendly

It's all about sharing at this simple, bright Greek restaurant where traditional recipes are given a modern twist to create vibrant, colourful and fresh tasting dishes. The garden terrace at the back is a charming spot in summer.

12-14 Hillgate St ✉ W8 7SR **MAP: 13-C3**
020 7229 3794 — **www**.mazi.co.uk
Notting Hill Gate

Menu £15 (weekday lunch) - Carte £28/43
Closed 24-25 December, 1-2 January and Monday lunch

LEDBURY ✿✿

Modern cuisine • Neighbourhood

Look around the smart but unshowy Ledbury and you may catch sight of a chef or two having dinner – that's because Aussie Brett Graham is considered a "chef's chef" and it's easy to see why. His cooking is informed by the seasonal ingredients available and his deep-rooted knowledge of husbandry and the close relationships he has formed with his suppliers are revealed throughout his menu.

Game and in particular the Sika deer – raised on their own small estate in Oxfordshire – are always highlights. Other signature dishes, such as beetroot baked in clay with English caviar, and brown sugar tart demonstrate how adept the kitchen is at harnessing the true flavours of ingredients, often with complementing layers. Like a gifted sportsman, it can sometimes look effortlessly easy but it takes great skill to make something with some depth look so simple. The service is personable and free from affectation; the wine list is strong across all regions; and the atmosphere hospitable and grown up.

FIRST COURSE

White beetroot baked in clay with English caviar and dried eel. • Tartare of sea bream with oyster and frozen wasabi.

MAIN COURSE

Sika deer with smoked bone marrow, rhubarb, red leaves and vegetables. • Lobster with shiitake, peas and lemon.

DESSERT

Brown sugar tart with stem ginger ice cream. • Roast pear ice cream with chestnut sponge, honey and bee pollen.

127 Ledbury Rd. ✉ W11 2AQ **MAP: 13-C2**
✆ 020 7792 9090 — **www.**theledbury.com
⊖ Notting Hill Gate

Menu £80/150
Closed 25-26 December, August bank holiday and lunch Monday-Tuesday

A/C

108 GARAGE ¶O

Modern British • Neighbourhood

A daily changing 6 course menu is offered, with a choice of main course; the modern dishes offer plenty of contrasts and originality. This former garage has a utilitarian look that's all bare brick, exposed ducting and polished concrete. Sit at the counter if you want to chat with the chefs.

■ 108 Golborne Rd ✉ W10 5PS **MAP: 13-B1**
✆ 020 8969 3769 — **www.**108garage.com
⊖ Westbourne Park
■ Menu £60 (dinner) - Carte £43/57
Closed 2 weeks August, 2 weeks Christmas, Sunday and Monday - booking essential
A/C

THE SHED ¶O

Modern British • Rustic

It's more than just a shed but does have a higgledy-piggledy charm and a healthy dose of the outdoors. One brother cooks, one manages and the third runs the farm which supplies the produce for the earthy, satisfying dishes.

■ 122 Palace Gardens Ter. ✉ W8 4RT **MAP: 13-C3**
✆ 020 7229 4024 — **www.**theshed-restaurant.com
⊖ Notting Hill Gate
■ Carte £26/38
Closed Monday lunch and Sunday

SIX PORTLAND ROAD ¶O

French • Neighbourhood

An intimate and personally run neighbourhood restaurant owned by Oli Barker, previously of Terroirs. The menu changes frequently and has a strong French accent; dishes are reassuringly recognisable, skilfully constructed and very tasty.

■ 6 Portland Rd ✉ W11 4LA **MAP: 13-B3**
✆ 020 7229 3130 — **www.**sixportlandroad.com
⊖ Holland Park
■ Menu £17 (weekday lunch) - Carte £32/55
Closed Christmas-New Year, last 2 weeks August, Sunday dinner and Monday
A/C

ZAIKA 🍴O

Indian • Contemporary décor

The cooking focuses on the North of India and the influences of Mughal and Nawabi, so expect rich and fragrantly spiced dishes. The softly-lit room makes good use of its former life as a bank, with its wood-panelling and ornate ceiling.

1 Kensington High St. ✉ W8 5NP **MAP: 13-D4**
020 7795 6533 — **www.**zaikaofkensington.com
⊖ High Street Kensington
Menu £23 (lunch) - Carte £28/65
Closed 25-26 December, 1 January and Monday lunch

ZAYANE 🍴O

Moroccan • Neighbourhood

An intimate neighbourhood restaurant owned by Casablanca-born Meryem Mortell and evoking the sights and scents of North Africa. Carefully conceived dishes have authentic Moroccan flavours but are cooked with modern techniques.

91 Golborne Rd ✉ W10 5NL **MAP: 13-B1**
020 8960 1137 — **www.**zayanerestaurant.com
⊖ Westbourne Park
Carte £25/42
Closed 10 days January, 26 August-3 September, Sunday and Monday

Remember, stars ✿ are awarded for cuisine only! Elements such as service and décor are not a factor.

GREATER LONDON

londongal_/iStock (bottom) • Eviled/Shutterstock.com (top)

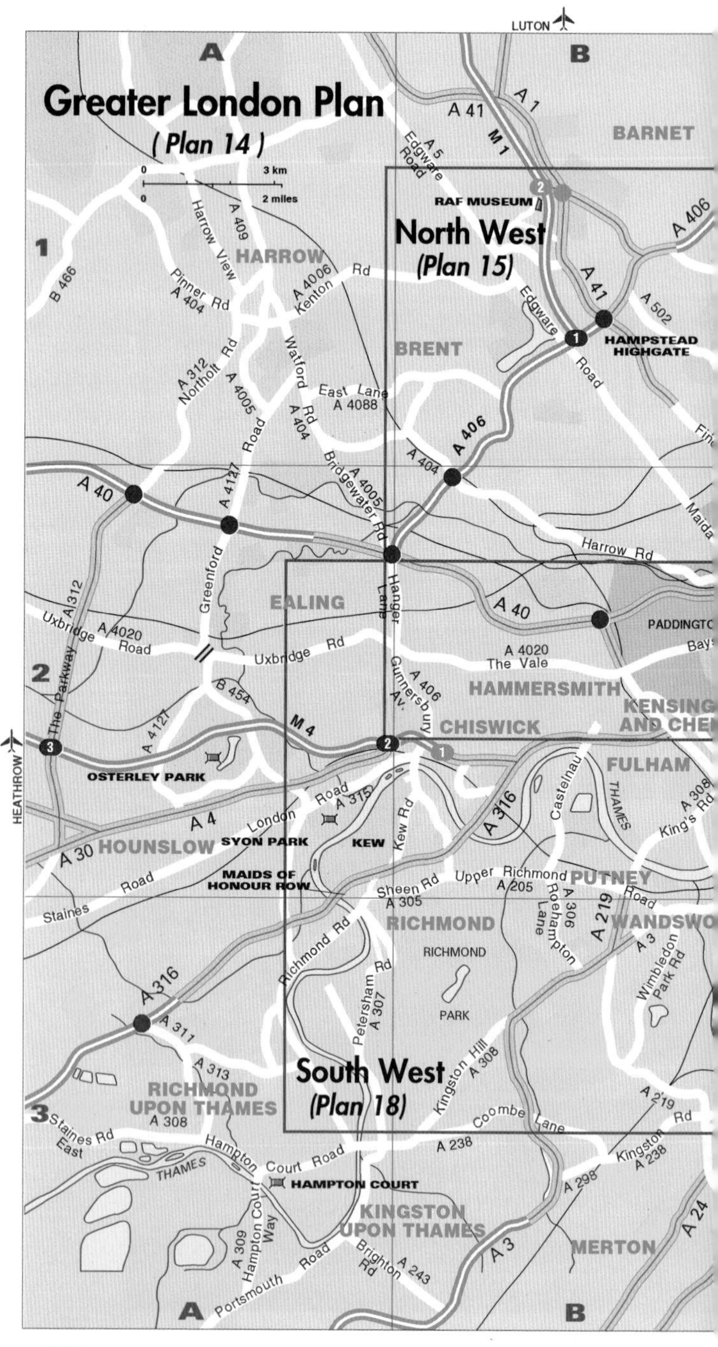
Greater London Plan
(Plan 14)
North West
(Plan 15)
South West
(Plan 18)
LUTON
HEATHROW
HARROW
BARNET
BRENT
EALING
HAMMERSMITH
CHISWICK
FULHAM
HOUNSLOW
PUTNEY
RICHMOND
RICHMOND UPON THAMES
KINGSTON UPON THAMES
MERTON
RAF MUSEUM
HAMPSTEAD HIGHGATE
OSTERLEY PARK
SYON PARK
KEW
MAIDS OF HONOUR ROW
RICHMOND PARK
HAMPTON COURT
PADDINGTON

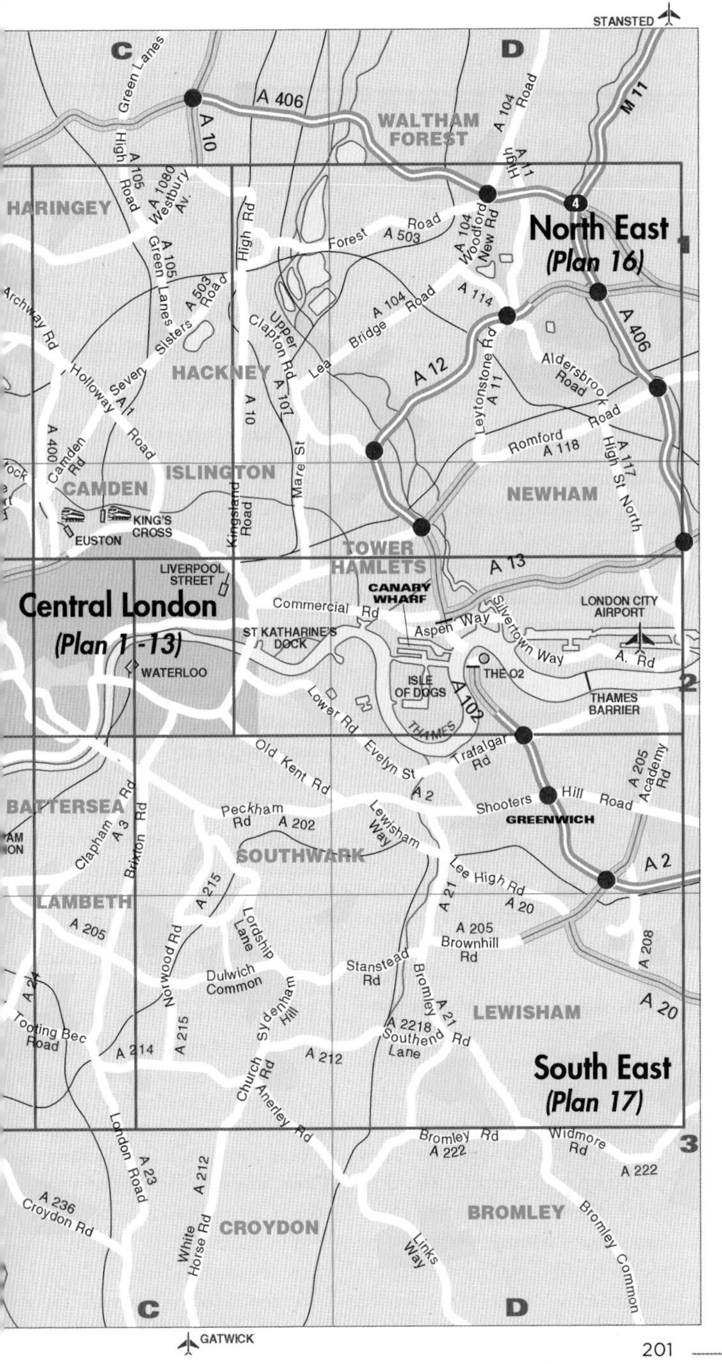
STANSTED
C
D
WALTHAM FOREST
HARINGEY
North East
(Plan 16)
HACKNEY
ISLINGTON
CAMDEN
NEWHAM
EUSTON
KING'S CROSS
TOWER HAMLETS
LIVERPOOL STREET
CANARY WHARF
Central London
(Plan 1-13)
ST KATHARINE'S DOCK
WATERLOO
LONDON CITY AIRPORT
ISLE OF DOGS
THE O2
THAMES BARRIER
BATTERSEA
GREENWICH
SOUTHWARK
LAMBETH
LEWISHAM
South East
(Plan 17)
BROMLEY
CROYDON
GATWICK

NORTH-WEST LONDON

Heading north from London Zoo and Regent's Park, the green baton is passed to two of the city's most popular and well-known locations: Hampstead Heath and Highgate Wood. In close proximity, they offer a favoured pair of lungs to travellers emerging from the murky depths of the Northern Line. Two centuries ago, they would have been just another part of the area's undeveloped high ground and pastureland, but since the building boom of the nineteenth century, both have become prized assets in this part of the metropolis.

People came to seek shelter in **Hampstead** in times of plague, and it's retained its bucolic air to this day. Famous names have always enjoyed its charms: Constable and Keats rested their brush and pen here, while the sculptors Henry Moore and Barbara Hepworth were residents in more recent times. Many are drawn to such delightful places as Church Row, which boasts a lovely Georgian Terrace. You know you're up high because the thoroughfares bear names like Holly Mount and Mount Vernon. The Heath is full of rolling woodlands and meadows; it's a great place for rambling, particularly to the crest of **Parliament Hill** and its superb city views. There are three bathing ponds here, one mixed, and one each for male and female swimmers, while up on the Heath's northern fringes, **Kenwood House,** along with its famous al fresco summer concerts, also boasts great art by the likes of Vermeer and Rembrandt. And besides all that, there's an ivy tunnel leading to a terrace with idyllic pond views.

Highgate Wood is an ancient woodland and conservation area, containing a leafy walk that meanders enchantingly along a former railway line to **Crouch End,** home to a band of thespians. Down the road at Highgate Cemetery, the likes of Karl Marx, George Eliot, Christina Rossetti and Michael Faraday rest in a great entanglement of breathtaking Victorian over-decoration. The cemetery is still in use – recent notables to be buried here include Douglas Adams and Malcolm McLaren.

Next door you'll find **Waterlow Park,** another fine green space, which, apart from its super views, also includes decorative ponds on three levels. Lauderdale House is here, too, a 16C pile which is now an arts centre; more famously, Charles II handed over its keys to Nell Gwynn for her to use as her North London residence. Head back south from here, and **Primrose Hill** continues the theme of glorious green space: its surrounding terraces are populated by media darlings, while its vertiginous mass is another to boast a famously enviable vista.

Of a different hue altogether is **Camden Town** with its buzzy edge, courtesy of a renowned indie music scene, goths, punks, and six earthy markets selling everything from tat to exotica. Charles Dickens grew up here, and he was none too complimentary; the area still relishes its seamy underside. A scenic route out is the **Regent's Canal,** which cuts its way through the market and ambles to the east and west of the city. Up the road, the legendary Roundhouse re-opened its arty front doors in 2006, expanding further the wide range of Camden's alt scene.

One of the music world's most legendary destinations, the **Abbey Road** studios, is also in this area and, yes, it's possible to join other tourists making their way over that zebra crossing. Not far away, in Maresfield Gardens, stands a very different kind of attraction. The Freud Museum is one of the very few buildings in London to have two blue plaques. It was home to Sigmund during the last year of his life and it's where he lived with his daughter Anna (her plaque commemorates her work in child psychiatry). Inside, there's a fabulous library and his working desk. But the pivotal part of the whole house is in another corner of the study – the psychiatrist's couch!

Greater London: North West

(Plan 15)

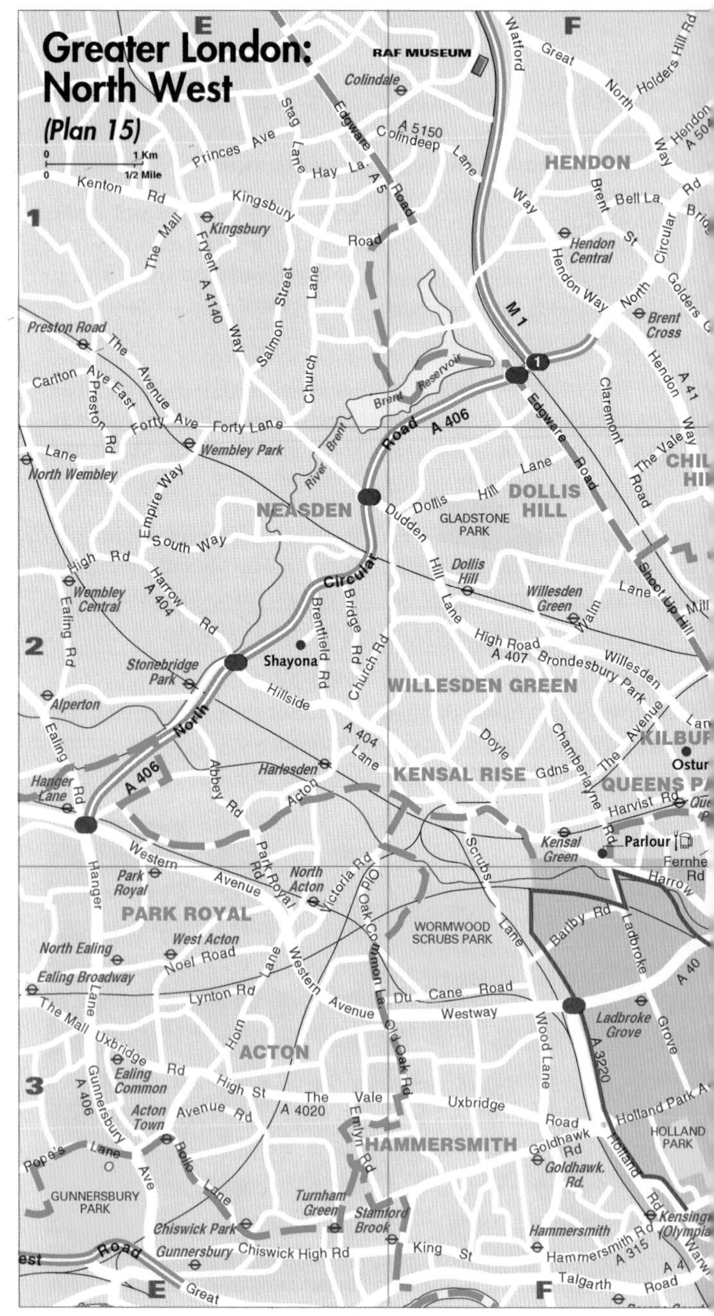

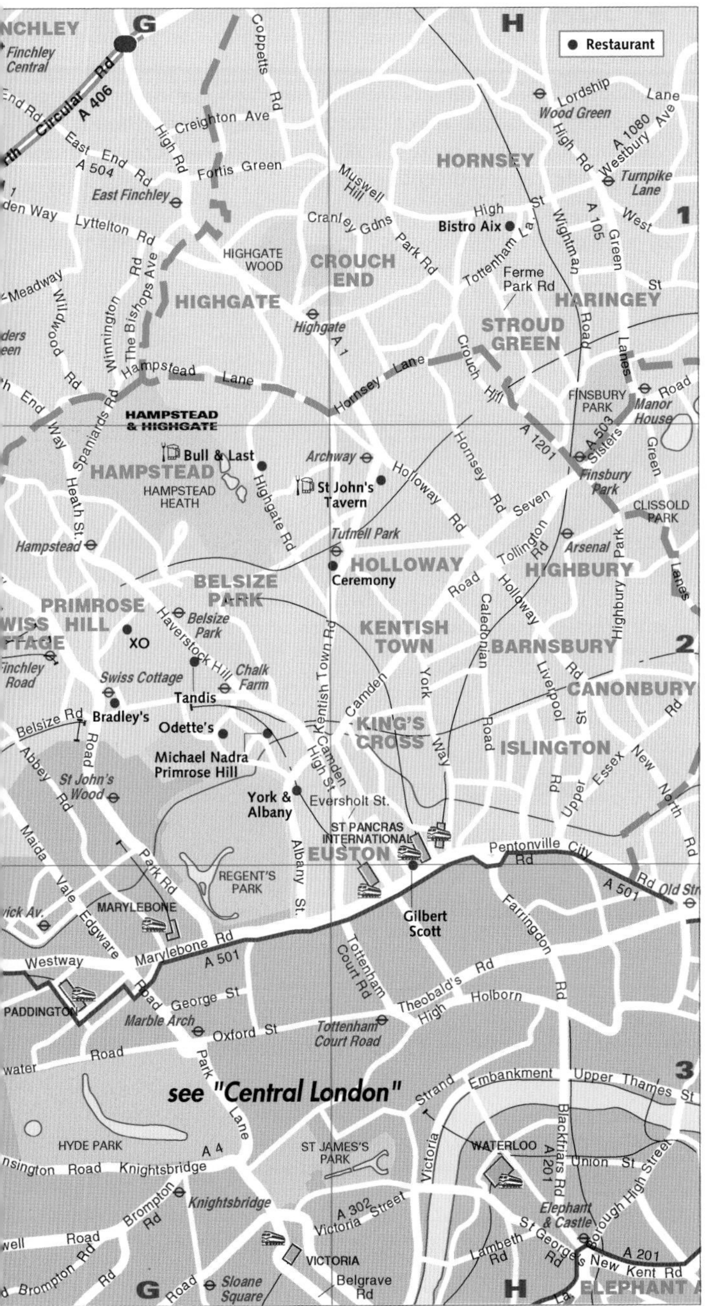

Restaurant
HORNSEY
CROUCH END
HIGHGATE
STROUD GREEN
HARINGEY
HAMPSTEAD & HIGHGATE
HAMPSTEAD
HAMPSTEAD HEATH
BELSIZE PARK
PRIMROSE HILL
HOLLOWAY
KENTISH TOWN
BARNSBURY
HIGHBURY
CANONBURY
KING'S CROSS
ISLINGTON
EUSTON
ST PANCRAS INTERNATIONAL
MARYLEBONE
REGENT'S PARK
PADDINGTON
HYDE PARK
ST JAMES'S PARK
WATERLOO
VICTORIA
Bistro Aix
Bull & Last
St John's Tavern
Ceremony
XO
Tandis
Bradley's
Odette's
Michael Nadra Primrose Hill
York & Albany
Gilbert Scott
see "Central London"

ST JOHN'S TAVERN

Modern cuisine • Pub

A Junction Road landmark with friendly service and a great selection of artisan beers. Tapas is served in the front bar; head to the vast, hugely appealing rear dining room for well-crafted British and Mediterranean dishes.

Archway — 91 Junction Rd ✉ N19 5QU **MAP: 15-H2**
✆ 020 7272 1587 — **www**.stjohnstavern.com
⊖ Archway.

Carte £23/36
Closed 25-26 December and Monday lunch

TANDIS

World cuisine • Neighbourhood

Persian and Middle Eastern food whose appeal stretches way beyond the Iranian diaspora. The specialities are the substantial and invigorating khoresh stew and the succulent kababs; end with Persian sorbet with rosewater.

Belsize Park — 73 Haverstock Hill ✉ NW3 4SL **MAP: 15-G2**
✆ 020 7586 8079 — **www**.tandisrestaurant.com
⊖ Chalk Farm

Carte £21/32
Closed 25 December

YORK & ALBANY

Modern cuisine • Inn

This handsome 1820s John Nash coaching inn was rescued by Gordon Ramsay a few years ago after lying almost derelict. It's a moot point whether it's still an inn or more a restaurant; the food is sophisticated and the service is bright.

Camden Town — 127-129 Parkway ✉ NW1 7PS **MAP: 15-G2**
✆ 020 7592 1227 — **www**.gordonramsayrestaurants.com/york-and-albany
⊖ Camden Town

Menu £25 (weekday lunch) - Carte £32/49

SHAYONA

Indian • Family

Opposite the striking Swaminarayan Temple is this simple, sattvic restaurant: it's vegetarian and 'pure' so avoids onion or garlic. Expect curries from the north, dosas from the south and Mumbai street food. No alcohol so try a lassi.

Church End — 54-62 Meadow Garth ✉ NW10 8HD **MAP: 15-E2**
☏ 020 8965 3365 — **www**.shayonarestaurants.com
⊖ Stonebridge Park

Menu £10 (weekday lunch) - Carte £12/19
Closed 27-28 October and 25 December

BISTRO AIX

French • Bistro

Dressers, cabinets and contemporary artwork lend an authentic Gallic edge to this bustling bistro, a favourite with many of the locals. Traditionally prepared French classics are the highlights of an extensive menu.

Crouch End — 54 Topsfield Par, Tottenham Ln ✉ N8 8PT **MAP: 15-H1**
☏ 020 8340 6346 — **www**.bistroaix.co.uk
⊖ Crouch Hill

Menu £25 (early dinner) - Carte £23/49
Closed 24, 26 December and 1 January - (dinner only and lunch Saturday-Sunday)

BULL & LAST

Traditional British • Neighbourhood

A busy Victorian pub with plenty of charm and character; the upstairs is a little quieter. Cooking is muscular, satisfying and reflects the time of year; charcuterie is a speciality.

Dartmouth Park — 168 Highgate Rd ✉ NW5 1QS **MAP: 15-G2**
☏ 020 7267 3641 — **www**.thebullandlast.co.uk
⊖ Tufnell Park.

Carte £34/47
Closed 23-25 December - booking essential

PARLOUR

Modern British • Pub

A fun, warmly run and slightly quirky neighbourhood hangout. The menu is a wonderfully unabashed mix of tradition, originality and reinvention, and dishes are beautifully fresh, full of flavour and such great value. Don't miss the cow pie which even Dan, however Desperate, would struggle to finish.

Kensal Green — 5 Regent St NW10 5LG **MAP: 15-F2**
020 8969 2184 — **www.**parlourkensal.com
Kensal Green

Menu £18 - Carte £18/42
Closed 1 week late August, 1 week Christmas-New Year and Monday

GILBERT SCOTT

Traditional British • Brasserie

Named after the architect of this Gothic masterpiece and run under the aegis of Marcus Wareing, this restaurant has the splendour of a Grand Salon but the buzz of a brasserie. The appealing menu showcases the best of British produce, whilst incorporating influences from further afield.

King's Cross St Pancras — St Pancras Renaissance Hotel, Euston Rd NW1 2AR **MAP: 15-H2/3**
020 7278 3888 — **www.**thegilbertscott.co.uk
King's Cross St Pancras

Menu £30 (lunch and early dinner) - Carte £28/61

MICHAEL NADRA PRIMROSE HILL

Modern cuisine • Neighbourhood

The menu resembles Michael Nadra's Chiswick operation, which means flavours from the Med but also the occasional Asian note. The bar offers over 20 martinis. The unusual vaulted room adds to the intimacy and service is very friendly.

Primrose Hill — 42 Gloucester Ave NW1 8JD **MAP: 15-G2**
020 7722 2800 — **www.**restaurant-michaelnadra.co.uk/primrose
Camden Town

Menu £23/39
Closed 24-28 December and 1 January

ODETTE'S

Modern cuisine • Neighbourhood

A long-standing local favourite. Warm and inviting interior, with chatty yet organised service. Robust and quite elaborate cooking, with owner passionate about his Welsh roots. Good value lunch menu.

Primrose Hill — 130 Regent's Park Rd. ✉ NW1 8XL **MAP: 15-G2**
✆ 020 7586 8569 — **www**.odettesprimrosehill.com
⊖ Chalk Farm

Menu £23 (lunch and early dinner) - Carte £34/53
Closed Christmas-New Year, Sunday dinner and Monday

OSTUNI

Italian • Neighbourhood

The cuisine of Puglia, the red hot heel in Italy's boot, is celebrated at this rustic local restaurant. Don't miss the olives, creamy burrata, fava bean purée, the sausages and bombette, or the orecchiette - the ear-shaped pasta.

Queens Park — 43-45 Lonsdale Rd ✉ NW6 6RA **MAP: 15-F2**
✆ 020 7624 8035 — **www**.ostuniristorante.co.uk
⊖ Queen's Park

Carte £24/45
Closed 24-25 December

BRADLEY'S

Modern cuisine • Neighbourhood

A stalwart of the local dining scene and ideal for visitors to the nearby Hampstead Theatre. The thoughtfully compiled and competitively priced set menus of mostly classical cooking draw in plenty of regulars.

Swiss Cottage — 25 Winchester Rd. ✉ NW3 3NR **MAP: 15-G2**
✆ 020 7722 3457 — **www**.bradleysnw3.co.uk
⊖ Swiss Cottage

Menu £24/30 - Carte £36/47
Closed Sunday dinner and bank holidays

Ⓝ CEREMONY

Vegetarian • Neighbourhood

Zinc-topped tables, a raised bar and a contemporary look - vegetarian restaurants never used to look like this. The small menu is full of interesting dishes, with influences from the Med and Asia; some even use produce from the garden at the back. The booths are the prized seats.

■ **Tufnell Park** — 131 Fortess Rd ✉ NW5 2HR **MAP: 15-H2**
✆ 020 3302 4242 — **www**.ceremonyrestaurant.london
⊖ Tufnell Park

■ Carte £27/33
Closed Christmas and Monday - booking essential - (dinner only and Sunday lunch)

Ⓝ HĀM

Modern cuisine • Neighbourhood

A bright, modern space that perfectly complements the style of cooking, which is light, seasonal and unfussy. The restaurant has a warm neighbourhood feel - its name means 'home' - and its brunches are also popular.

■ **West Hampstead** — 238 West End Ln ✉ NW6 1LG **MAP: 15-G2**
✆ 020 7813 0168 — **www**.hamwesthampstead.com
⊖ West Hampstead

■ Carte £35/46
Closed Sunday dinner, Monday and Tuesday

The sun is out — let's eat alfresco! Look for 🏠.

CAMDEN LOCK
CAMDEN
LOCK
MARKET

NORTH-EAST LONDON

If northwest London is renowned for its leafy acres, then the area to its immediate east has a more urban, brick-built appeal. Which has meant, over the last decade or so, a wholesale rebranding exercise for some of its traditionally shady localities. A generation ago it would have been beyond the remit of even the most inventive estate agent to sell the charms of Islington, Hackney or Bethnal Green. But then along came Damien Hirst, Tracey Emin et al, and before you could say 'cow in formaldehyde' the area's cachet had rocketed.

Shoreditch and **Hoxton** are the pivotal points of the region's hip makeover. Their cobbled brick streets and shabby industrial remnants were like heavenly manna to the artists and designers who started to colonise the old warehouses thirty years ago. A fashionable crowd soon followed in their footsteps, and nowadays the area around **Hoxton Square** positively teems with clubs, bars and galleries. Must-sees include Rivington Place, a terrific gallery that highlights visual arts from around the world, Deluxe (digital installations) and Hales (contemporary art). Before the area was ever trendy, there was the Geffrye Museum. A short stroll up Hoxton's **Kingsland Road,** it's a jewel of a place, set in elegant 18C almshouses, and depicting English middle-class interiors from 1600 to the present day. Right behind it is St. Mary's Secret Garden, a little oasis that manages to include much diversity including a separate woodland and herb area, all in less than an acre. At the southern end of the area, in Folgate Street, Dennis Severs' House is an original Huguenot home that recreates 18 and 19C life in an original way – cooking smells linger, hearth and candles burn, giving you the impression the owners have only just left the place. Upstairs the beds remain unmade: did a certain local artist pick up any ideas here?

When the Regent's Canal was built in the early 19C, **Islington's** fortunes nose-dived, for it was accompanied by the arrival of slums and over-crowding. But the once-idyllic village managed to hold onto its Georgian squares and handsome Victorian terraces through the rough times, and when these were gentrified a few years ago, the area ushered in a revival. **Camden Passage** has long been famed for its quirky antique emporiums, while the slinky Business Design Centre is a flagship of the modern Islington. Cultural icons established themselves around the Upper Street area and these have gone from strength to strength. The **Almeida** Theatre has a habit of hitting the production jackpot with its history of world premieres, while the King's Head has earned itself a reputation for raucous scene-stealing; set up in the seventies, it's also London's very first theatre-pub. Nearby, the Screen on the Green boasts a wonderful old-fashioned neon billboard.

Even in the 'bad old days', Islington drew in famous names, and at Regency smart **Canonbury Square** are the one-time homes of Evelyn Waugh (no.17A) and George Orwell (no.27). These days it houses the Estorick Collection of Modern Italian Art; come here to see fine futuristic paintings in a Georgian villa. To put the history of the area in a proper context, head to St. John Street, south of the City Road, where the Islington Museum tells the story of a colourful and multi-layered past.

Further up the A10, you come to **Dalston,** a bit like the Islington of old but with the buzzy Ridley Road market and a vibrant all-night scene including the blistering Vortex Jazz Club just off Kingsland Road. A little further north is **Stoke Newington,** referred to, a bit unkindly, as the poor man's Islington. Its pride and joy is Church Street, which not only features some eye-catching boutiques, but also lays claim to Abney Park Cemetery, an enchanting old place with a wildlife-rich nature reserve.

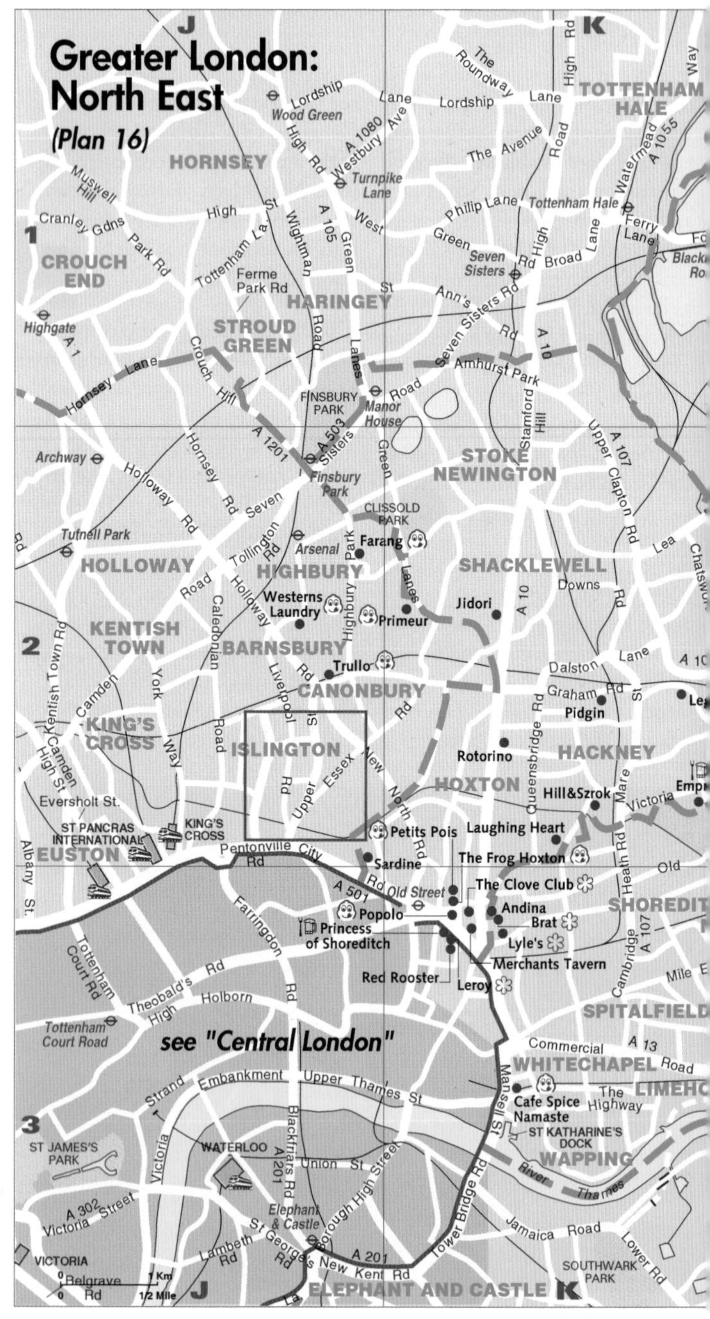
Greater London: North East
(Plan 16)
J
K
1
2
3
HORNSEY
CROUCH END
HARINGEY
STROUD GREEN
TOTTENHAM HALE
STOKE NEWINGTON
HOLLOWAY
HIGHBURY
SHACKLEWELL
KENTISH TOWN
BARNSBURY
CANONBURY
KING'S CROSS
ISLINGTON
HACKNEY
HOXTON
EUSTON
SHOREDITCH
SPITALFIELDS
WHITECHAPEL
WAPPING
ELEPHANT AND CASTLE
Wood Green
Turnpike Lane
Tottenham Hale
Seven Sisters
Highgate
Finsbury Park
Manor House
Archway
Tufnell Park
Arsenal
CLISSOLD PARK
Farang
Westerns Laundry
Primeur
Jidori
Trullo
Pidgin
Rotorino
Hill&Szrok
Petits Pois
Laughing Heart
Sardine
The Frog Hoxton
The Clove Club
Old Street
Popolo
Andina
Brat
Princess of Shoreditch
Lyle's
Merchants Tavern
Red Rooster
Leroy
Cafe Spice Namaste
ST PANCRAS INTERNATIONAL
KING'S CROSS
Tottenham Court Road
see "Central London"
ST KATHARINE'S DOCK
ST JAMES'S PARK
WATERLOO
Elephant & Castle
VICTORIA
SOUTHWARK PARK
River Thames
Commercial Road
The Highway
Jamaica Road
Pentonville Rd
City Rd
Holborn
Theobald's Rd
Upper Thames St
Embankment
Strand
Tower Bridge Rd
New Kent Rd
Borough High Street
Blackfriars Rd
Upper St
Essex Rd
New North Rd
Seven Sisters Rd
Holloway Rd
Caledonian Road
Camden Rd
York Way
Hornsey Lane
Amhurst Park
Stamford Hill
Upper Clapton Rd
Dalston Lane
Graham Rd
Queensbridge Rd
Mare St
Victoria Park Rd
Cambridge Heath Rd
0 1 Km
0 1/2 Mile

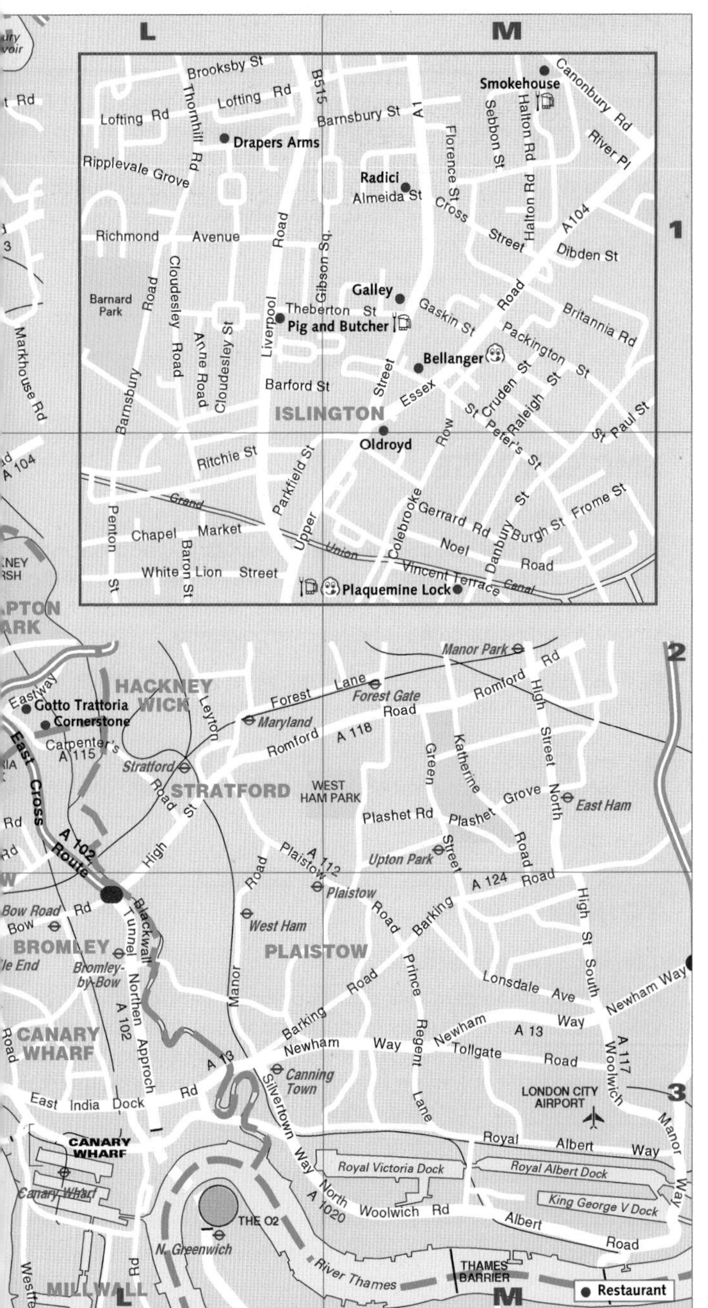
L
M
1
2
3
Brooksby St
Lofting Rd
Thornhill Rd
B515
Barnsbury St
A1
Smokehouse
Canonbury Rd
Sebbon St
Halton Rd
River Pl
Drapers Arms
Ripplevale Grove
Radici
Almeida St
Florence St
Cross Street
A104
Dibden St
Richmond Avenue
Road
Gibson Sq.
Barnard Park
Cloudesley Road
Galley
Theberton St
Gaskin St
Pig and Butcher
Britannia Rd
Packington St
Liverpool
Anne Road
Cloudesley St
Bellanger
Barnsbury
Barford St
Street
Essex
Cruden St
Raleigh St
ISLINGTON
Oldroyd
Row
St Peter's St
St Paul St
Ritchie St
Parkfield St
Grand
Colebrooke
Gerrard Rd
Frome St
Penton St
Chapel Market
Baron St
Upper
Union
Noel
Danbury St
Burgh St
Road
White Lion Street
Plaquemine Lock
Vincent Terrace
Canal
Markhouse Rd
A 104
Manor Park
Rd
Forest Lane
Forest Gate
Romford
HACKNEY WICK
Eastway
Gotto Trattoria
Cornerstone
Leyton
Maryland
Road
Romford
A 118
Carpenter's
A 115
Stratford
High Street
Green
Katherine
STRATFORD
WEST HAM PARK
Road
St
Plashet Rd
Plashet Grove
North
East Ham
East Cross
A 102 Route
High
Plaistow
A 112
Upton Park
Street
Road
Road
A 124
Road
Plaistow
Road
Bow Road
Rd
Bow
Blackwall Tunnel
Barking
High St South
West Ham
BROMLEY
Bromley-by-Bow
PLAISTOW
Prince Regent Lane
Lonsdale Ave
Newham Way
Manor
Northern Approch
A 102
Road
Barking
CANARY WHARF
Newham Way
Newham Way
A 13
Way
A 117 Woolwich
A 13
Tollgate Road
Canning Town
East India Dock Rd
Silvertown Way
LONDON CITY AIRPORT
CANARY WHARF
Royal Albert Way
Manor Way
Royal Victoria Dock
Royal Albert Dock
Canary Wharf
North
A 1020
King George V Dock
Woolwich Rd
THE O2
Albert Road
N. Greenwich
River Thames
THAMES BARRIER
MILLWALL
Restaurant

PRIMEUR

Modern cuisine • Simple

A relaxed neighbourhood restaurant whose concertina doors fold back to reveal a quirky interior with counter seating around the edges and a huge communal table. Plates are small and designed for sharing; understated but packed with flavour - simplicity is key, allowing the ingredients to really shine.

Canonbury — 116 Petherton Rd ✉ N5 2RT **MAP: 16-K2**
020 7226 5271 — **www**.primeurn5.co.uk
⊖ Canonbury
Carte £21/38
Closed Christmas, Sunday dinner, Monday and lunch Tuesday-Thursday

---

SMOKEHOUSE

Modern cuisine • Pub

You can smell the oak chips in the smoker as you approach this warm, modern pub. Meat is the mainstay - the peppered ox cheeks are a firm favourite - but whilst flavours are gutsy, the smoking and barbecuing is never overpowering.

Canonbury — 63-69 Canonbury Rd ✉ N1 2DG **MAP: 16-M1**
020 7354 1144 — **www**.smokehouseislington.co.uk
⊖ Highbury & Islington.
Carte £29/35
Closed 24-26 December and lunch Monday-Thursday except bank holidays

---

TRULLO

Italian • Neighbourhood

A neighbourhood gem split over two floors; its open kitchen serving an ingredient-led daily menu. Harmonious, tried-and-tested combinations create rustic, full-flavoured Italian dishes, including meats and fish cooked on the charcoal grill and delicious fresh pasta, hand-rolled before each service.

Canonbury — 300-302 St Paul's Rd ✉ N1 2LH **MAP: 16-J2**
020 7226 2733 — **www**.trullorestaurant.com
⊖ Highbury & Islington
Carte £25/48
Closed 24 December-1 January and Sunday dinner - booking essential
A/C

JIDORI ¶O

Japanese • Bistro

A sweet, unadorned yakitori-style restaurant serving succulent skewers of chicken, cooked on a charcoal-fired Kama-Asa Shoten grill imported from Japan. Charming staff and a good selection of cocktails, sake and craft beers.

Dalston — 89 Kingsland High St ✉ E2 8BP **MAP: 16-K2**
✆ 020 7686 5634 — **www**.jidori.co.uk
⊖ Dalston Kingsland
Carte £17/28
Closed 25-26 December, 1 January, bank holiday Mondays and Sunday - bookings not accepted - (dinner only and lunch Wednesday-Friday)

ROTORINO ¶O

Italian • Simple

A stylish yet down to earth Italian serving Southern Italian specialities like caponata, gnudi and Sasso chicken. Staff are welcoming and knowledgeable; ask for one of the booths at the back.

Dalston — 434 Kingsland Rd ✉ E8 4AA **MAP: 16-K2**
✆ 020 7249 9081 — **www**.rotorino.com
⊖ Dalston Junction
Menu £19 (early dinner) - Carte £22/34
Closed Christmas-New Year - (dinner only and Sunday lunch)
A/C

LAUGHING HEART ¶O

Modern cuisine • Wine bar

A wine bar for our age and as joyful as the name suggests. It comes with a great vibe, lovely service and a flexible menu of cleverly paired seasonal ingredients with occasional Asian flavours. Natural wines are the focus of the wine list and the small wine shop downstairs.

Hackney — 277 Hackney Rd ✉ E2 8NA **MAP: 16-K2**
✆ 020 7686 9535 — **www**.thelaughingheartlondon.com
⊖ Hoxton
Carte £20/38
Closed 12-26 August, 1-6 January and Sunday - (dinner only)

LEGS

Modern British • Neighbourhood

An urban, no-frills bistro with a lively atmosphere, charming staff and food bursting with freshness and flavour. Dinner is a daily selection of small plates for sharing - and they also serve brunch on Saturdays. The wine list focuses on organic wines from small producers.

Hackney — 120 Morning Ln ✉ E9 6LH **MAP: 16-K2**
020 3441 8765 — **www**.legsrestaurant.com
Hackney Central

Carte £15/31
Closed Sunday dinner, Monday and Tuesday - (dinner only and lunch Saturday-Sunday)

CORNERSTONE

Seafood • Neighbourhood

Fish dishes - which change according to seasons and catches - are the highlight here, which is hardly surprising as the owner-chef was Nathan Outlaw's chef at The Capital. Save room for the Cornish burnt cream. The pared-back room is dominated by a large open kitchen.

Hackney Wick — 3 Prince Edward Rd ✉ E9 5LX **MAP: 16-L2**
020 8986 3922 — **www**.cornerstonehackney.com
Hackney Wick (Rail)

Carte £26/46
Closed 23 December-2 January, 23-30 July, Sunday and Monday - booking essential

A/C

GOTTO TRATTORIA

Italian • Simple

The sister to Soho's Mele e Pere is a modern trattoria in a canal-side setting. The imported Italian ingredients are treated with respect and some of the recipes - such as for the ever-present lasagne - are family secrets. Many of the cocktails use their homemade vermouth.

Hackney Wick — 27 East Bay Ln ✉ E15 2GW **MAP: 16-L2**
020 3424 5035 — **www**.gotto.co.uk
Hackney Wick (Rail)

Carte £18/26

FARANG

Thai • Friendly

Seb and Dan had a series of pop-ups for their Thai street food before moving into this permanent home. Dishes have an authentic heart and use a mix of Thai and British produce. The small menu is supplemented by a number of specials, while the 'Feasting' menus are great for larger groups.

Highbury — 72 Highbury Pk ✉ N5 2XE **MAP: 16-J2**
020 7226 1609 — **www**.faranglondon.co.uk
Arsenal
Carte £20/40
Closed Sunday and Monday - (dinner only and Saturday lunch)

WESTERNS LAUNDRY

Modern British • Fashionable

Sister to Primeur and with the same industrial feel; set on the ground floor of a former laundry, with a pleasant front terrace. Sit at the kitchen counter or at one of the communal tables. The fish-focused menu is accompanied by natural wines and the confidently executed dishes are full of flavour.

Holloway — 34 Drayton Pk ✉ N5 1PB **MAP: 16-J2**
020 7700 3700 — **www**.westernslaundry.com
Holloway Road
Carte £26/35
Closed Monday, lunch Tuesday-Thursday and Sunday dinner - booking essential

---

THE FROG HOXTON

Modern cuisine • Brasserie

In 2018 Adam Handling moved his Frog from Spitalfields to bigger premises here in Hoxton Square. The three operations under one roof all have their own identity: a coffee shop and deli, a large bar and a casual restaurant specialising in well-priced, creative sharing plates.

Hoxton — 45-47 Hoxton Sq ✉ N1 9PD **MAP: 16-K2**
020 3813 9832 — **www**.thefroghoxton.com
Old Street
Carte £17/31
A/C

Ⓝ PETIT POIS

Modern British • Neighbourhood

Some restaurants just have a certain honesty about them. The small, even cramped, dining room is full of life and the service team take it in their stride. The flavoursome cooking is all about allowing the main ingredient to shine. The chocolate mousse is scooped at the table.

Hoxton — 9 Hoxton Sq ✉ N1 6NU **MAP: 16-K2**
020 7613 3689 — **www**.petitpoisbistro.com
Old Street

Menu £14 (weekday lunch) - Carte £28/36
Closed 24-26 December

SARDINE

French • Fashionable

A trendy, compact restaurant with a communal table at the heart of proceedings. The food comes from Southern France, and dishes are rustic, unfussy and very tasty; try the lamb à la ficelle, cooked over an open fire.

Hoxton — Parasol Art Gallery, 15 Micawber St ✉ N1 7TB **MAP: 16-J2**
020 7490 0144 — **www**.sardine.london
Old Street

Menu £16 (lunch and early dinner) - Carte £27/40
Closed Christmas-New Year and Monday lunch - booking essential

A/C

BELLANGER

French • Brasserie

All-day brasserie, with the sumptuous style of an authentic grand café, modelled on those opened in Paris by the Alsatians at the turn of the century. Regional French and Alsatian-inspired fare is served from breakfast until late.

Islington — 9 Islington Grn ✉ N1 2XH **MAP: 16-M1**
020 7226 2555 — **www**.bellanger.co.uk
Angel

Menu £16 (lunch) - Carte £22/40

A/C

DRAPERS ARMS

Traditional British • Neighbourhood

An imposing neighbourhood pub with warming fires, shabby-chic styling, a relaxed, unpretentious feel, a bevy of eager-to-please staff and a courtyard garden. They offer gutsy and satisfying seasonal British dishes, a great selection of regional ales and a well-thought-out wine list.

Islington — 44 Barnsbury St ✉ N1 1ER **MAP: 16-L1**
☎ 020 7619 0348 — **www**.thedrapersarms.com
⊖ Highbury & Islington.

Carte £24/37
Closed 25-26 December

GALLEY

Seafood • Brasserie

A smart, colourful seafood restaurant with a brasserie feel; there's a bar at the front and a few prized booths, but the best seats in the house are at the kitchen counter. The hot or cold seafood platters are great to share.

Islington — 105-106 Upper St ✉ N1 1QN **MAP: 16-M1**
☎ 020 7684 2538 — **www**.galleylondon.co.uk
⊖ Highbury & Islington

Carte £27/42
Closed 1 January

A/C

OLDROYD

Modern British • Intimate

The eponymous Oldroyd is Tom, who left his role with the Polpo group to open this busy little bistro. It's all about small plates - ingredients are largely British, influences are from within Europe and dishes are very easy to eat.

Islington — 344 Upper St ✉ N1 0PD **MAP: 16-M1**
☎ 020 8617 9010 — **www**.oldroydlondon.com
⊖ Angel

Menu £19 (weekday lunch) - Carte £16/35
Closed 25-26 December and 1 January

PIG AND BUTCHER

Traditional British • Pub

Dating from the mid-19C, when cattle drovers taking livestock to Smithfield Market would stop for a swift one, and now fully restored. There's a strong British element to the daily menu; meat is butchered and smoked in-house.

Islington — 80 Liverpool Rd ✉ N1 0QD **MAP: 16-L1**
020 7226 8304 — **www**.thepigandbutcher.co.uk
Angel

Carte £28/50
Closed 24-26 December - (dinner only and lunch Friday-Sunday)

PLAQUEMINE LOCK

Creole • Cosy

A unique and very colourful pub named after a small city in Louisiana and with a menu centred around Creole and Cajun traditions. Dishes like gumbo with okra, blackened chicken, and crawfish with corn and potatoes are carefully cooked and packed with flavour. Big Easy style cocktails add to the fun.

Islington — 139 Graham St ✉ N1 8LB **MAP: 16-M2**
020 7688 1488 — **www**.plaqlock.com
Angel

Carte £21/35
Closed 25 December

RADICI

Italian • Rustic

Its name means roots and cooking is based around hearty Southern Italian classics inspired by chef Francesco Mazzei's childhood. The room has a rustic look, a wood-fired oven for pizzas and a wine lounge packed with Italian bottles.

Islington — 30 Almeida St ✉ N1 1AD **MAP: 16-M1**
020 7354 4777 — **www**.radici.uk
Angel

Menu £18 - Carte £28/36

HILL & SZROK

Meats and grills • Neighbourhood

Butcher's shop by day; restaurant by night, with a central marble-topped table, counters around the edge and a friendly, lively feel. Daily blackboard menu of top quality meats, including steaks aged for a minimum of 60 days. No bookings.

London Fields — 60 Broadway Market ✉ E8 4QJ **MAP: 16-K2**
✆ 020 7254 8805 — **www**.hillandszrok.co.uk
⊖ Bethnal Green
Carte £17/34
Closed 23 December-2 January - bookings not accepted - (dinner only and Sunday lunch)

PIDGIN

Modern British • Neighbourhood

A cosy, single room restaurant with understated décor and a lively atmosphere, tucked away on a residential Hackney street. The no-choice four course menu of modern British dishes changes weekly, as does the interesting wine list.

London Fields — 52 Wilton Way ✉ E8 1BG **MAP: 16-K2**
✆ 020 7254 8311 — **www**.pidginlondon.com
⊖ Hackney Central
Menu £49
Closed Christmas-New Year and Monday - booking essential - (dinner only and lunch Friday -Sunday) - (tasting menu only)

ANDINA

Peruvian • Simple

Andina may be smaller and slightly more chaotic that its sister Ceviche, but this friendly picantería with live music is equally popular. The Peruvian specialities include great salads and skewers, and ceviche that packs a punch.

Shoreditch — 1 Redchurch St ✉ E2 7DJ **MAP: 16-K3**
✆ 020 7920 6499 — **www**.andinarestaurants.com
⊖ Shoreditch High Street
Carte £15/31
Closed 24-26 December and 1 January - booking essential
A/C

Ⓝ BRAT ✿

Traditional British • Neighbourhood

It takes a lot of skill, experience and confidence to make something look effortlessly simple. When it came to opening his own place, Tomos Parry, late of Kitty Fisher's, took inspiration from the cooking styles found in the Basque country, and in particular the town of Getaria. This is about cooking over fire - the stove, grill and oven, hand-built to his own specification, provide the focal point of the room, which is on the first floor of an old pub.

'Brat' is the Old English word for turbot and this is the house speciality, a whole turbot grilled in a handmade basket over lump wood charcoal with a sauce made from the released collagen and gelatine. There are plenty of other dishes to enjoy first, some of which are inspired by his Welsh roots, such as pork and laverbread salami, or baby peas with Carmarthen ham.

It's all about wonderful ingredients and natural flavours - and there is something very joyful about it. You don't just eat at Brat - you tuck in.

FIRST COURSE	MAIN COURSE	DESSERT
Soused red mullet. • Spider crab with cabbage and fennel.	Herdwick lamb. • Whole turbot roasted on the fire.	Burnt cheesecake with rhubarb. • Lemon tart.

Shoreditch — 4 Redchurch St (1st Floor) ✉ E1 6JL **MAP: 16-K3**
www.bratrestaurant.com
⊖ Shoreditch High Street

Carte £23/40
Closed 24-26 December, Easter, Sunday dinner and Monday - booking essential

THE CLOVE CLUB ✿

Modern cuisine • Trendy

Chefs perform centre stage in the smart, blue-tiled kitchen of the Grade II listed Shoreditch Town Hall, whose sparse dining room has been softened slightly by the introduction of window blinds and foliage; sit here rather than in the adjacent bar so you don't miss out on the buzz. And be prepared for their online pre-pay booking system.

Cooking has a Scandic style, with a set menu at dinner – this is a kitchen fanatical about sourcing top-notch British produce so expect scallops from Orkney, mackerel from Cornwall and veal from Dorset. The meal starts with a few canapés which set the tone: there is originality, verve and flair but flavours are always expertly judged and complementary, with seafood dishes a highlight. Wonderfully simple-looking dishes often have a deceptive depth to them, with full-on flavours extracted from the humblest of produce.

FIRST COURSE	MAIN COURSE	DESSERT
Hot-smoked wild Irish trout with almond milk sauce and Oscietra caviar. • Penjar tomatoes with ginger, sardine pressing, ham and aromatic herbs.	Aylesbury duck with red cabbage, blackcurrant purée and beetroot. • Cornish turbot with spruce shoots, oyster and caviar sauce.	Loquat sorbet, loquat kernel mousse, with puffed amaranth and popcorn. • Warm potato mousse with coffee and caramel ice cream.

■ **Shoreditch** — 380 Old St ✉ EC1V 9LT **MAP: 16-K3**
✆ 020 7729 6496 — **www.**thecloveclub.com
⊖ Old Street

■ Menu £75/110
Closed 2 weeks Christmas-New Year, August bank holiday, Monday lunch and Sunday - booking essential

Ⓝ LEROY ✿

Modern British • *Neighbourhood*

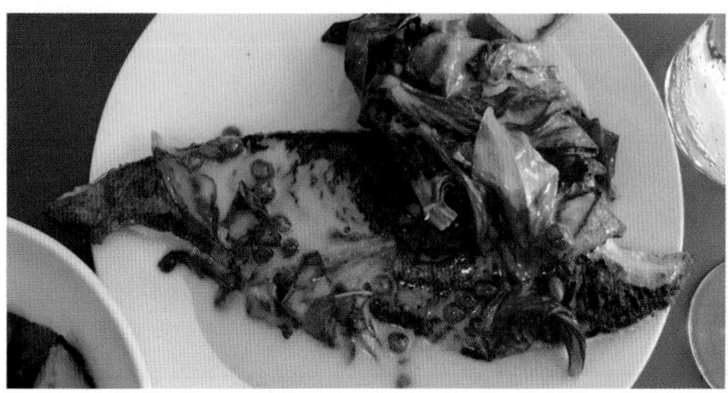

Fans of Ellory must have rejoiced when they heard the owners were reopening in 2018 in a more accessible location. The result was Leroy and it's clear the move paid off. Putting all their experience to bear, they have created a restaurant with a relaxed, easy vibe and great food. How can you not fall for a place where the first thing you see is a couple of shelves of vinyl?

They now have a local demand for lunch and are busier for dinner, so the increased turnover means the quality of the ingredients they can use is even better. As Sam the chef says "We can now buy brill or turbot instead of mackerel and calf's sweetbreads instead of liver". The core ingredient shines through in every dish – whether that's razor clams with garlic and parsley, boudin noir with watercress or the delicious skewers of honeyed quail. There's no clear division between starters and main courses – just order a few dishes to share and marvel at how much skill must go into making something so unshowy.

FIRST COURSE

Peas, lardo, mint and slow-cooked egg yolk. • Monk's beard with brown shrimp and lemon butter.

MAIN COURSE

Brill, beurre blanc, borage and sorrel. • Lamb sweetbreads with pancetta, peas and horseradish.

DESSERT

Sauternes crème caramel. • Strawberries and rosé granita.

Shoreditch — 18 Phipp St ✉ EC2A 4NU **MAP: 16-K3**
✆ 020 7739 4443 — **www**.leroyshoreditch.com
⊖ Old Street

Menu £20 (weekday lunch) - Carte £29/48
Closed 24-30 December, Monday lunch and Sunday

LYLE'S ✿

Modern British • Simple

The building was once owned by Lipton, the tea people, and the pared-down, ersatz industrial look is bang on trend. With its tiles and concrete floor, the space may be more about functionality than comfort but help is at hand from the open kitchen which is very much part of the room and adds colour and animation. Warmth and personality also come from the young service team, who share the passion of the kitchen, offer great advice and really know their menu.

One glance at that menu tells immediately of the influence of Fergus Henderson – and sure enough, the young chef-owner previously ran the kitchen at St John Bread and Wine. Cooking is refreshingly unadorned and the use of superb seasonal British ingredients results in flavours that are clean, natural, unadulterated and a joy to experience. Only a set menu is offered at dinner but at lunch you can choose from an array of dishes in smaller sizes. Combinations are largely classically based but come with a modern touch.

FIRST COURSE	MAIN COURSE	DESSERT
Peas with Ticklemore cheese. • Beetroot with cured Gloucester Old Spot belly.	Dexter rib, broccoli leaf and anchovy. • Monkfish with turnips and preserved lemon.	Caramel ice cream with espresso meringue. • Florence strawberries with rye and honey.

Shoreditch — Tea Building, 56 Shoreditch High St ✉ E1 6JJ **MAP: 16-K3**
✆ 020 3011 5911 — **www.**lyleslondon.com
⊖ Shoreditch High Street

Menu £59 (dinner) - Carte lunch £34/48
Closed Sunday and bank holidays

A/C

MERCHANTS TAVERN

Traditional British • Brasserie

The 'pub' part - a Victorian warehouse - gives way to a large restaurant with the booths being the prized seats. The cooking is founded on the sublime pleasures of seasonal British cooking, in reassuringly familiar combinations.

Shoreditch — 36 Charlotte Rd ✉ EC2A 3PG **MAP: 16-K3**
020 7060 5335 — **www**.merchantstavern.co.uk
Old Street
Carte £30/60
Closed 12-26 August, 24-27 December and 1 January

POPOLO

Mediterranean cuisine • Trendy

Skimmed concrete floors and exposed brick walls give this restaurant a utilitarian feel; sit at the counter and chat to the chefs as they work. Italian, Spanish and North African influences feature on the menu of small plates. Pasta is a highlight and classic, simply cooked dishes allow the ingredients to shine.

Shoreditch — 26 Rivington St ✉ EC2A 3DU **MAP: 16-K3**
020 7729 4299 — **www**.popoloshoreditch.com
Old Street
Carte £19/39
Closed Sunday - bookings not accepted - (dinner only)

PRINCESS OF SHOREDITCH

Traditional British • Pub

There has been a pub on this corner site since 1742 but it is doubtful many of the previous incarnations were as busy or as pleasant as the Princess is today. The best dishes are those with a rustic edge, such as goose rillettes or chicken pie.

Shoreditch — 76-78 Paul St ✉ EC2A 4NE **MAP: 16-K3**
020 7729 9270 — **www**.theprincessofshoreditch.com
Old Street
Carte £26/40
Closed 24-26 December - booking essential

N RED ROOSTER 🍴

American • Fashionable

An outpost of Marcus Samuelsson's famed Harlem restaurant. His Southern soul food classics include "Sammy's chicken 'n' waffles" and "Ol' man shrimp 'n' grits"; the "Bird Royale Feast" is proving popular. There's live music at night and a gospel choir to accompany Sunday brunch.

Shoreditch — The Curtain Hotel, 45 Curtain Rd ✉ EC2A 3PT **MAP: 16-K3**
020 3146 4545 — **www**.redroosterldn.com
⊖ Old Street

Carte £31/45
Closed Sunday dinner - (dinner only and Sunday lunch)

EMPRESS 🍴

Traditional British • Pub

An 1850s neighbourhood pub with a short, simple and pleasingly seasonal menu of traditional British dishes with the occasional Mediterranean influence. Service is friendly and you can bring your own bottle on Tuesday nights.

South Hackney — 130 Lauriston Rd, Victoria Park ✉ E9 7LH **MAP: 16-K2**
020 8533 5123 — **www**.empresse9.co.uk
⊖ Homerton.

Carte £21/42
Closed 25-27 December and Monday lunch except bank holidays

GRAND TRUNK ROAD 🍴

Indian • Contemporary décor

Named after one of Asia's oldest and longest routes, which provided inspiration for the menu. Dishes are well-balanced and original with a modern touch; breads come from a charcoal-fired tandoor and vegetable dishes are a highlight.

South Woodford — 219 High Rd ✉ E18 2PB
020 8505 1965 — **www**.gtrrestaurant.co.uk
⊖ South Woodford

Menu £20 (weekday lunch) - Carte £30/57
Closed 25-26 December, 1 January and Monday - booking essential at dinner

PROVENDER

French • Bistro

A welcoming and busy neighbourhood bistro, courtesy of experienced restaurateur Max Renzland. The fairly priced French cooking is pleasingly rustic and satisfying; the classic dishes are the ones to go for. Look out for the good value menus during the week.

- **Wanstead** — 17 High St E11 2AA
  020 8530 3050 — **www**.provenderlondon.co.uk
  Snaresbrook
- Menu £17 (lunch and early dinner) - Carte £20/45

Look for our symbol
restaurants opening for (a good) breakfast.

A. HUDSON
RNISHING BRASSFOUND

SOUTH-EAST LONDON

Once considered not only the wrong side of the tracks, but also most definitely the wrong side of the river, London's southeastern chunk has thrived in recent times courtesy of the Docklands Effect. As the gleaming glass peninsula of **Canary Wharf** (ironically, just north of the Thames) sprouted a personality of its own – with bars, restaurants, slinky bridges and an enviable view, not to mention moneyed residents actually putting down roots – the city's bottom right hand zone began to achieve destination status on a par with other parts of London. You only have to stroll around the glossy and quite vast **Limehouse Basin** – a slick marina that was once a hard-grafting East End dock – to really see what's happened here.

Not that the area hasn't always boasted some true gems in the capital's treasure chest. **Greenwich,** with fabulous views across the water to the docklands from its delightfully sloping park, has long been a favourite of kings and queens: Henry VIII and Elizabeth I resided here. The village itself bustles along with its market and plush picturehouse, but most visitors make their way to the standout attractions, of which there are many. The **Royal Observatory** and the Meridian Line draw star-gazers and hemisphere striders in equal number, while the palatial Old Royal Naval College is a star turn for lovers of Wren, who designed it as London's answer to Versailles. On the northern edge of Greenwich Park, the **National Maritime Museum** has three floors of sea-faring wonders; down by the pier, the real thing exists in the shape of the **Cutty Sark**. Up on the peninsula, the O2 Arena's distinctive shape has become an unmistakable landmark, but if you fancy a contrast to all things watery, the Fan Museum on Crooms Hill has more hand-held fans (over 3,000 of them) than anywhere else on earth. Strolling south from Greenwich park you reach **Blackheath,** an alluring suburban village, whose most striking feature is the towering All Saints' Church, standing proud away from the chic shops and restaurants.

Of slightly less spectacular charms, but a real crowd-pleaser nevertheless, is **Dulwich Village,** hidden deeper in the southeastern enclaves. It's a leafy oasis in this part of the world, with a delightful park that boasts at its western end, next to the original buildings of the old public school, the Dulwich Picture Gallery. This was designed in 1811, and its pedigree is evident in works by the likes of Rembrandt, Rubens, Van Dyck and Canaletto. Half an hour's walk away across the park is the brilliant Horniman Museum, full of natural history and world culture delights – as well as a massive aquarium that seems to take up much of southeast London.

A bit further east along the South Circular, there's the unexpected gem of Eltham Palace, originally the childhood home of Henry VIII with a magnificent (and still visible) Great Hall. What makes it unique is the adjacent Art Deco mansion built for millionaires in the 1930s in Ocean Liner style. It's the closest you'll ever get to a setting fit for hog roast and champagne. Heading back towards London, a lifestyle of bubbly and banquets has never really been **Peckham**'s thing, but it boasts a couple of corkers in the shape of the South London Gallery with its zeitgeist-setting art shows, and the Peckham Library, a giant inverted 'L' that looks like a lot of fun to go into.

Back in the luxury flat-lands of the **Docklands, Wapping** has become an interesting port of call, its new-build architecture mixing in with a still Dickensian feel, in the shape of glowering Victorian warehouses and Wapping New Stairs, where pirates were hanged from a gibbet until seven tides had showered their limp bodies. You can catch a fascinating history of the whole area in the nearby Museum Of London Docklands.

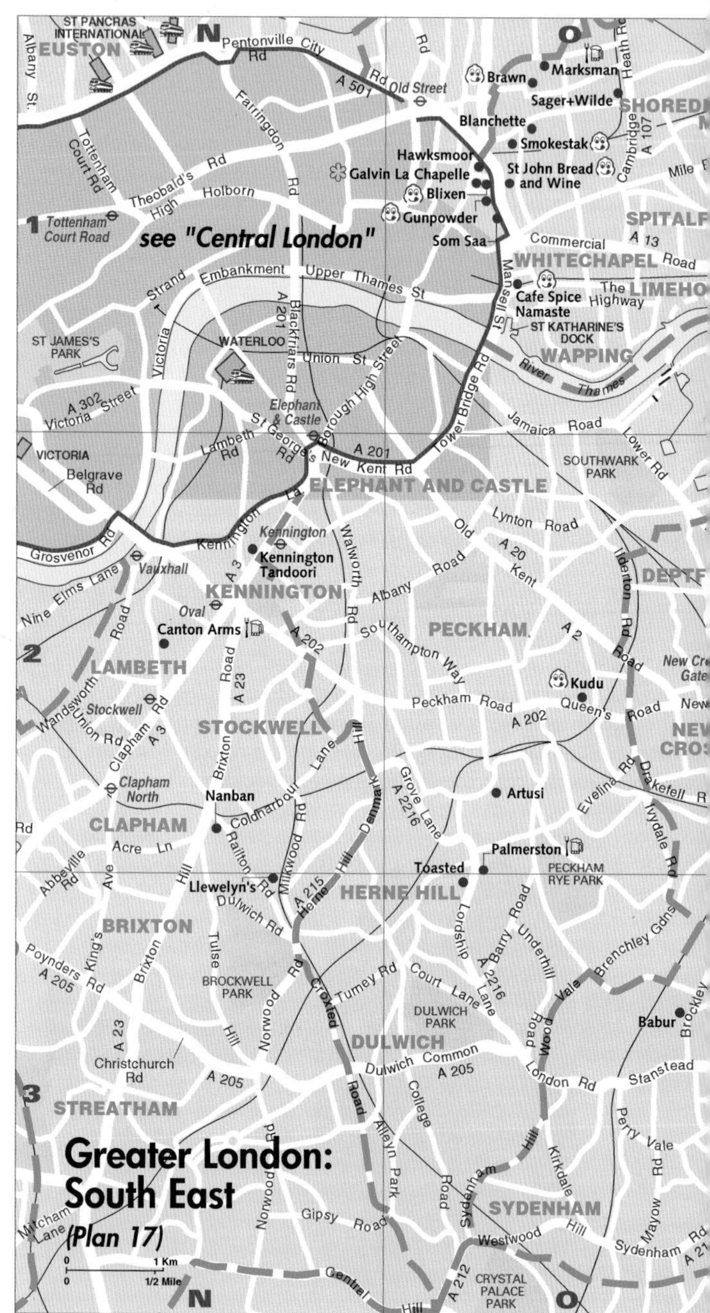
Greater London:
South East
(Plan 17)
see "Central London"
EUSTON
SHOREDITCH
SPITALFIELDS
WHITECHAPEL
WAPPING
ELEPHANT AND CASTLE
KENNINGTON
PECKHAM
LAMBETH
STOCKWELL
CLAPHAM
BRIXTON
HERNE HILL
DULWICH
STREATHAM
SYDENHAM
Brawn
Marksman
Sager+Wilde
Blanchette
Smokestak
Hawksmoor
Galvin La Chapelle
St John Bread and Wine
Blixen
Gunpowder
Som Saa
Cafe Spice Namaste
Kennington Tandoori
Canton Arms
Kudu
Artusi
Nanban
Palmerston
Toasted
Llewelyn's
Babur

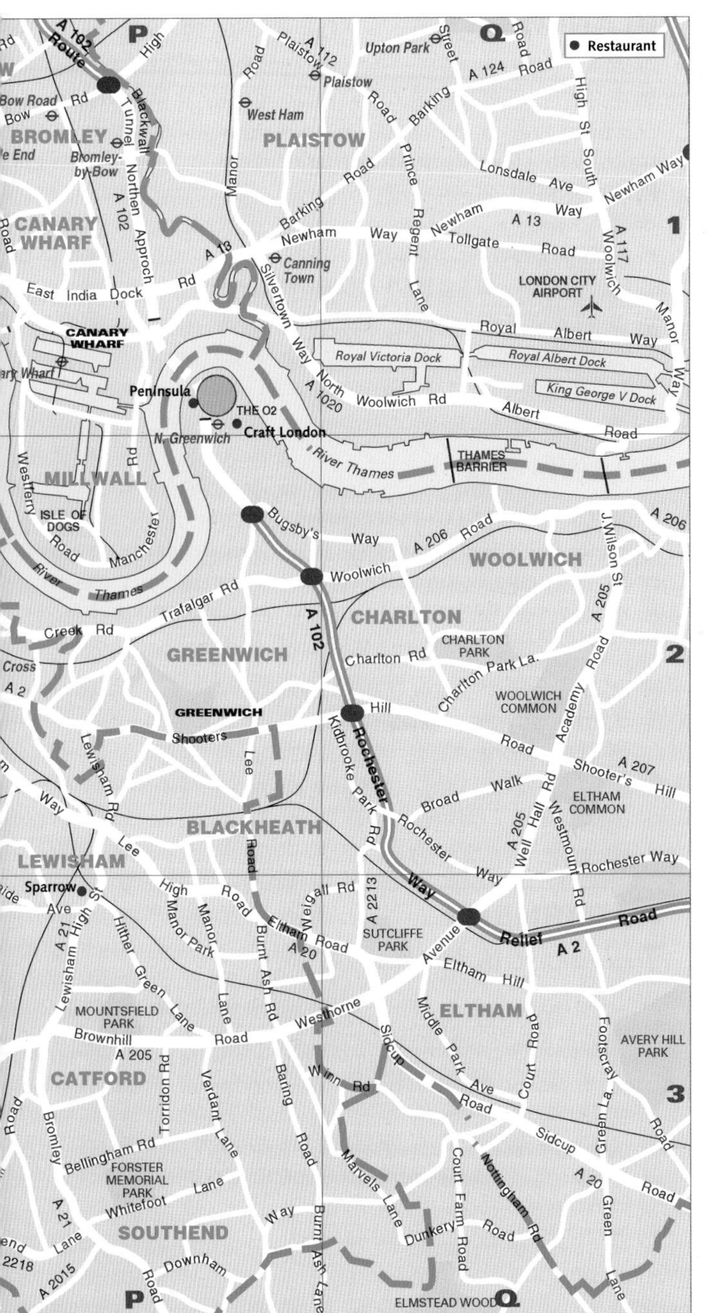
Restaurant
P
Q
1
2
3
A 102 Route
High
Bow Road
Rd
Bow
BROMLEY
Bromley-by-Bow
Blackwall Tunnel Northen Approch
A 102
CANARY WHARF
East India Dock Rd
A 13
Manor Road
West Ham
PLAISTOW
Plaistow
A 112
Plaistow Road
Upton Park
Street
A 124 Road
Barking Road
Prince Regent Lane
High St South
Lonsdale Ave
Newham Way
A 13
Tollgate Road
A 117 Woolwich
Newham Way
Canning Town
Silvertown Way
LONDON CITY AIRPORT
Royal Albert Way
Manor Way
Royal Victoria Dock
Royal Albert Dock
King George V Dock
North Woolwich Rd
A 1020
Albert Road
Peninsula
THE O2
Craft London
N. Greenwich
River Thames
THAMES BARRIER
MILLWALL
Westferry Road
ISLE OF DOGS
Manchester Rd
Bugsby's Way
A 206 Road
A 206
WOOLWICH
J. Wilson St
Woolwich
Trafalgar Rd
Creek Rd
CHARLTON
A 102
GREENWICH
Charlton Rd
CHARLTON PARK
Charlton Park La.
A 205
Academy Road
WOOLWICH COMMON
GREENWICH
Shooters Hill Road
Rochester
Kidbrooke Park Rd
Lee
Lewisham Rd
A 207
Shooter's Hill
ELTHAM COMMON
Broad Walk
Rochester Way
A 205 Well Hall Rd
Westmount Rd
BLACKHEATH
LEWISHAM
Lee High Road
Road
Sparrow
A 21 Lewisham High St
Manor Park
Manor Lane
Burnt Ash Rd
Neigall Rd
A 2213
Eltham Road
A 20
SUTCLIFFE PARK
Avenue
Relief Road
A 2
Eltham Hill
Hither Green Lane
MOUNTSFIELD PARK
Brownhill Road
A 205
Westhorne
ELTHAM
Middle Park Ave
Court Road
Footscray Road
AVERY HILL PARK
CATFORD
Torridon Rd
Verdant Lane
Baring Road
Winn Rd
Sidcup Road
Green La.
Bromley Road
Bellingham Rd
FORSTER MEMORIAL PARK
Whitefoot Lane
Marvels Lane
Court Farm Road
Nottingham Rd
A 20
Green Lane
A 21 Lane
SOUTHEND
Way
Burnt Ash Lane
Dunkery Road
Downham Road
A 2015
2218
ELMSTEAD WOOD

BLANCHETTE

French • Bistro

Sister to the Soho original with the same lively buzz, funky music and tasty French dishes, but this time the menu heads further south, with a few North African influences too. 3 or 4 plates per person should suffice.

Bethnal Green — 204 Brick Ln ✉ E1 6SA **MAP: 17-O1**
✆ 020 7729 7939 — **www**.blanchettelondon.co.uk
⊖ Shoreditch High Street

Menu £20 (lunch) - Carte £23/36
Closed 24-26 December

BRAWN

Modern cuisine • Neighbourhood

Unpretentious and simply kitted out, with a great local atmosphere and polite, helpful service. The name captures the essence of the cooking perfectly: it is rustic, muscular and makes very good use of pig. Interesting wine list with a focus on natural and organic wines.

Bethnal Green — 49 Columbia Rd. ✉ E2 7RG **MAP: 17-O1**
✆ 020 7729 5692 — **www**.brawn.co
⊖ Bethnal Green

Carte £27/43
Closed Christmas-New Year, Sunday dinner, Monday lunch and bank holidays

---

MARKSMAN

Traditional British • Friendly

With its quirky, brown-tiled façade, this pub has long been a local landmark; the wood-panelled bar retains the feel of a traditional boozer, while the first floor dining room is more modern. Simply cooked, seasonal British dishes are wonderfully fresh, well-balanced and full of flavour.

Bethnal Green — 254 Hackney Rd ✉ E2 7SJ **MAP: 17-O1**
✆ 7739 7393 — **www**.marksmanpublichouse.com
⊖ Hoxton.

Menu £26 (lunch) - Carte £28/39
Closed 25-30 December - (dinner only and lunch Friday-Sunday)

SAGER + WILDE

Mediterranean cuisine • Rustic

Friendly neighbourhood restaurant - a former wine bar - set underneath a railway arch. Tasty, well-priced, creative dishes have a Mediterranean heart and an eye-catching modern style, with some interesting combinations.

Bethnal Green — 250 Paradise Row ✉ E2 9LE **MAP: 17-O1**
020 7613 0478 — **www**.sagerandwilde.com
Bethnal Green
Carte £21/30
Closed Monday lunch

SMOKESTAK

Meats and grills • Rustic

A buzzing barbecue restaurant with an open kitchen and an industrial feel. Highlights include the brisket and ribs: these are brined, oak-smoked, coated with a sweet and sour BBQ sauce and chargrilled - the results being unctuous and incredibly satisfying. The charming staff are happy to guide you.

Bethnal Green — 35 Sclater St ✉ E1 6LB **MAP: 17-O1**
020 3873 1733 — **www**.smokestak.co.uk
Shoreditch High Street
Carte £16/31

PALMERSTON

Mediterranean cuisine • Pub

A brightly run Victorian pub that has a comfortable, lived-in feel and lies at the heart of the local community. The cooking has a satisfying, gutsy edge with meat dishes, especially game, being the highlight.

East Dulwich — 91 Lordship Ln ✉ SE22 8EP **MAP: 17-O2**
020 8693 1629 — **www**.thepalmerston.co.uk
East Dulwich (Rail).
Menu £16 (weekday lunch) - Carte £27/44
Closed 25-26 December and 1 January

BABUR

Indian • Neighbourhood

Good looks and innovative cooking make this passionately run and long-established Indian restaurant stand out. Influences from the south and north west feature most and seafood is a highlight - look out for the 'Treasures of the Sea' menu.

Forest Hill — 119 Brockley Rise SE23 1JP **MAP: 17-O3**
020 8291 2400 — **www**.babur.info
Honor Oak Park

Menu £33/39 - Carte £27/36
Closed 26 December

CRAFT LONDON

Modern British • Design

Chef Stevie Parle has created a striking space beside the O2 that includes a coffee shop, a cocktail bar, and a restaurant championing seasonal British produce. They do their own curing and smoking, and roast their own coffee.

Greenwich — Peninsula Sq SE10 0SQ **MAP: 17-P1**
020 8465 5910 — **www**.craft-london.co.uk
North Greenwich

Menu £32 - Carte £27/43
Closed Christmas-New Year, Sunday and Monday - (dinner only and Saturday lunch)

N PENINSULA

Modern cuisine • Elegant

Don't be put off by its being in a somewhat corporate hotel - the floor-to-ceiling windows ensure great views across the river. The menu is also creative and ambitious, with the occasional Nordic touch; the dishes are skilfully executed and attractively presented.

Greenwich — InterContinental London Hotel - The O2 (2nd floor), 1 Waterview Dr, Greenwich Peninsula SE10 0TW **MAP: 17-P1**
020 8463 6913 — **www**.iclondon-theo2.com
North Greenwich

Menu £35 (early dinner) - Carte £39/58
Closed 1-14 January, 1 week summer and Sunday - (dinner only)

LLEWELYN'S

Traditional British • Neighbourhood

A neighbourhood restaurant in a village-like location. Cooking is British with Mediterranean influences and dishes to share are a feature. Expect quality ingredients in hearty portions, with no unnecessary elaboration.

Herne Hill — 293-295 Railton Rd ✉ SE24 0JP **MAP: 17-N3**
020 7733 6676 — **www**.llewelyns-restaurant.co.uk
Herne Hill
Carte £24/33
Closed 22 December-4 January, Sunday dinner and Monday

KENNINGTON TANDOORI

Indian • Neighbourhood

Kowsar Hoque runs this contemporary Indian restaurant with great pride and his eagerness and professionalism filters through to his staff. The food is prepared with equal care - try the seasonal specialities and the excellent breads.

Kennington — 313 Kennington Rd ✉ SE11 4QE **MAP: 17-N2**
020 7735 9247 — **www**.kennigtontandoori.com
Kennington
Carte £20/34
Closed 25-26 December - (dinner only and lunch Saturday-Sunday)

SPARROW

Modern British • Friendly

A bright and buzzing neighbourhood spot whose name symbolises the culinary diversity of its globally influenced menus, as well as one of the owners' Sri Lankan heritage. Weekend brunches also offer an eclectic choice of dishes.

Lewisham — 2 Rennell St ✉ SE13 7HD **MAP: 17-P3**
020 8318 6941 — **www**.sparrowlondon.co.uk
Lewisham
Carte £27/35
Closed Sunday dinner, Monday and lunch Tuesday

ARTUSI

Italian • Neighbourhood

An enthusiastically run Italian restaurant which shows Peckham is on the rise. The kitchen displays clear respect for the seasonal ingredients, dishes are kept honest and the prices are more than fair.

Peckham — 161 Bellenden Rd ✉ SE15 4DH **MAP: 17-O2**
020 3302 8200 — **www**.artusi.co.uk
Peckham Rye
Carte £21/35
Closed 1 week Christmas - booking essential at dinner

KUDU

Modern cuisine • Neighbourhood

Run by a young husband and wife team who have attracted a fun and young local clientele. Patrick's South African roots are evident in dishes like the mussel potjie and the 'braai' lamb neck; the brioche-style bread with bacon butter is memorable. Amy and her service team are delightful.

Peckham — 119 Queen's Rd ✉ SE15 2EZ **MAP: 17-O2**
020 3950 0226 — **www**.kudu-restaurant.com
Queens Road Peckham (Rail).
Carte £20/40
Closed Monday, Tuesday and lunch Wednesday-Thursday.

BLIXEN

Mediterranean cuisine • Fashionable

A charmingly run and good-looking restaurant with lots of natural light; set in a former bank. The appealing European menu offers keenly priced modern dishes. Service is enthusiastic, the atmosphere's buzzing and you'll want to return for breakfast, or cocktails in the basement bar.

Spitalfields — 65a Brushfield St ✉ E1 6AA **MAP: 17-O1**
020 7101 0093 — **www**.blixen.co.uk
Liverpool Street
Carte £27/50
Closed Sunday dinner

GALVIN LA CHAPELLE ✿

French • Elegant

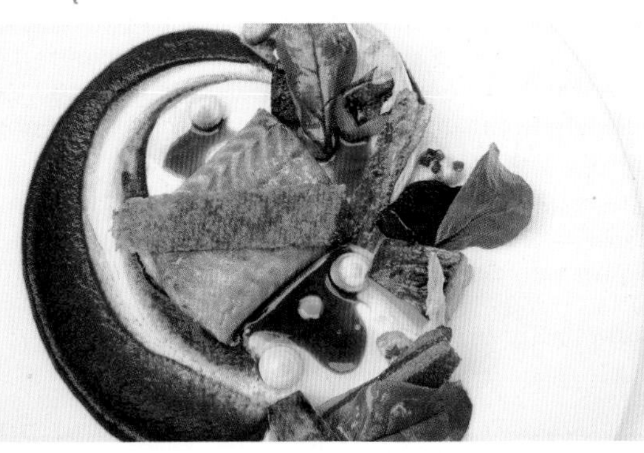

Built in 1890 as a girls' school, this splendid Grade II listed structure with its vaulted ceiling, arched windows and marble pillars was an inspired choice for a venue, and remains as impressive now as when it first opened back in 2009. It lends itself effortlessly to its role as a glamorous restaurant: a magnificent open space with a mezzanine for private dining, and plenty of tables, whether in booths, in the wings or right in the middle of the action. The sommelier is knowledgeable, service is professional and the atmosphere, relaxed and unstuffy.

Cooking is assured and precise, with a classical French foundation and a sophisticated modern edge. There are no unnecessary fripperies – just three courses of reassuringly familiar combinations with the emphasis on bold, harmonious flavours and, whilst dishes may sound complicated, they are anything but. Must-tries include the tagine of Bresse pigeon and the tarte Tatin.

FIRST COURSE	MAIN COURSE	DESSERT
Lasagne of Dorset crab with beurre Nantais & pea shoots. • Carpaccio of Cumbrian beef with pickled shimeji and truffle emulsion.	Roast loin and slow-cooked venison with butternut, chestnuts and sauce grand veneur. • Icelandic cod, Jersey Royals, asparagus and hazelnuts.	Banoffee cheesecake with chocolate ice cream. • Gariguette strawberry soufflé with milk ice cream.

Spitalfields — 35 Spital Sq ✉ E1 6DY **MAP: 17-O1**
✆ 020 7299 0400 — **www**.galvinrestaurants.com
⊖ Liverpool Street

Menu £34 (lunch and early dinner) - Carte £53/78
Closed 25-26 December and 1 January

GUNPOWDER ㊽

Indian • Simple

A loud, buzzy restaurant with just ten tightly packed tables, serving vibrant small plates from across the Indian regions. The name is a reference to the chef's daily-made spice mix and his menu takes its influence from old family recipes. Standout dishes include deep-fried crab and crispy pork ribs.

Spitalfields — 11 White's Row ✉ E1 7NF **MAP: 17-O1**
☎ 020 7426 0542 — **www**.gunpowderlondon.com
⊖ Liverpool Street

Carte £16/39
Closed Sunday - bookings not accepted

HAWKSMOOR

Meats and grills • Friendly

A buzzy, relaxed restaurant with friendly staff. It's not really about the starters or the puds here - the star is the great British beef, hung for 35 days, which comes from Longhorn cattle in the heart of the Yorkshire Moors.

Spitalfields — 157a Commercial St ✉ E1 6BJ **MAP: 17-O1**
☎ 020 7234 9940 — **www**.thehawksmoor.com
⊖ Shoreditch High Street

Menu £25 (lunch and early dinner) - Carte £26/86
Closed 25-26 December and 1 January - booking essential

A/C

Good quality cooking at a great price?
Look out for the Bib Gourmand.

ST JOHN BREAD AND WINE

Traditional British • Bistro

An appealing restaurant with a stripped back style. The highly seasonal menu offers starter-sized dishes perfect for sharing and the cooking is British, uncomplicated and very satisfying. Breakfast includes a wonderful rare breed bacon sandwich.

Spitalfields – 94-96 Commercial St ✉ E1 6LZ **MAP: 17-O1**
✆ 020 7251 0848 – **www**.stjohngroup.uk.com
⊖ Liverpool Street

Carte £21/43
Closed 25-26 December and 1 January

SOM SAA

Thai • Rustic

Som Saa's success took it from pop-up to permanent restaurant, with a lively atmosphere and a rustic, industrial look. Menus show-case the diversity of Thai cuisine. 4 or 5 dishes between two are recommended - and do try a cocktail or two!

Spitalfields – 43a Commerical St ✉ E1 6BD **MAP: 17-O1**
✆ 020 7324 7790 – **www**.somsaa.com
⊖ Aldgate East

Carte £19/32
Closed Christmas, bank holiday Mondays, Sunday and lunch Monday

CANTON ARMS

Traditional British • Pub

An appreciative crowd of all ages come for the earthy, robust and seasonal British dishes which suit the relaxed environment of this pub so well. Staff are attentive and knowledgeable.

Stockwell — 177 South Lambeth Rd ✉ SW8 1XP **MAP: 17-N2**
✆ 020 7582 8710 — **www**.cantonarms.com
⊖ Stockwell.

Carte £22/38
Closed Monday lunch, Sunday dinner and bank holidays - bookings not accepted

---

CAFE SPICE NAMASTE

Indian • Neighbourhood

Fresh, vibrant and fairly priced Indian cuisine from Cyrus Todiwala, served in a colourfully decorated room that was once a magistrate's court. Engaging service from an experienced team.

Whitechapel — 16 Prescot St. ✉ E1 8AZ **MAP: 17-O1**
✆ 020 7488 9242 — **www**.cafespice.co.uk
⊖ Tower Hill

Menu £18 (lunch) - Carte £26/38
Closed Saturday lunch, Sunday and bank holidays

The symbol indicates a private dining room option.

SOUTH-WEST LONDON

Meandering like a silver snake, **The Thames** coils serenely through south-west London, adding definition to the area's much-heralded middle-class enclaves and leafy suburbs. It's the focal point to the annual **university boat race** from **Putney** to **Mortlake,** and it serves as the giant glass pond attractively backing countless bank-side pubs. This area has long been regarded as the cosy bourgeois side of town, though within its postcode prowls the lively and eclectic **Brixton,** whose buzzing street markets and lauded music venues add an urban lustre and vibrant edge.

In most people's minds, though, south-west London finds its true colours in the beautiful terrace view from the top of **Richmond Hill,** as the river bends majestically through the meadows below. Or in the smart **Wimbledon Village,** its independent boutiques ranged prettily along its own hill, with the open spaces of the Common for a back garden. Or, again, in the Italianate architecture that makes **Chiswick House** and grounds a little corner of the Mediterranean close to the Great West Road.

Green space is almost as prolific in this zone as the streets of Victorian and Edwardian villas. **Richmond Park** is the largest royal park in the whole of London and teems with kite flyers, cyclists and deer – though not necessarily in that order. From here, round a southerly bend in the river, delightful grounds surround **Ham House,** which celebrated its 400th birthday in 2010, although not so excessively as during the seventeenth century when it was home to Restoration court life. Head slightly north to **Kew Gardens** whose world famous 300 acres can be viewed from above – the treetop walkway takes you 60 feet up to offer some breath-taking views. Just across the river from here is another from the historical hitlist: **Syon Park,** which boasts water meadows still grazed by cattle, giving it a distinctly rural aspect. Syon House is considered one of architect Robert Adam's finest works; it certainly appealed to Queen Victoria, who spent much of her young life here. Up the road in bourgeoning Brentford, two unique museums bring in hordes of the curious: the Musical Museum includes a huge Wurlitzer theatre organ (get lucky and watch it being played), while almost next door, the London Museum of Water & Steam shows off all things steamy on a grand scale, including massive beam engines which pumped London's water for over a century.

Hammersmith may be known for its bustling Broadway and flyover, but five minutes' walk from here is the Upper Mall, which has iconic riverside pubs and Kelmscott House, the last home of artistic visionary William Morris: down in the basement and coach house are impressive memorabilia related to his life plus changing exhibitions of designs and drawings. From here, it's just a quick jaunt across **Hammersmith Bridge** and down the arrow-straight Castelnau to the Wetland Centre in Barnes, which for nearly two decades has lured wildlife to within screeching distance of the West End. **Barnes** has always revelled in its village-like identity – it juts up like an isolated peninsula into the Thames and boasts yummy boutiques and well-known restaurants. The Bulls Head pub in Lonsdale Road has featured some of the best jazz in London for over half a century.

In a more easterly direction, the urbanised areas of **Clapham** and **Battersea** have re-established themselves as desirable places to live over the last decade. **Clapham Common** is considered prime southwest London turf, to the extent that its summer music festivals are highly prized. It's ringed by good pubs and restaurants, too. Battersea used to be famous for its funfair, but now the peace pagoda in the park lends it a more serene light. And if you're after serenity on a hot day, then a cool dip in the wondrous **Tooting** Lido is just the thing.

viadyan/iStock

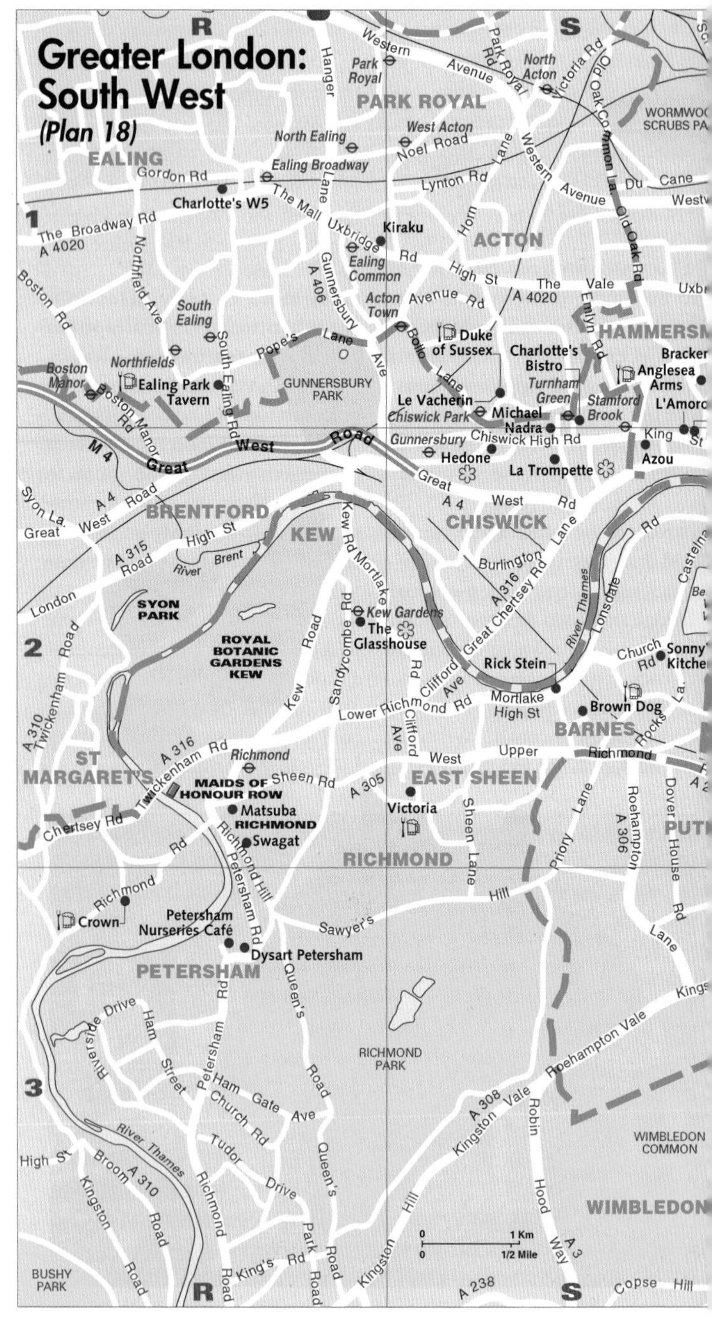

Greater London: South West
(Plan 18)
EALING
PARK ROYAL
ACTON
BRENTFORD
KEW
CHISWICK
BARNES
EAST SHEEN
RICHMOND
ST MARGARET'S
PETERSHAM
WIMBLEDON
ROYAL BOTANIC GARDENS KEW
SYON PARK
GUNNERSBURY PARK
RICHMOND PARK
WIMBLEDON COMMON
BUSHY PARK
WORMWOOD SCRUBS PARK
MAIDS OF HONOUR ROW
Charlotte's W5
Kiraku
Ealing Park Tavern
Duke of Sussex
Charlotte's Bistro
Le Vacherin
Michael Nadra
Hedone
La Trompette
Anglesea Arms
L'Amorosa
Azou
The Glasshouse
Rick Stein
Brown Dog
Sonny's Kitchen
Victoria
Matsuba
Swagat
Crown
Petersham Nurseries Café
Dysart Petersham
0 1 Km
0 1/2 Mile

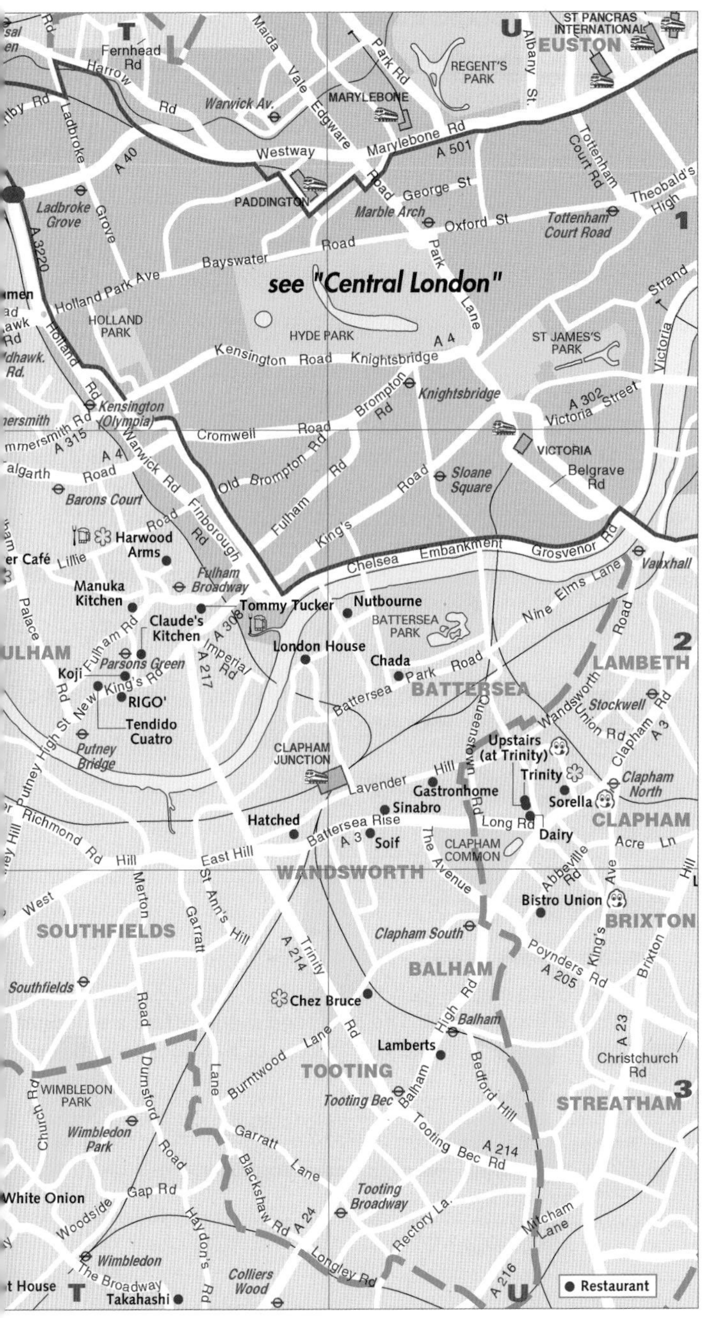

see "Central London"
ST PANCRAS INTERNATIONAL
EUSTON
REGENT'S PARK
MARYLEBONE
PADDINGTON
Warwick Av.
Ladbroke Grove
Marble Arch
Tottenham Court Road
Westway
Marylebone Rd
A 501
George St
Oxford St
Theobald's
High
Bayswater Road
Holland Park Ave
HOLLAND PARK
HYDE PARK
Park Lane
Strand
ST JAMES'S PARK
Kensington Road
Knightsbridge
A 4
Brompton Rd
Knightsbridge
Victoria Street
A 302
Victoria
Kensington (Olympia)
Cromwell Road
Hammersmith Rd
A 315
VICTORIA
Belgrave Rd
Sloane Square
Old Brompton Rd
Fulham Rd
King's Road
Talgarth Road
Barons Court
Warwick Rd
Finborough Rd
Lillie Road
Harwood Arms
Chelsea Embankment
Grosvenor Rd
Vauxhall
Fulham Broadway
Manuka Kitchen
Tommy Tucker
Nutbourne
BATTERSEA PARK
Nine Elms Lane
Claude's Kitchen
Fulham Rd
A 308
Imperial Rd
London House
Chada
Battersea Park Road
FULHAM
Parsons Green
Koji
New King's Rd
RIGO'
Tendido Cuatro
A 217
BATTERSEA
LAMBETH
Stockwell
Wandsworth Rd
Union Rd
Clapham Rd
A 3
Putney Bridge
Putney High St
CLAPHAM JUNCTION
Queenstown Rd
Upstairs (at Trinity)
Trinity
Sorella
Clapham North
Lavender Hill
Gastronhome
Sinabro
Long Rd
Dairy
CLAPHAM
Richmond Rd
Hatched
Battersea Rise
A 3
Soif
The Avenue
CLAPHAM COMMON
Acre Ln
East Hill
WANDSWORTH
Abbeville Rd
Bistro Union
BRIXTON
West Hill
SOUTHFIELDS
Merton Road
Garratt
St Ann's Hill
Trinity
A 214
Clapham South
King's Ave
BALHAM
Poynders Rd
A 205
Brixton
Southfields
Chez Bruce
High Rd
Balham
Lamberts
Burntwood Lane
A 23
Christchurch Rd
TOOTING
Bedford Hill
STREATHAM
WIMBLEDON PARK
Church Rd
Durnsford Road
Wimbledon Park
Tooting Bec
Balham
Tooting Bec Rd
A 214
Garratt Lane
Blackshaw Rd
A 24
Tooting Broadway
Gap Rd
White Onion
Woodside
Haydon's Rd
Rectory La.
Mitcham Lane
Wimbledon
The Broadway
Longley Rd
A 216
Colliers Wood
Takahashi
Restaurant
1
2
3

DUKE OF SUSSEX

Mediterranean cuisine • Pub

Bustling Victorian pub, whose striking dining room was once a variety theatre complete with proscenium arch. Stick to the Spanish dishes; stews and cured meats are the specialities. BYO on Mondays.

Acton Green — 75 South Par ✉ W4 5LF **MAP: 18-S1**
020 8742 8801 — **www**.thedukeofsussex.co.uk
Chiswick Park.

Carte £19/54

LE VACHERIN

French • Brasserie

Authentic feel to this comfortable brasserie, with its brown leather banquette seating, mirrors and belle époque prints. French classics from snails to duck confit; beef is a speciality.

Acton Green — 76-77 South Par ✉ W4 5LF **MAP: 18-S1**
020 8742 2121 — **www**.levacherin.com
Chiswick Park

Menu £25 (weekdays) - Carte £25/53
Closed Monday lunch

A/C

BROWN DOG

Modern British • Pub

Concealed in a maze of residential streets is this homely, relaxed pub with a lived-in feel. The balanced menu offers traditional and flavoursome fare like venison pie or haddock fishcake; all done 'properly'.

Barnes — 28 Cross St ✉ SW13 0AP **MAP: 18-S2**
020 8392 2200 — **www**.thebrowndog.co.uk
Barnes Bridge (Rail).

Carte £25/32
Closed 25 December

RICK STEIN

Seafood • Fashionable

In a stunning spot beside the Thames; its glass extension offering the best views. Dishes from the celebrity chef's travels inform the menu, so expect Indonesian seafood curry alongside old favourites like cod and chips with mushy peas.

Barnes — Tideway Yard, 125 Mortlake High St ✉ SW14 8SN — **MAP: 18-S2**
020 8878 9462 — **www**.rickstein.com

Menu £20 (weekday lunch) - Carte £28/91
Closed 25 December

SONNY'S KITCHEN

Mediterranean cuisine • Neighbourhood

A longstanding and much-loved neighbourhood spot with a bright, relaxed feel and some striking art on the walls; co-owned by Barnes residents Rebecca Mascarenhas and Phil Howard. Menus are all-encompassing and portions generous.

Barnes — 94 Church Rd ✉ SW13 0DQ — **MAP: 18-S2**
020 8748 0393 — **www**.sonnyskitchen.co.uk

Menu £23 (lunch and early dinner) - Carte £27/55
Closed 25-26 December, 1 January and bank holiday Mondays

A/C

GASTRONHOME

Modern French • Intimate

A cosy restaurant run by two young Frenchmen. Bi-monthly changing menus offer regional French dishes which come with a very modern, almost Scandic touch. The Gallic wine list has prices right across the scale.

Battersea — 59 Lavender Hill ✉ SW11 5QN — **MAP: 18-U2**
020 3417 5639 — **www**.gastronhome.co.uk

Menu £35 (lunch) - Carte £44/55
Closed Monday-Wednesday lunch - booking essential at dinner

Ⓝ HATCHED

Modern British • Neighbourhood

The large open kitchen is the focus of this relaxed and simply styled room. The ethos is about using quality ingredients, prepared with skill, and with the addition of some international flavours which reflect the chef-owner's travels. Gnocchi is a standout.

Battersea — 189 St John's Hill SW11 1TH **MAP: 18-T2**
020 7738 0735 — **www**.hatchedsw11.com
Clapham Junction

Carte £30/51
Closed 1 week January, 1 week June, 1 week August, Monday, Tuesday, Sunday dinner and lunch Wednesday-Thursday

---

LONDON HOUSE

Modern British • Neighbourhood

One doesn't always associate neighbourhood restaurants with Gordon Ramsay but London House is an appealing place. It's comfortable and well run and the classically-based dishes come with modern touches and ingredients that marry well.

Battersea — 7-9 Battersea Sq, Battersea Village SW11 3RA **MAP: 18-T2**
020 7592 8545 — **www**.gordonramsayrestaurants.com/london-house
Clapham Junction

Menu £20 (weekdays)/30 - Carte £35/55

NUTBOURNE

Modern British • Neighbourhood

The 3rd restaurant from the Gladwin brothers; named after the family farm and vineyards in West Sussex. British produce drives the eclectic daily menu, with meats cooked on the open fire; dishes are hearty, wholesome and full of flavour.

Battersea — Unit 29, Ransomes Dock, 35-37 Parkgate Rd SW11 4NP **MAP: 18-U2**
020 7350 0555 — **www**.nutbourne-restaurant.com

Carte £25/45
Closed 23 December-2 January, Easter, Sunday dinner and Monday

SINABRO

Modern cuisine • Neighbourhood

The main room feels almost kitchen-like, courtesy of a wall of stainless steel; sit at the wooden counter - made by the chef-owner's father. Confidently prepared dishes rely largely on classic French flavours but are modern in style.

Battersea — 28 Battersea Rise SW11 1EE **MAP: 18-U2**
020 3302 3120 — **www**.sinabro.co.uk
Clapham Junction
Menu £29/49
Closed 12-27 August, 25-26 December, 1 January, Sunday and Monday
A/C

SOIF

French • Neighbourhood

A busy bistro-cum-wine-shop with a great atmosphere. The satisfying French food takes regular excursions across the border into Italy and the thoughtfully compiled wine list includes plenty of natural wines from artisan winemakers.

Battersea — 27 Battersea Rise SW11 1HG **MAP: 18-U2**
020 7223 1112 — **www**.soif.co
Clapham Junction
Carte £29/39
Closed Christmas, New Year, Sunday dinner, Monday lunch and bank holidays - booking essential at dinner
A/C

NANBAN

Japanese • Simple

A ramen-bar-cum-izakaya, tucked away at the back of Brixton Market and owned by former MasterChef winner, Tim Anderson. Food is fresh and full of flavour; the spicy, super-crispy chicken karaage will have you coming back for more.

Brixton — 426 Coldharbour Ln SW9 8LF **MAP: 17-N2**
020 7346 0098 — **www**.nanban.co.uk
Brixton
Carte £21/35
Closed 25 December and Monday lunch
A/C

CHARLOTTE'S BISTRO

Modern cuisine • Neighbourhood

A friendly, brightly decorated and unpretentious bistro, with a well-priced menu of flavoursome, well-prepared and quite rustic dishes of largely European provenance. Sister to Charlotte's W5 in Ealing.

Chiswick – 6 Turnham Green Terr ✉ W4 1QP **MAP: 18-S1**
020 8742 3590 – **www**.charlottes.co.uk
Turnham Green
Menu £25/35

MICHAEL NADRA

Modern cuisine • Neighbourhood

Half way down a residential side street is this intimate little place where the closely set tables add to the bonhomie. Dishes are modern, colourful and quite elaborate in their make-up; it's worth going for the sensibly priced set menu and the chosen wines.

Chiswick – 6-8 Elliott Rd ✉ W4 1PE **MAP: 18-S1/2**
020 8742 0766 – **www**.restaurant-michaelnadra.co.uk
Turnham Green
Menu £28/39
Closed 24-28 December, 1 January and Monday

BISTRO UNION

Modern British • Neighbourhood

The little sister to Trinity restaurant is fun and affordable, with a welcoming feel and sweet staff. The menu is appealingly flexible, whether you're here for brunch or a full dinner; eschew starters in favour of their great 'snacks'.

Clapham Common – 40 Abbeville Rd ✉ SW4 9NG **MAP: 18-U3**
020 7042 6400 – **www**.bistrounion.co.uk
Clapham South
Carte £23/49
Closed 24-27 December

HEDONE ✿

Modern cuisine • Design

Named after the goddess of sensual pleasure, Hedone is a restaurant where diners put themselves entirely in the hands of the kitchen. Lawyer-turned-chef-owner Mikael Jonsson is passionate about seeking out the best possible ingredients and does things his own way. So, don't expect to be presented with a printed menu when you sit down; instead, dishes you'll be served will be governed entirely by what ingredients are in their prime. Whether that's scallops from Mull, pigeon from the Vendée or asparagus from The Luberon, these ingredients are some of the finest around and they are treated with considerable respect to ensure their natural flavours come through.

To accompany them are thoughtfully considered wine pairings. The open kitchen takes centre-stage in the room, which is run in an engaging way, with just the right balance of efficiency and relaxed informality.

FIRST COURSE	MAIN COURSE	DESSERT
Isle of Mull scallops with San Danielle consommé and Amontillado foam. • Asparagus with morels, hollandaise and asparagus vinaigrette.	Roast rack of lamb, Komatsuna leaves, seaweed and mustard jus. • Smoked eel and black rice with wasabi flowers and oil.	Warm chocolate mousse, passion fruit and mascarpone ice cream. • Tarte Tatin with caramel cream, cinnamon ice cream and quince purée.

Chiswick — 301-303 Chiswick High Rd ✉ W4 4HH **MAP: 18-S2**
✆ 020 8747 0377 — **www**.hedonerestaurant.com
⊖ Chiswick Park

Menu £65/95
Closed 2 weeks Christmas-New Year - booking essential - (dinner only) - (surprise menu only)

A/C

LA TROMPETTE ✿

Modern British • Neighbourhood

It's little wonder this neighbourhood restaurant comes with a loyal following: it has a grounded head chef who ensures that the food continues to satisfy, a well-chosen wine list with something to appeal to any enthusiast, and service that is as discreet as it is free of undue pomp. This is a restaurant that seems happy in Chiswick and never gives the impression it would prefer to be in Mayfair; the locals repay the compliment by creating a warm, relaxed atmosphere and have every right to look so pleased with themselves.

The menu changes twice a day and there's little difference between the style of dishes served at lunch and at dinner. The set price menu is balanced and appealing and, while the influences are varied, its heart is French with occasional nods to the Mediterranean. The dishes themselves are free of unnecessary adornment, so the focus remains on the top quality ingredients.

FIRST COURSE	MAIN COURSE	DESSERT
Home-cured Mangalitsa with ricotta, celeriac and pear. • Dorset crab with pink grapefruit, kohlrabi and ice lettuce.	Cod with pumpkin gnocchetti, chanterelles and hazelnut pesto. • Roast guinea hen with spätzle, turnip, grilled calçots and black truffle butter.	Muscovado custard tart with Earl Grey ice cream and dates. • Caramelised banana soufflé with gingerbread and passion fruit ice cream.

Chiswick — 3-7 Devonshire Rd ✉ W4 2EU **MAP: 18-S2**
✆ 020 8747 1836 — **www**.latrompette.co.uk
⊖ Turnham Green

Menu £35 (weekday lunch)/55
Closed 24-26 December and 1 January - booking essential

DAIRY

Creative British • Rustic

The rustic, easy-to-eat food, which comes as small sharing plates, is driven by seasonality - some of the produce comes from their own farm. The higgledy-piggledy, homemade look of this fun, lively neighbourhood restaurant adds to its charm.

Clapham Common — 15 The Pavement ✉ SW4 0HY **MAP: 18-U2**
020 7622 4165 — **www**.the-dairy.co.uk
⊖ Clapham Common

Menu £28 (weekday lunch) - Carte £25/37
Closed 24-27 December, Sunday dinner and Monday - booking essential at dinner

---

Ⓝ SORELLA

Italian • Bistro

The cooking found in Italy's Amalfi region inspired this 'sister' to The Dairy. Expect a great buzz, fair prices and enthusiastic service. 4-5 sharing plates per couple should do it; be sure to include some pasta. Dishes may look simple but the kitchen infuses them with bags of flavour.

Clapham Common — 148 Clapham Manor St ✉ SW4 6BX **MAP: 18-U2**
020 7720 4662 — **www**.sorellarestaurant.co.uk
⊖ Clapham Common

Carte £25/45
Closed 1 week Christmas, Sunday dinner, Monday and lunch Tuesday - booking essential at dinner

---

UPSTAIRS (AT TRINITY)

Modern British • Fashionable

The open-plan kitchen is the focus of this more relaxed room upstairs from Trinity. It's all about sharing the visually appealing, flavoursome and reasonably priced plates, which bring a hint of the Mediterranean with them.

Clapham Common — 4 The Polygon ✉ SW4 0JG **MAP: 18-U2**
020 3745 7227 — **www**.trinityrestaurant.co.uk
⊖ Clapham Common

Carte £19/43
Closed 24-30 December, 1 January, Sunday and Monday - (dinner only)

TRINITY ✿

Modern cuisine • Fashionable

The joy of genuine neighbourhood restaurants is that customers tend to be treated less like numbers and chefs listen more to their opinions. This is certainly true at chef-owner Adam Byatt's Clapham restaurant, which has built its considerable reputation on giving locals exactly what they want. Even a change to a 4-course dinner menu went smoothly, largely because it came with in-built flexibility so that guests could virtually create their own tasting menus.

The skilled kitchen wisely avoids reinventing the wheel. Dishes boast classic combinations and are refreshingly free from unnecessary decorative flourishes so that the focus remains firmly on the primary ingredient, whether that's roast cod served with a squid ink linguine or Bresse pigeon with rainbow chard. Don't miss the crispy pig's trotter with sauce Gribiche and it's well worth pre-ordering the tarte Tatin with prune and Armagnac ice cream for two.

FIRST COURSE

Beef tartare with pickled mushrooms, smoked bone marrow and caviar. • Soused Cornish mackerel with white gazpacho, grapes and tarragon.

MAIN COURSE

Brill cooked in sea urchin butter with asparagus and sauce Maltaise. • Pork jowl with roast langoustines, peas, apple and black garlic.

DESSERT

Salt caramel custard tart with salt caramel ice cream. • Peach savarin.

Clapham Common — 4 The Polygon ✉ SW4 0JG **MAP: 18-U2**
✆ 020 7622 1199 — **www**.trinityrestaurant.co.uk
⊖ Clapham Common

Menu £40/68
Closed 24-30 December and 1-2 January

CHARLOTTE'S W5

Modern cuisine • Neighbourhood

It's all about flexibility at this converted stable block - you can come for a drink, a snack or a full meal. Every dish is available in a choice of three sizes and every bottle of wine is offered by the glass or carafe. The charming service team add to the buzz.

Ealing — Dickens Yard, Longfield Ave ✉ W5 2UQ **MAP: 18-R1**
✆ 020 3771 8722 — **www**.charlottes.co.uk
⊖ Ealing Broadway

Menu £18/30 - Carte £28/49

KIRAKU

Japanese • Friendly

The name of this cute little Japanese restaurant means 'relax and enjoy' - easy with such charming service. Extensive menu includes zensai, skewers, noodles, rice dishes and assorted sushi; ask if you want them in a particular order.

Ealing — 8 Station Par, Uxbridge Rd. ✉ W5 3LD **MAP: 18-R1**
✆ 020 8992 2848 — **www**.kiraku.co.uk
⊖ Ealing Common

Carte £14/35
Closed Christmas-New Year

VICTORIA

Modern British • Pub

A proper local, with a lived-in feel, especially in the bars; if you're here to eat head for the conservatory, which overlooks a terrace. The appealing menu offers a good range of dishes and comes with a distinct Mediterranean slant, with Middle Eastern influences never far away.

East Sheen — 10 West Temple ✉ SW14 7RT **MAP: 18-S2**
✆ 020 8876 4238 — **www**.victoriasheen.co.uk
⊖ Mortlake (Rail).

Menu £14 (weekday lunch) - Carte £25/41

CLAUDE'S KITCHEN

Modern cuisine • Bistro

Two operations in one converted pub: 'Amuse Bouche' is a well-priced champagne bar; upstairs is an intimate dining room with a weekly changing menu. The cooking is colourful and fresh, with the odd challenging flavour combination.

Fulham — 51 Parsons Green Ln ✉ SW6 4JA **MAP: 18-T2**
✆ 020 3813 3223 — **www**.amusebouchelondon.com
⊖ Parsons Green.

Menu £23 - Carte £31/36
Closed 24-26 December, Sunday and Monday - booking essential - (dinner only)

A/C

KOJI

Japanese • Wine bar

A fun, contemporary wine bar serving Japanese food. The menu mixes the modern and the classic, with tempura and dishes from the robata grill particularly popular; food is full of flavour and the kitchen clearly know their craft.

Fulham — 58 New King's Rd ✉ SW6 4LS **MAP: 18-T2**
✆ 020 7731 2520 — **www**.koji.restaurant
⊖ Parsons Green

Carte £45/78
Closed 25-26 December and Monday

A/C

MANUKA KITCHEN

Modern cuisine • Rustic

The two young owners run their simple little restaurant with great enthusiasm and their prices are keen. Like the magical Manuka honey, the chef is from New Zealand; his menu is varied and his food is wholesome and full of flavour.

Fulham — 510 Fulham Rd ✉ SW6 5NJ **MAP: 18-T2**
✆ 020 7736 7588 — **www**.manukakitchen.com
⊖ Fulham Broadway

Menu £15 (weekday lunch) - Carte £24/33
Closed 25-26 December, Sunday dinner and Monday lunch

A/C

HARWOOD ARMS ❀

Modern British • Pub

It may be a very handsome pub in a smart postcode and have all its tables laid up for dining but there's nothing stuck-up or snooty about this place – in fact, the only thing that's superior is the cooking. It's British to its core, with its reassuringly concise, daily changing menu resolutely governed by our country's own seasonal produce.

Cornish fish, Herdwick lamb, Cumbrian chicken and Wiltshire pork can all feature and game, whether grouse or Hampshire muntjac, is a strength. Dishes have real depth and flavours are bold. Service is assured and comes courtesy of a young yet experienced team and the well-chosen wine list offers a good choice of mature claret. If you're sitting beneath the skylight then look up and you'll spot the rooftop vegetable and herb 'garden'. As this is still a pub, you can just pop in for a drink at the bar but if you do then be sure to order some of the great bar snacks like game rissoles or a venison scotch egg.

FIRST COURSE

Wood pigeon and prune faggots with onion cream and thyme. • Coronation quail salad with almond and apricot.

MAIN COURSE

Roast fallow deer with baked crapaudine beetroot, smoked bone marrow and walnut. • Pollock with melted leeks, cockles and bacon.

DESSERT

Rhubarb and sherry trifle. • Poached cherries with vanilla cream and a brandy snap.

Fulham — Walham Grove ✉ SW6 1QP **MAP: 18-T2**
✆ 020 7386 1847 — **www**.harwoodarms.com
⊖ Fulham Broadway.

Menu £33 (weekday lunch)/50
Closed 24-26 December, lunch 27 December and 1 January and Monday lunch except bank holidays - booking essential

Ⓝ RIGO'

Creative • Design

The Italian chef-owner uses his international experience to create menus that are made up of quite delicate compositions. While there's plenty of pasta and Italian produce like Fassona beef, you are also just as likely to see, say, some Japanese influences. Service is quite formal.

Fulham — 277 New King's Rd ✉ SW6 4RD **MAP: 18-T2**
020 7751 3293 — **www**.rigolondon.com
Parsons Green

Menu £46
Closed 23 December-3 January, 11-25 August and Sunday - (dinner only and lunch Friday-Saturday)

A/C

TENDIDO CUATRO

Spanish • Neighbourhood

Along with tapas, the speciality is paella. Designed for a hungry two, they vary from seafood to quail and chorizo; vegetarian to cuttlefish ink. Vivid colours used with abandon deck out the busy room.

Fulham — 108-110 New Kings Rd ✉ SW6 4LY **MAP: 18-T2**
020 7371 5147 — **www**.cambiodetercio.co.uk
Parsons Green

Carte £26/47
Closed 2 weeks Christmas

A/C

TOMMY TUCKER

Traditional British • Pub

The old Pelican pub was revamped by the owners of nearby Claude's Kitchen. It's bright and open plan, with an unstructured menu divided under headings of 'meat', 'fish' and 'fruit and veg'. The cooking is rustic and satisfying.

Fulham — 22 Waterford Rd ✉ SW6 2DR **MAP: 18-T2**
020 7736 1023 — **www**.thetommytucker.com
Fulham Broadway.

Carte £21/42

A/C

L'AMOROSA

Italian • Neighbourhood

Former Zafferano head chef Andy Needham has created a warm and sunny Italian restaurant - one that we'd all like to have in our high street. The quality of the produce shines through and homemade pasta dishes are a highlight.

Hammersmith — 278 King St W6 0SP **MAP: 18-S1**
020 8563 0300 — **www**.lamorosa.co.uk
Ravenscourt Park
Carte £25/39
Closed 1 week August, 1 week Christmas, Sunday dinner, Monday and bank holidays
A/C

ANGLESEA ARMS

Modern British • Neighbourhood

One of the daddies of the gastropub movement. The seasonal menu gives the impression it's written by a Brit who occasionally holidays on the Med - along with robust dishes are some that display a pleasing lightness of touch.

Hammersmith — 35 Wingate Rd W6 0UR **MAP: 18-S1**
020 8749 1291 — **www**.angleseaarmspub.co.uk
Ravenscourt Park
Carte £24/36
Closed 24-26 December and lunch Monday-Thursday

AZOU

North African • Neighbourhood

Silks, lanterns and rugs add to the atmosphere of this personally run, North African restaurant. Most come for the very filling tajines, served with triple steamed couscous. Many of the dishes are designed for sharing.

Hammersmith — 375 King St W6 9NJ **MAP: 18-S2**
020 8563 7266 — **www**.azou.co.uk
Stamford Brook
Carte £20/37
Closed 1 January and 25 December - booking essential - (dinner only)
A/C

BRACKENBURY

Mediterranean cuisine • Neighbourhood

A much loved neighbourhood restaurant given a new lease of life. The kitchen looks to Italy, France and the Med for inspiration and doesn't waste time on presentation; dishes feel instinctive and flavours marry well.

Hammersmith — 129 - 131 Brackenbury Rd W6 OBQ **MAP: 18-S1**
020 8741 4928 — **www**.brackenburyrestaurant.co.uk
Ravenscourt Park

Menu £18 (weekday lunch) - Carte £23/35
Closed Christmas, New Year, Easter, August bank holiday, Sunday and Monday

---

INDIAN ZING

Indian • Neighbourhood

Chef-owner Manoj Vasaikar seeks inspiration from across India. His cooking balances the traditional with the more contemporary and delivers many layers of flavour - the lamb dishes and breads are particularly good. The restaurant is always busy yet service remains courteous and unhurried.

Hammersmith — 236 King St. W6 ORF **MAP: 18-S2**
020 8748 5959 — **www**.indianzing.co.uk
Ravenscourt Park

Menu £19 (lunch) - Carte £23/44

DYSART PETERSHAM

Modern cuisine • Intimate

A pub built in the 1900s as part of the Arts and Crafts movement but now run as quite a formal restaurant. The kitchen uses top-notch ingredients and adds subtle Asian tones to a classical base. Occasional music recital suppers.

Richmond — 135 Petersham Rd TW10 7AA **MAP: 18-R3**
020 8940 8005 — **www**.thedysartpetersham.co.uk

Menu £28 (weekdays) - Carte £40/75
Closed Sunday dinner, Monday and Tuesday

RIVER CAFÉ ✿

Italian • Fashionable

It's more than thirty years since the River Café opened but the ethos here is still very much the same, with superlative ingredients at the centre of everything they do. The team here seem like one big happy family, with servers who welcome you as if into their own home and all the chefs on show in what must be one of the calmest kitchens in London.

The menu is written anew for each service and bursts with authentic Italian flavours; there's a vigour and honesty to the cooking and dishes like wood-roasted Anjou pigeon with speck or veal shin slow-cooked in chardonnay are made with top-class produce and come in hearty portions. Pasta is a must-have, as is the perennial Chocolate Nemesis; one bite of the latter and you'll understand why it never comes off the menu. This iconic restaurant's location on the banks of the Thames is as much part of the experience as the cooking – ask for a seat on the riverside terrace, or failing that, sit by the window.

FIRST COURSE	MAIN COURSE	DESSERT
Asparagus with anchovy butter and parmesan. • Wood-roasted Scottish langoustines with chilli and oregano.	Anjou pigeon with Allegrini Valpolicella and green beans 'in umido'. • Turbot wood-roasted over potatoes with Amalfi lemon and zucchini.	Nespole and almond tart. • Pressed chocolate cake with zabaglione ice cream.

Hammersmith — Thames Wharf, Rainville Rd ✉ W6 9HA **MAP: 18-T2**
✆ 020 7386 4200 — **www.**rivercafe.co.uk
⊖ Barons Court

Carte £64/70
Closed Christmas-New Year and Sunday dinner – booking essential

THE GLASSHOUSE ✿

Modern cuisine • Fashionable

2019 sees the 20th birthday of this very model of a modern neighbourhood restaurant. The quirkily-shaped room comes with textured walls and some vibrant artwork and, as the name implies, it's a bright spot, with floor-to-ceiling windows at the front. Tables may be rather formally laid but the service is undertaken by a team who are sociable and engaging and the atmosphere, thanks largely to the high number of locals who call this place their own, is never less than animated.

The last change of chef resulted in the cooking reverting to a more natural, unfussy style - and it's all the better for it. The kitchen concentrates on recognisable combinations and flavours that complement one another - ox cheek with mushrooms, rabbit with broad beans, hake with potted shrimps - and a strong sense of seasonality. A wonderful panna cotta with strawberries is the perfect example of what this place is all about.

FIRST COURSE

Salmon sashimi, with pickled rhubarb, ginger and white soy. • Warm rabbit salad with globe artichokes, asparagus, tarragon and truffle cream.

MAIN COURSE

Venison haunch and pie with smoked creamed potato, rainbow chard and pickled walnuts. • Cornish hake with potted shrimp butter and crisp potatoes.

DESSERT

Chocolate and hazelnut pavé with milk ice cream. • Mascarpone ice cream sandwich with poached apricots and champagne jelly.

Kew — 14 Station Par. ✉ TW9 3PZ **MAP: 18-R2**

✆ 020 8940 6777 — **www**.glasshouserestaurant.co.uk

⊖ Kew Gardens

Menu £38/58

Closed 24-26 December, 1 January, Sunday dinner and Monday except bank holidays

A/C ✿

MATSUBA ¶○

Japanese • Design

Family-run Japanese restaurant with just 11 tables; understated but well-kept appearance. Extensive menu offers wide range of Japanese dishes, along with bulgogi, a Korean barbecue dish.

Richmond — 10 Red Lion St ✉ TW9 1RW **MAP: 18-R2**
020 8605 3513 — **www**.matsuba-restaurant.com
⊖ Richmond
Carte £30/45
Closed 25-26 December, 1 January, Sunday and Monday
A/C

PETERSHAM NURSERIES CAFÉ ¶○

Modern cuisine • Rustic

On a summer's day there can be few more delightful spots for lunch, whether that's on the terrace or in the greenhouse. The kitchen uses the freshest seasonal produce in unfussy, flavoursome dishes that have a subtle Italian accent.

Richmond — Church Ln (off Petersham Rd) ✉ TW10 7AB **MAP: 18-R3**
020 8940 5230 — **www**.petershamnurseries.com
Carte £39/51
Closed 24-27 December and Monday - booking essential - (lunch only)

SWAGAT ¶○

Indian • Bistro

A very likeable little Indian restaurant, run by two friends who met while training with Oberoi hotels in India. One partner organises the warm service; the other prepares dishes with a pleasing degree of lightness and subtlety.

Richmond — 86 Hill Rise ✉ TW10 6UB **MAP: 18-R2**
020 8940 7557 — **www**.swagatindiancuisine.co.uk
⊖ Richmond
Carte £18/30
Closed 25 December - booking essential - (dinner only)
A/C

SHIKUMEN

Chinese • Intimate

Impressive homemade dim sum at lunch and excellent Peking duck are the standouts at this unexpectedly sleek Cantonese restaurant in an otherwise undistinguished part of Shepherd's Bush.

Shepherd's Bush — 58 Shepherd's Bush Grn ✉ W12 8QE **MAP: 18-T1**
020 8749 9978 — **www**.shikumen.co.uk
⊖ Shepherd's Bush

Carte £22/63
Closed 25 December

EALING PARK TAVERN

Modern British • Trendy

An impressive Arts and Crafts property, dating from 1886 and brought up to date thanks to a splendid refurbishment from the Martin Brothers. Cooking is robust yet with a refined edge. The pub also boasts its own brewery at the back.

South Ealing — 222 South Ealing Rd ✉ W5 4RL **MAP: 18-R1**
020 8758 1879 — **www**.ealingparktavern.com
⊖ South Ealing

Carte £22/30
Closed 25 December

CROWN

Traditional British • Pub

Relaxed, stylish pub with parquet floors and feature fireplaces; sit in the airy, elegant rear restaurant, with its high vaulted ceiling and garden view. Global, bound-to-please menus offer fresh, tasty, amply-sized dishes.

Twickenham — 174 Richmond Rd, St Margarets ✉ TW1 2NH **MAP: 18-R3**
020 8892 5896 — **www**.crowntwickenham.co.uk
⊖ St Margarets (Rail).

Carte £16/44
Closed 26 December

CHEZ BRUCE ✿

French • Brasserie

There are few restaurants that engender such loyalty from their regulars as Chez Bruce. Maybe that's because they get to enjoy top quality cooking without having to schlep up to the West End; or perhaps it's because they like to be surrounded by the same familiar faces every time they come here. Add in sprightly and enthusiastic service and more than fair prices and you realise that the longevity of this restaurant is no accident.

The cooking of Chef Matt Christmas, who has worked with owner Bruce Poole for over a decade, is all about flavour and balance; the plates are never over-crowded and ingredients are not required to fight for supremacy. The base is largely classical French but with a pronounced Mediterranean influence – this is a kitchen where things are done the traditional way. Equal effort also goes into the make-up of the cheeseboard and the wine list.

FIRST COURSE

Grilled tuna with lemon dressing, aioli and aubergine. • Home-made cavatelli with Italian sausage, broccoli, chilli, anchovy, pecorino and almonds.

MAIN COURSE

Pig's cheek and pork belly with boudin noir, celeriac and mustard. • Roast cod with olive oil mash, Provençale tomato and gremolata.

DESSERT

Buttermilk pudding with rhubarb, lemon and pistachio. • Hot chocolate pudding with praline parfait.

Wandsworth — 2 Bellevue Rd ✉ SW17 7EG **MAP: 18-U3**
✆ 020 8672 0114 — **www**.chezbruce.co.uk
⊖ Tooting Bec

Menu £38/58
Closed 24-26 December and 1 January - booking essential

LIGHT HOUSE

Mediterranean cuisine • Neighbourhood

A neighbourhood favourite offering Mediterranean cooking in smart, comfortable surroundings. The food is wholesome and confident, with plenty of bold flavours; Italian dishes and puddings are the highlights and staff are calm and cheery.

Wimbledon — 75-77 Ridgway ✉ SW19 4ST **MAP: 18-T3**
020 8944 6338 — **www**.lighthousewimbledon.com
Wimbledon
Menu £23 (weekday dinner) - Carte £25/44
Closed 25-26 December, 1 January and Sunday dinner

TAKAHASHI

Japanese • Friendly

The eponymous chef-owner of this sweet spot is a Nobu alumnus and his wife runs the service with a personal touch. Mediterranean ingredients bring a creative edge to the pure, delicately flavoured dishes. Sushi and sashimi are a highlight.

Wimbledon — 228 Merton Rd ✉ SW19 1EQ **MAP: 18-T3**
020 8540 3041 — **www**.takahashi-restaurant.co.uk
South Wimbledon
Menu £30/78
Closed Monday and Tuesday - booking essential - (dinner only and lunch Saturday-Sunday)

WHITE ONION

Modern cuisine • Bistro

A relaxed bistro deluxe with a handsome marble-topped bar and an attentive young team. Flavoursome classic French cooking has clever modern touches. Great value set lunch and a terrific selection of wine by the glass and carafe.

Wimbledon — 67 High St ✉ SW19 5EE **MAP: 18-T3**
020 8947 8278 — **www**.thewhiteonion.co.uk
Wimbledon
Menu £24 (lunch) - Carte dinner £32/46
Closed 5-14 August, 25 December-9 January, Monday, lunch Tuesday-Thursday and Sunday dinner

INDEXES

ekash/iStock (bottom) • gilaxia/iStock (top)

ALPHABETICAL LIST OF RESTAURANTS

C

D

G

H

I

J

K

L

M

N

O

P

Q

R

S

W

X

Y

Z

STARRED RESTAURANTS

✿✿✿

✿✿

✿

BIB GOURMAND

J - K

L - M

P

S

T

U - W

RESTAURANTS BY CUISINE TYPE

CREATIVE

CREATIVE BRITISH

CREATIVE FRENCH

CREOLE

FISH AND CHIPS

FRENCH

FUSION

GREEK

INDIAN

ITALIAN

JAPANESE

MEATS AND GRILLS

MEDITERRANEAN CUISINE

MEXICAN

MIDDLE EASTERN

MODERN BRITISH

MODERN FRENCH

MODERN CUISINE

MOROCCAN

NORTH AFRICAN

PERUVIAN

POLISH

PORTUGUESE

PROVENÇAL

SCANDINAVIAN

SCOTTISH

SEAFOOD

SOUTH INDIAN

SPANISH

THAI

TRADITIONAL BRITISH

VEGETARIAN

VIETNAMESE

WORLD CUISINE

THE BEST PUBS

RESTAURANTS WITH OUTSIDE DINING

M

N

O

P

R

S

T

V

Y

Z

RESTAURANTS OPEN FOR BREAKFAST

INDEX OF MAPS

CENTRAL LONDON

GREATER LONDON

LONDON TRANSPORT
BAKERLOO
CENTRAL
CIRCLE
DISTRICT
JUBILEE
Ruislip Gardens
South Ruislip
Northolt
Greenford
Perivale
Hanger Lane
North Ealing
EALING BROADWAY
West Ealing
Hanwell
Southall
Hayes & Harlington
Ealing Common
Acton Central
ACTON TOWN
South Ealing
Northfields
Boston Manor
Osterley
Hounslow Central
Hounslow East
Hatton Cross
Hounslow West
HEATHROW TERMINALS 2 & 3
HEATHROW TERMINAL 5
HEATHROW TERMINAL 4
South Harrow
Sudbury Hill
Sudbury Town
Alperton
Park Royal
West Acton
North Acton
East Acton
WHITE CITY
WOOD LANE
South Acton
Chiswick Park
Turnham Green
Stamford Brook
Ravenscourt Park
HAMMERSMITH
Barons Court
Gunnersbury
Kew Gardens
RICHMOND
South Kenton
North Wembley
WEMBLEY CENTRAL
Stonebridge Park
Harlesden
WILLESDEN JUNCTION
Kensal Rise
Kensal Green
Acton Main Line
Ladbroke Grove
Latimer Road
Shepherd's Bush Market
SHEPHERD'S BUSH
Goldhawk Road
KENSINGTON (OLYMPIA)
Holland Park
West Kensington
WEST BROMPTON
Fulham Broadway
Parsons Green
Putney Bridge
East Putney
Northwick Park
Preston Road
Kingsbury
WEMBLEY PARK
Neasden
Dollis Hill
Willesden Green
Kilburn
Brondesbury Park
Brondesbury
Kilburn High Road
Queen's Park
Kilburn Park
Maida Vale
Warwick Avenue
Westbourne Park
Royal Oak
Bayswater
PADDINGTON
Queensway
NOTTING HILL GATE
HIGH STREET KENSINGTON
Lancaster Gate
Marble Arch
EDGWARE ROAD
Edgware Road
Marylebone
South Hampstead
Finchley Road & Frognal
WEST HAMPSTEAD
FINCHLEY ROAD
Swiss Cottage
Hyde Park Corner
Knightsbridge
Gloucester Road
Sloane Square
EARL'S COURT
SOUTH KENSINGTON
VICTORIA
Imperial Wharf
River Thame
Wandsworth Road
CLAPHAM JUNCTION
CLAPHAM NORTH
Clapham South
Brent Cross
Golders Gree
Hampstead
Hampstead Heath
Belsi
Chalk
St. John's Wo
BAKER STREET
Regent's Park
BOND ST.
OXFORD CIRCUS
GREEN PARK
PICCADIL CIRCUS
CHARING CRO
EMBAN
WESTMINST
St. James's Park
Pimlico
Vauxha
CLAPH HIGH ST
HAMMERSM & CITY

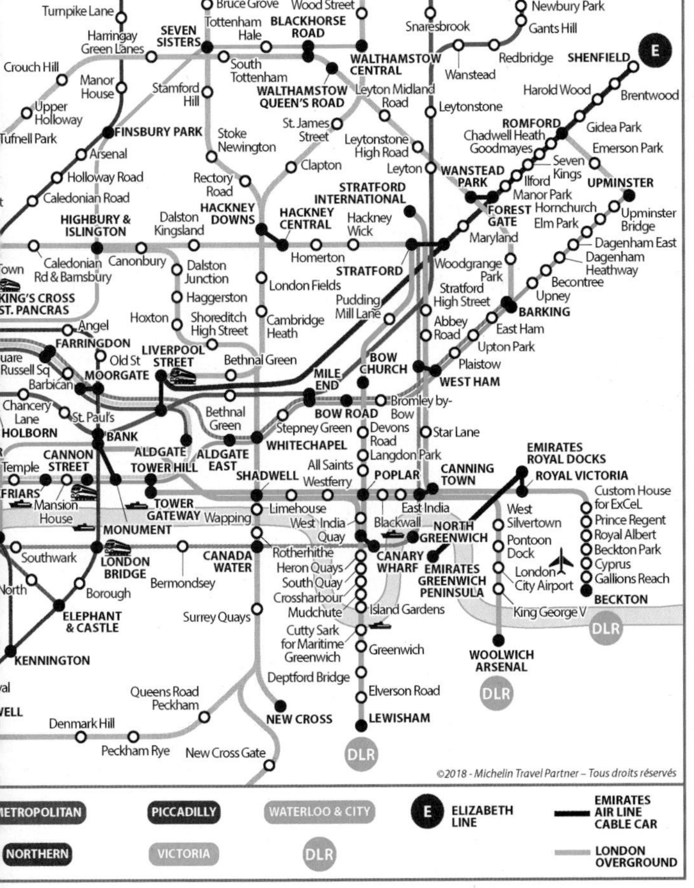
Turnpike Lane
Harringay Green Lanes
SEVEN SISTERS
Bruce Grove
Tottenham Hale
BLACKHORSE ROAD
Wood Street
Snaresbrook
Newbury Park
Gants Hill
Crouch Hill
Manor House
Stamford Hill
South Tottenham
WALTHAMSTOW CENTRAL
WALTHAMSTOW QUEEN'S ROAD
Leyton Midland Road
Wanstead
Redbridge
SHENFIELD
Upper Holloway
Tufnell Park
FINSBURY PARK
Stoke Newington
St. James Street
Leytonstone
Harold Wood
Brentwood
ROMFORD
Gidea Park
Chadwell Heath
Goodmayes
Emerson Park
Seven Kings
Ilford
Arsenal
Holloway Road
Caledonian Road
Rectory Road
Clapton
Leytonstone High Road
Leyton
WANSTEAD PARK
Manor Park
UPMINSTER
HIGHBURY & ISLINGTON
Dalston Kingsland
HACKNEY DOWNS
HACKNEY CENTRAL
Hackney Wick
STRATFORD INTERNATIONAL
FOREST GATE
Hornchurch
Upminster Bridge
Elm Park
Maryland
Dagenham East
Caledonian Rd & Barnsbury
Canonbury
Dalston Junction
Homerton
STRATFORD
Woodgrange Park
Dagenham Heathway
Becontree
KING'S CROSS ST. PANCRAS
Haggerston
London Fields
Stratford High Street
Upney
BARKING
Hoxton
Shoreditch High Street
Cambridge Heath
Pudding Mill Lane
Abbey Road
East Ham
Angel
FARRINGDON
LIVERPOOL STREET
Old St
Bethnal Green
Upton Park
Russell Sq
MOORGATE
BOW CHURCH
Plaistow
Barbican
MILE END
WEST HAM
Chancery Lane
St. Paul's
Bethnal Green
BOW ROAD
Bromley by-Bow
HOLBORN
BANK
Stepney Green
Devons Road
Star Lane
WHITECHAPEL
ALDGATE
ALDGATE EAST
Langdon Park
EMIRATES ROYAL DOCKS
CANNON STREET
Temple
TOWER HILL
SHADWELL
All Saints
POPLAR
CANNING TOWN
ROYAL VICTORIA
Westferry
Custom House for ExCeL
FRIARS
Mansion House
TOWER GATEWAY
Wapping
Limehouse
East India
West Silvertown
Prince Regent
West India Quay
Blackwall
NORTH GREENWICH
Royal Albert
MONUMENT
Pontoon Dock
Beckton Park
Southwark
LONDON BRIDGE
CANADA WATER
Rotherhithe
CANARY WHARF
London City Airport
Cyprus
Heron Quays
EMIRATES GREENWICH PENINSULA
Gallions Reach
Bermondsey
South Quay
BECKTON
Borough
Crossharbour
ELEPHANT & CASTLE
Mudchute
Island Gardens
King George V
Surrey Quays
DLR
Cutty Sark for Maritime Greenwich
Greenwich
KENNINGTON
WOOLWICH ARSENAL
Deptford Bridge
DLR
Queens Road Peckham
Elverson Road
NEW CROSS
LEWISHAM
Denmark Hill
Peckham Rye
New Cross Gate
DLR
©2018 - Michelin Travel Partner – Tous droits réservés
METROPOLITAN
PICCADILLY
WATERLOO & CITY
E
ELIZABETH LINE
EMIRATES AIR LINE CABLE CAR
NORTHERN
VICTORIA
DLR
LONDON OVERGROUND